Enterprise Games

Using Game Mechanics to Build a Better Business

Michael Hugos

Center for Systems Innovation [c4si]
CHICAGO

ENTERPRISE GAMES
by Michael Hugos

Copyright © 2012 Center for Systems Innovation. All rights reserved.

Printing History:

    September 2012:   First Edition.

Revision History for the First Edition:

    2012-09-07:   First release

    2013-06-11   Revised release

May be purchased for educational, business, or sales promotional use. Online editions are also available. For more information, contact our corporate/institutional sales department: (312) 771-1354 or admin@michaelhugos.com.

Applying game mechanics to the great game of business

Many of the designations used by manufacturers and sellers to distinguish their products are claimed as trademarks. Where those designations appear in this book, and Center for Systems Innovation was aware of a trademark claim, the designations have been printed in caps or initial caps.

While every precaution has been taken in the preparation of this book, the publisher and author(s) assume no responsibility for errors or omissions, or for damages resulting from the use of the information contained herein.

To my wife, Venetia.

Contents

Preface	vii	
1	Transformation of the Great Game of Business	1
2	Feedback in the Real-Time Economy (Why Games Matter)	11
3	Feedback Systems Drive Business Agility	23
4	New Paradigms and Operating Principles	37
5	Gamification	47
6	A Continuum of Functionality: Simulations to Serious Games	63
7	Massively Multiplayer Online Games and Real-Time Collaboration	79
8	Driving the Great Game of Sales	93
9	Game Mechanics in Products, Services, and User Interfaces	105
10	Environments of Decision	117

11	A Novel Encounter with Big Data	129
12	Game Layer on Top of the World	147
13	Games for Change	163
14	The Future of Work	175
Index	193

Preface

WE ARE LIVING IN a time of big changes. We face changes driven by powerful forces like world population growth; rising prices for food, fuel, and raw materials; depletion of natural resources; and increasing levels of greenhouse gases in the atmosphere. And at the very same time, we are also surrounded by the rapid spread of new technologies such as social media, mobile consumer devices like smartphones and tablet computers, and cloud computing and software apps. Clearly, the path forward involves finding ways to use the potentials of the latter to address the challenges of the former.

The magnitude of the challenges we face now is unlike anything we have experienced since the early years of the last century. At that time a hundred years ago, work and society were transformed by the spread of industrial technology and the resulting mass migration of people from farms and small towns to factories and big cities.

The first decades of the last century saw a transition from the practices of an earlier age—the Victorian Age—to the practices of a new age—the Industrial Age. In the countries where industrial activity was concentrated, there was conflict between those who paid wages and those who earned wages, and yet ultimately, that conflict was channeled in socially constructive ways that resulted in the growth of a large middle class sustained by lifetime employment in companies offering jobs with career paths, benefits, and pensions. This economic model of employment became a worldwide standard during the last half of the twentieth century.

Challenges and Opportunities

Now, industrial activity has spread around the world. And we see traditional practices that once sustained the middle class are disappearing in countries everywhere, and conflict between wage payers and wage earners is returning. High rates of change in technology and volatility in the prices of everything from basic commodities to finished products make it hard for companies to predict demand for their products, and even harder for them to create long-term business plans. A major result of this is the fluid nature of employment these days.

People are employed one month and unemployed the next, and it is usually for reasons beyond their control that have little to do with their personal performance. Companies hire and fire as needed to respond to market volatility and rapid rates of change. Twentieth-century traditions of lifetime employment and jobs with career paths, benefits, and pensions are harder and harder to maintain.

The personal and economic stress and dislocation this causes makes us yearn to revive or reinvigorate business practices from the last century so as to recapture the stability and benefits they once provided. But that yearning will go unrequited because those practices no longer fit the realities of our real-time, global economy.

Games and the associated technology we currently refer to as video games offer us more than just diversion and escape from difficult times. They offer us field-tested models to use for organizing companies and performing complex and creative tasks. They offer clear and compelling examples for how people can work together, build their careers, and earn a living in rapidly changing and unpredictable environments.

The very notion that games could have anything in common with work will trigger some to reject these ideas out of hand. For the rest, this book offers a set of grounding concepts, case studies, and a big-picture view of the use of games and game-like operating models in business. As one person who helped me with this book said, "There is a huge game-shaped opportunity in modern business practices."

Audience for This Book

This book is written for people who are interested in exploring the use of games to address the challenges we face. It is written to be accessible to a broad base of readers from business, professional, and technical backgrounds. It is written for change-minded business executives, and for people who advise them and deliver new ideas and services to them. It is written for people who design games and are curious about new opportunities that arise from the merging of games and business, and for people whose work is already taking on a game-like quality and who want further insight into what is happening.

Footnotes and references are provided for readers who wish to explore in more detail the particular technologies, methodologies, and business practices that are presented. This is not a book that concentrates on any one game topic such as the practice currently known as "gamification." Nor is this a prescriptive cookbook that lays out a predefined set of steps for applying a specific game technique to a particular business situation.

My intent is to arm and inspire those who are in a position to influence or change the way businesses and organizations operate. I draw on my own experience as well as on the writings and experiences of others in business and game design in order to present real-world examples of the merging of games and business. These examples outline salient features of an operating model for companies and economies that can deliver broad-based and sustainable prosperity. I hope this sparks your own creativity. I hope you build on the examples and concepts presented here as you experiment with them in your own company and your own career.

Structure of This Book

The book is loosely divided into three parts. The first part, Chapters 1–4, presents the challenges and opportunities for redesigning work to fit the realities of our real-time economy. It puts forth ideas and case studies to illustrate how games can provide operating models to follow for redesigning work.

The second part consists of Chapters 5–9, and is a discussion of games and game mechanics that are relevant to rethinking the way work is done. This part provides specific examples, pictures, and case studies to show how game techniques and technologies can be applied to the design of new business systems and workflows.

The third and last part, Chapters 10–14, describes business and social impacts of combining technology from video games with in-house corporate systems and the rapidly spreading technologies that make up social media, consumer technology, and cloud computing. The book concludes with a discussion about where this is all going and what it might mean for the future of work.

I welcome hearing from you with thoughts, comments, and questions. You can contact me via email at *mhugos@yahoo.com* or visit my website at *www.MichaelHugos.com*.

MICHAEL HUGOS

Center for Systems Innovation [c4si]
Chicago, Illinois
June 2013

Acknowledgments

Thank you to the game designers and developers who have so expanded the state of the art over the last 25 years and more. They brought the design and the technology of video games, social games, massively multiplayer games, and alternate reality games to their present state of sophistication. They keep pushing the envelope.

Thank you to the thinkers and visionaries who have practiced, written, and spoken about the techniques and potentials of games. I have read the works of many of them and spoken in person with some of them. Throughout this book, I footnote relevant works and comments of people who influenced me in formulating my ideas and writing this book. Interested readers owe it to themselves to follow up on these footnotes and learn more about these people and their work.

Thank you to the reviewers of this book, who helped me clarify my message and who pointed out errors in my original manuscript and offered suggestions for improvement.

We'd Like to Hear from You

Please address comments and questions concerning this book to Michael Hugos at mhugos@yahoo.com

Center for Systems Innovation
1319 W Granville, Suite 101
Chicago, IL 60660-1910
+1 (312) 771-1354

PREFACE

To comment or ask technical questions about this book, send email to:

mhugos@yahoo.com

For more information about our books, courses, conferences, and news, see our website at *http://www.michaelhugos.com*.

Twitter: *http://twitter.com/MichaelHugos*
YouTube: *https://www.youtube.com/user/mhugos*

1

Transformation of the Great Game of Business

USING GAMES AND GAME mechanics might be as powerful a model for organizing knowledge and creative work as the assembly line was for organizing industrial and repetitive work.

Because we have been taught that play is the opposite of work and that a game is the opposite of a job, we believe that play and games are frivolous. Thus, many of us instinctively reject the idea that games or play can be part of that serious activity we call work. But maybe we should think again.

We all have a sense of what a game is. Regardless of whether we are talking about sports games or card games or board games or video games, we can see they all share a core set of traits in common. Games are skills based, results oriented, and structured by rules. Games have been described as having four defining traits: a *goal*, *rules*, a *feedback system*, and *voluntary participation*.[1]

The goal of a game defines what the game is about, its purpose. Rules place limitations on how the players can accomplish the goal, and they channel the activities of the players into directions that are supportive of the game. Rules are what make the game work. A feedback system is what keeps the players constantly informed on how well they are doing and their progress toward accomplishment of the goal. Voluntary participation means that people in the game understand and willingly accept the goal, the rules, and the feedback system. This willing acceptance creates the common ground that unites all the players in a game and makes it possible for them to play or work together.

---

1 Jane McGonigal, *Reality is Broken: Why Games Make Us Better and How They Can Change the World* (New York: The Penguin Press, 2011), 21. Watch a video of a talk she gave titled "Gaming Can Make a Better World" at http://www.ted.com/talks/jane_mcgonigal_gaming_can_make_a_better_world.html.

When these four traits are employed effectively, they create a self-reinforcing dynamic that helps us focus and engage in a series of activities that is so engrossing and satisfying that it induces a state of mind known as "flow."[2] Flow is that place where people lose their self-consciousness, where time becomes distorted, and where the pleasure and satisfaction people get from the experience is an end in itself. What would happen if work flowed?

In 2005, the *Washington Post* ran a story reporting on the results of an extensive survey on worker engagement run by the Gallup Organization. Curt W. Coffman, the global practice leader in charge of this survey, reported on some of the findings as follows, "We know that 55 percent of all U.S. employees are not engaged at work. They are basically in a holding pattern. They feel like their capabilities aren't being tapped into and utilized and therefore, they really don't have a psychological connection to the organization."[3]

Now, in the midst of a difficult economy, a lot of employees are just thankful to have a job—whether it's boring or not. But that still does not mean these employees are any more engaged with their companies or that their talents are any more effectively tapped into. They're still restless and bored. What a waste of time, talent, and potential.

Perhaps the source of energy and creativity that will drive the next sustained increase in economic productivity, personal satisfaction and the growth of a widespread global middle class is standing right in front of us, waiting for us to see it.

Boredom comes from our lack of meaningful engagement with each other and from the lack of opportunity to utilize our full talents in our jobs. Boredom leaves us feeling isolated, stressed, and alienated. And that leads inevitably to the state of being called depression.

Perhaps our boredom and depression is a direct result of the way our companies are designed and the way they operate. Maybe systems and procedures that worked well enough during last century's industrial age

---

[2] Mihaly Csikszentmihalyi, *Creativity: Flow and the Psychology of Discovery and Intervention* (New York:HarperCollins, 1996), 110 - 113. Watch a video of a talk he did titled "Flow - the Secret to Happiness" at *http://www.ted.com/talks/mihaly_csikszentmihalyi_on_flow.html*.

[3] Amy Joyce, "Boredom Numbs the Working World," *Washington Post*, August 10, 2005, *http://www.washingtonpost.com/wp-dyn/content/article/2005/08/09/AR2005080901395.html*.

are now obsolete and need to be redesigned. Maybe games could be a significant part of that redesign.

In her book *Reality Is Broken*, a prominent game designer and developer, Jane McGonigal, describes games as "an opportunity to focus our energy, with relentless optimism, at something we're good at (or getting better at) and enjoy. In other words, gameplay is the direct emotional opposite of depression."[4]

Professor Byron Reeves and venture capitalist J. Leighton Read, working together through the business school at Stanford University, make a case for using games to change the way companies operate. They state in their book *Total Engagement*, "We believe the highest use of games will be to redesign work so that it is more like a game and to allow work to be conducted within games."[5] They believe work will be "hopelessly confused with play and the result a possible win-win for the players and the businesses that sponsored them."[6]

Look at what young people are doing in every country and every culture and you will see a huge common activity that cannot be ignored. They are using mobile devices like smartphones and laptops to tap into social networks and they are communicating with each other all the time. Look at what working people are doing in every country and every culture and again you will see a huge common activity that cannot be overlooked. They are using smartphones, tablet computers, and PCs to tap into ecommerce networks, and they are transacting business all the time. The four traits of games are rapidly emerging in all of these networks.

Games are coming. Resistance is futile. You will be assimilated.

Games Could Make Work Flow

Great changes are happening in the world, and at a relentless pace. Whether we know what to do or not, changes keep coming and they keep challenging our personal ability and the ability of our companies, governments, and institutions to respond effectively. We need new models for

---

4 McGonigal, *Reality is Broken*, 28. Find out more at her website: *http://janemcgonigal.com/*.

5 Byron Reeves and J. Leighton Read, *Total Engagement: Using Games and Virtual Worlds to Change the Way People Work and Businesses Compete* (Boston: Harvard Business Press, 2009), 13. Watch a video of a virtual interview with Byron Reeves titled "Total Engagement - Gaming the Workplace" at *http://www.metanomics.net/show/total_engagement_-_gaming_the_workplace/*.

6 Ibid., 10. Find out more at their website: *http://www.totalengagement.org/*.

how to organize and carry out work. The industrial model of organizing work as expressed in the linear, sequential process of the assembly line still has its strengths, but it is no longer the all-encompassing solution it once seemed to be. More and more, we are faced with situations that defy effective application of the assembly line model. These are situations that happen without warning and that cannot be broken down into linear sequences of discrete tasks. And because they are not linear sequences of tasks, it is hard for centralized groups of managers to exert control in the traditional top-down hierarchical manner that most companies still use.

Traditional boundaries between work and the rest of life are blurring, and have been for a while now. Often, it is work that's invading every other part of our lives. So how do we balance this out? Maybe we let play and games become part of work. It might just make work a lot more fun and productive. If we're spending so much time on work anyway, why not give it a try?

There is a growing body of research and real-world experience that shows games to be a fertile source of ideas for how to address the kind of unpredictable and complex situations that challenge us now. The answers we seek may well be right before our eyes in the form of games and their online manifestations currently known as video games. Video games are literally a rapidly evolving and field-tested body of best practices for attracting and engaging people in complex activities involving both competition and collaboration.

In this book, we'll explore the practices and potentials of games and discuss how the merging of games with business operations will affect you, your company, and your career. This book provides a framework to understand, discuss, and participate in what is happening as games blend with business.

We'll start our exploration of games and their potential by painting a big-picture view of what games are and how they can act as a model for organizing work. The point of this is to establish a broad framework and a deep foundation for a wide-ranging discussion of how games can be used to transform work. The purpose is to present a set of concepts, principles, and examples that you can use to spark your own thinking about how work can be revamped and reenergized through the application of game mechanics.

Many of the concepts for using gaming techniques and technologies in business are illustrated by case studies that come from my own experience and from the experiences of other business executives, entrepreneurs and game designers who are actively researching and applying game mechanics to solve business problems. The intent of these case studies is to provide practical examples of applying game mechanics to solve real problems in business. Hopefully, they will be models for you to follow as you address similar situations in your own company.

Game designers strive to create games that address what Jane McGonigal describes as the four essential human cravings.[7] Those cravings are satisfying work, the experience or hope of success, social connection, and meaningful work defined as a chance to be part of something larger than ourselves. When situations provide us with opportunities to respond to these essential cravings, we can feel how they call forth in us the desire and drive that energizes us and enables us to tackle big challenges. This is what makes work fun. This is what takes business to a new level.

Many people feel their jobs are not fair, and they do not connect with them precisely because their jobs lack the four defining traits of a game. Their jobs lack a clear goal, the rules are hard to understand and change all the time, they do not get useful feedback in a timely manner, and they have little control over what jobs they perform, so voluntary or enthusiastic participation is often hard to come by.

Yet, game-like operating models (operating models that incorporate the four game traits) are being used by a small but growing number of companies, and this enables them to succeed in spite of tough economic times and larger, more entrenched competitors. These companies are creating a way of doing business that gets everyone involved and creates companies of entrepreneurs who are deeply committed to accomplishing company goals. These companies have operating models that leverage the four game traits. They appeal to the cravings people have for satisfying work, to be successful, to have social connections, and to find meaning in being part of something larger.

At the same time a growing body of experience is demonstrating the effectiveness of this game-like operating model, there is a parallel development taking place in technology that further strengthens and accelerates the merging of games and business. Early research indicates this technology can be applied to amplify the inherent strengths of game-like business models. This technology is composed of social media, cloud computing, software as a service (SaaS), and mobile consumer IT devices such as

---

7   Ibid., 49.

smartphones, tablet computers, and ebook readers.[8] We'll call this new wave of technology "social technology."

The opportunity for companies today is to find ways to merge game-like operating models with the power of social technology. Those organizations that figure this out will benefit from a new level of productivity and responsiveness to change that is needed for success in today's economy. At the beginning of the last century, there occurred a great merging of business operating models with technology. Companies learned to combine business operations with assembly line technology to maximize their efficiency. The resulting productivity was the foundation for the rise of the consumer economy in which we live today. Something of equal or even greater impact is happening now.

Capitalism as Shared Opportunity

Two companies that have been applying game-like operating models for more than 20 years are well documented. One is an American company named Springfield ReManufacturing and the other is a Brazilian company named Semco. The CEOs of both companies have written books that explain how they operate: Jack Stack, the CEO of Springfield ReManufacturing, wrote *The Great Game of Business*,[9] and Ricardo Semler, CEO of Semco, wrote *Maverick: The Success Story Behind the World's Most Unusual Workplace*.[10]

These two companies and other companies experimenting with game-like operating models share some key characteristics. These characteristics align closely with the four defining traits of a game. I would summarize them as:

---

8 For this book, we'll define cloud computing as the ability to deliver computing power and software applications over the Internet as a metered, pay-as-you-go utility service. I explore the impact of cloud computing in my book *Business in the Cloud: What Every Business Needs to Know about Cloud Computing* (Hoboken: John Wiley & Sons, 2010). The book page is on my website at *http://michaelhugos.com/business-in-the-cloud/*.

9 Jack Stack, *The Great Game of Business* (New York: Currency/Doubleday, 1992). The Springfield ReManufacturing website is *http://srcreman.com/*. It describes their products and business model. They offer training in their "open book" business model through seminars on *The Great Game of Business* (*http://greatgame.com/*).

10 Ricardo Semler, *Maverick: The Success Story Behind the World's Most Unusual Workplace* (New York: Grand Central Publishing, 1995). The Semco company website offers insights into their business model that they call "The Semco Way" (*http://www.semco.com.br/en/content.asp?content=3*).

Goals
> All employees participate in setting company goals and have a personal and financial stake in accomplishing those goals.

Rules
> Employees understand the rules that govern company operations; they understand what is fair and what is not fair, and how to score points.

Feedback system
> Everybody learns to read financial statements and they know how their company is doing and how they as individuals are doing; they see the results of their actions in real time or near real time.

Voluntary participation
> People get the training they need to do their jobs well, and they can move into other jobs in the company that interest them as they develop the skills and demonstrate the competence needed for those jobs.

Business practices and the game of capitalism itself—as it has been handed down to us from the last century—are mostly about money-motivated behavior that recognizes no other higher good beyond profits. This was once a clear and simple goal to use for guiding behavior, but it is now causing excessive concentration of wealth, environmental destruction, structural unemployment, and alienation of large numbers of people in companies and society generally. The economic game as we have known it for the last hundred years needs to evolve into something more inclusive and appropriate for our present circumstances.

Capitalism needs to evolve just as another great game that is central to our way of life has also evolved. That other great game is democracy. Imagine what our lives would be like if democracy was still practiced as it was a hundred years ago. At that time in the United States, only men had the right to vote. And a hundred years prior that, democracy was a game where the vote was even further restricted—it was often available only to property-owning white men. Democracy had to become more inclusive in order to remain relevant to our evolving circumstances, and capitalism too must evolve to remain relevant.

Game-Like Operating Models Drive Growth and Profits

Mike Chakos is a Chicago-based serial entrepreneur[11] in a tough line of business—industrial services. His present company provides protective coatings (paint and fireproofing) and related maintenance services to the industrial market.[12] His educational degrees include a B.A. in accounting and an M.B.A. in finance, and he is a certified public accountant. He is in his fifties and has owned and managed various businesses in the industrial services market. These experiences have led him to a business model and philosophy that has been extremely successful. He calls it "human-based capitalism."

Mike has led management teams that have successfully started up or turned around five companies over the last two decades. These companies all grew to become more profitable than their industry peers. And Mike has defined a set of operating principles that he applies to achieve these results. They cover the way people are motivated to engage with each other and participate in the business, and they cover the way his companies are organized. What strikes me is how closely Mike's operating principles align with the four traits of a game. In particular, let's take a look at one of the techniques Mike uses to get people's enthusiastic engagement in doing what it takes to make the business successful.

As Mike explains it, his main idea has been to build an organization that teaches employees the attributes of a successful company and rewards them with the success they generate. He wants to unlock the potential of the people who work for him and get them focused on making things happen. He believes that being in business is just too hard when all the responsibility is on one person or just a few people. But when you get a whole company involved, then things happen. Mike likes to say, "You can stop one guy, but you can't stop a hundred guys when they're all focused on getting something done."

He describes his philosophy of business as follows: "We share the opportunity with qualified people to do the job they like to do; have fun working; be part of something bigger than themselves; earn as much money

---

11 We are also related by marriage—Mike Chakos is my wife's brother. The link for his LinkedIn profile is *http://www.linkedin.com/pub/michael-chakos/38/1b2/455*.

12 North American Coatings, LLC (*http://www.nacoatings.com/Home.aspx*) is headquartered in a suburb of Chicago and has regional offices in five locations around the United States.

as they are capable of earning; and live the entrepreneurial experience." Does this sound like the elements of a game are being employed to guide and motivate people? He creates companies that directly appeal to the four essential human cravings and that also incorporate the four game traits into the way they operate.

Mike gets enthusiastic participation from the people who work in his companies because he shares the opportunity to be a successful entrepreneur with a larger group than is the norm in most companies today. He has separated equity ownership from earning potential. People who are not equity owners still have the potential to earn as much or more annual income than equity owners.

This is possible because of the bonus programs and the transparency he uses to keep people informed of company performance and their bonus payouts. Over his years of experience, he has evolved a basic company bonus plan that pays out a percentage of pretax earnings every year to people in the bonus pool. This pool consists of nonequity owners in the company and includes people from regional VPs, project managers, and superintendents to crew foremen and office support staff.

Mike feels it is best that new workers in the field are not initially in the bonus pool. He feels that they should earn their way into the bonus pool as they demonstrate they have developed the needed skills. Yet even for people not in the bonus pool, Mike's company keeps field workers engaged through the opportunity of year-round employment and by offering paid overtime work where many of their competitors offer only seasonal employment and little overtime.

The company accrues and pays out the entire bonus pool every year. It's set each year at somewhere between 20 to 25 percent of pretax income. Mike does this not to be good or generous, but because it gets the results he wants.

The bonus plan has evolved to promote team success as opposed to individual success. Mike has found that the bonus plan works best when everybody has a single common set of performance objectives and everybody shares in the group's success. This creates an environment of sharing and helping, as well as a good dose of peer group pressure that keeps people focused on doing their best.

Employees in the bonus pool are paid a base salary at the low end of acceptable—just as if they were starting their own businesses. In Mike's current company, over the last several years, people have been earning annual bonuses averaging more than 50 percent of their base salaries during these tough economic times. This bonus plan is backed up with a full set of financial statements that are made available to every bonus pool member every month.

This bonus program is the vehicle Mike uses to set up and perpetuate a feedback system that engages company employees. It keeps them focused month after month and year after year on operating the company efficiently and doing what they need to do to achieve company performance and sales objectives.

People are taught to read monthly financial statements so they can assess for themselves how they are doing, how their team and other teams are doing, and how the company as a whole is doing. This use of transparency and clear rules has created a game-like effect that makes the company's operating model quite successful. Without this financial transparency, there would be no trust and no commitment.

Mike's present company, North American Coatings, is an example of the results that his operating principles and bonus program produces. Founded in 2004, in its first four years the company grew to $34 million in annual sales and over 200 employees. In the next three years, the company's revenue grew to over $45 million (which is a 15 percent compound annual growth rate) during the most difficult years since the Great Depression. And they have generated consistent operating profits that are 2 to 6 percent higher than the industry averages for their lines of work.

Because Mike's experience comes from mid-sized companies working in mature industries and competitive markets, they provide an example that is relevant to many other companies in the United States and around the world. Their results from applying game-like operating principles are an indication of what other companies can achieve by adopting similar operating principles.

In the chapters that follow, we'll explore the techniques and technologies that make games work and discuss how they can be applied to business to create effective game-like operating models—models that enable companies to be both competitive and profitable in the great game of business.

Perhaps the best place to start is with feedback systems. Games have much to teach companies about the design and the effective use of feedback systems.

2

Feedback in the Real-Time Economy (Why Games Matter)

WELCOME TO THE REAL-TIME world. It's a place where cause and effect follow each other so quickly that everything seems to be speeding up. We work longer and harder every day just to keep up with the pace of activity. This real-time world is a place where, in many cases, it is no longer easy or effective to organize work using the linear, sequential, centrally controlled model of the assembly line. A new organizational model is needed.

The quickening pace of activity in individual companies and in the whole world economy is happening because of the feedback loops generated by the two billion (soon to be four billion and more) of us all over the world who are sharing information and opinions via social media accessed through consumer IT devices such as smartphones, netbooks, and tablet computers. This fast feedback real-time world sometimes makes people yearn for a return to simpler slower times, but the genie is out of the bottle, and there's no going back.[1]

The way forward is all about harnessing the power of feedback loops. The economy of the industrial world was based on the assembly line, a strict linear process that put everything in its place and maximized efficiency. The economy of the real-time world is driven by the feedback loop, a flexible circular process that maximizes responsiveness to continuous change. And powerful examples for how to harness feedback loops come from video games. Video games are examples of how to integrate technology, process, and people into operating models that generate the feedback needed to thrive in our real-time economy.

---

1   This opening section was first published as a post titled "Feedback in the Real-Time Economy (Why Games Matter)" on my blog called *Doing Business in Real Time* at CIO.com on January 3, 2012, at *http://blogs.cio.com/blog/doing-business-in-real-time*.

A game is an engagement engine—it attracts and engages players. You can measure the success of a game by the number of players it attracts and the level of engagement it gets from its players. Games are specifically designed to attract and engage people through the application of the four traits introduced in Chapter 1: goals, rules, feedback systems, and voluntary participation. Looking at these four traits you could say that the combination of the first three traits is what creates the fourth trait.

The goals of a game are what the game is about; they are what attract people. Rules define how players go about achieving the goals; they are the challenge of the game. And feedback systems are the user interfaces that engage the players. They present a continuous flow of information that shows people how they are doing and whether they are getting closer to or further from accomplishing the goals. The right combination of these three traits is what induces voluntary participation.

Maybe the best definition of a business these days is to say that it too is an engagement engine—it attracts and engages customers and employees. Perhaps a company in the real-time economy should no longer operate like an assembly line focused on efficiency. Perhaps it should operate instead in a more game-like manner—more like a feedback system guided by goals and rules focused on generating voluntary participation as measured by repeat customers and dedicated employees. This is illustrated in Figure 2-1.

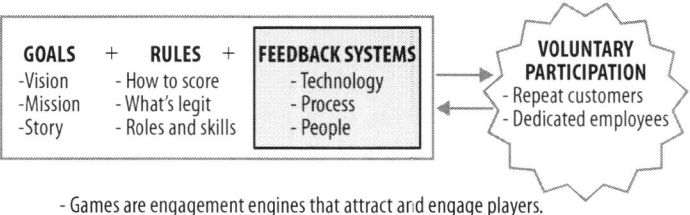

GOALS	+	RULES	+	FEEDBACK SYSTEMS	VOLUNTARY PARTICIPATION
-Vision		- How to score		- Technology	- Repeat customers
-Mission		- What's legit		- Process	- Dedicated employees
-Story		- Roles and skills		- People	

- Games are engagement engines that attract and engage players.
- *Companies are engagement engines that attract and engage target audiences.*
- Both are feedback systems guided by goals and rules.

Figure 2-1. Games generate continuous feedback

The driving force for success in the real-time economy is a continuous response to change so as to maintain the voluntary participation of customers and employees. Businesses that fail to do this go the way of once great companies whose names were household words but who have since faded away.[2] Such companies were once very efficient at what they did, but as the economy shifted from industrial to real time, they lost the participation of their customers and employees. Their goals, rules, and feedback systems failed to interest and engage people. And their senior managers attempted to address this problem by applying industrial measures to increase efficiency such as cutting headcount, selling off business units, and squeezing suppliers. This mostly just alienated people and accelerated the loss of the voluntary participation they so desperately needed.

Feedback Systems Are the New Highest Calling of Information Technology

In the industrial economy, the purpose of technology was to increase efficiency and productivity, and information technology was applied with that end in mind. Many companies still view IT as primarily a tool to increase efficiency (and those that persist in this point of view are headed the way of other once great companies that could not change with the times). It is not possible to cost cut and downsize your way to success in the real-time economy. Companies have to find ways to maintain or increase voluntary participation of their customers and employees or they will simply fade away like a melting block of ice.

The explosive growth of social media and business networks from Facebook to Foursquare, LinkedIn, and Google is fueled by their increasing use of traits and techniques borrowed from video games. An increasing number of companies are using techniques from video games such as leaderboards, progress bars, and badges as feedback mechanisms to engage people and induce higher levels of participation. This trend is known as "gamification" (see Chapter 5 for more on gamification) and this is only the start of the inevitable merging of games and business.

Games offer organizing and motivating models that are far more powerful than just points and badges. The opportunity exists for substantial

---

[2] Some recent examples of such companies are Kodak, Motorola, and Sears. These companies once dominated their respective markets and were part of people's daily lives. Kodak struggled to remain relevant in the digital photography world and ultimately declared bankruptcy after selling off its film business and failing to make money selling PC printers and supplies. At the turn of this century, Motorola practically owned the global mobile phone market but has now sold off what remained of its mobile phone business to Google and retreated into smaller, more predictable markets. Sears is becoming a shadow of its former self as it continues to close stores and shed employees in response to declining sales and customer interest.

and deliberate application of game traits and mechanics to business operations, and the driving force for this opportunity is the development of more and more sophisticated and engaging feedback systems. Engaging business feedback systems can combine company in-house systems with social media and cloud computing-based applications and leverage mobile consumer IT devices like smartphones and tablet computers for their user interfaces. They can be built on top of and communicate with existing transaction processing systems that companies already have—systems such as ERP, CRM, Supply Chain, and HR/Payroll.

Real-time business intelligence systems and analytics can be added to provide data transparency and reporting. Simulation and "what if" modeling can be added to support training and decision making. And real-time communication systems using text, audio, and video can support a whole new level of collaboration and problem solving between companies, customers, and employees. These technologies already exist.

As companies strive to find their way in this confusing real-time economy, the good news is this: video games provide a rapidly increasing body of field-tested best practices for using technology to create feedback systems to attract and engage huge numbers of people. So instead of hiring more financial analysts and management consultants to cut costs, maybe companies would get better results by hiring some good game designers to reach out to customers and business partners and increase participation.

Game Mechanics Applied to Business

Let's do a thought experiment that will illustrate how the creation of a feedback system can trigger the start of a game to accomplish an important business goal. We'll also look at how the goal and rules of the game can be used to guide the conduct of the players and achieve the business results that companies want. This experiment will provide ideas and techniques you can work with and apply to similar situations in your own company.

Imagine you are the chief information officer (CIO) who is suddenly, as often happens these days, confronted with a situation that calls for a creative response. Depending on how you respond, it could result in a big growth opportunity for your company. In the middle of the summer just as things seem to be slowing down, a very important customer summons you and other senior people at your company to a meeting at their headquarters. The VP of Sales, the Account Sales Director, and you all fly out to meet with them.

Imagine this company accounts for a scary large chunk of your annual revenue. Your company delivers a wide range of products and services to thousands of stores operated by this customer. They have been a demanding customer, but they have a right to be. Now it sounds like they want your company to do something that just doesn't seem possible. And they are giving you only 90 days notice to get it done. Time to send in the A Team because failure, as they say, is not an option.[3]

When you arrive at their headquarters, you and the others sign in at the front desk and clip security badges onto your blazers. You don't say much as you wait for the meeting to start. Someone comes out and leads you back through a maze of hallways and work areas, and up a wide staircase to a meeting room where a collection of people from the customer's purchasing and store operations groups are waiting for you.

The new purchasing manager in charge of inventory for their annual holiday promotions has just joined the company. His name is Hank and he clearly intends to make a name for himself with his new employer. He informs you that in previous years there was typically about five percent excess inventory amounting to more than half a million dollars left over at the end of the holiday season in the form of supplies and other special print items that had the holiday theme for that year printed on them. They can't use that inventory again the following year because each year always has a different holiday theme. So they donate excess inventory to charity and write it off. Hank tells you this year he intends to cut excess inventory by at least 50 percent. And he wants to know how you are going to help him make that happen.

OK, think quick (you're the analytic on the team). The VP of Sales buys you a bit of time by launching into a long-winded answer full of appeasing words like "absolutely" and "highest priority" and "our full commitment." But nothing comes, your heart is racing and your head is empty; nobody has any ideas. "We'll get back to you on this," says the sales director in charge of the account at your company.

On the flight back home, you sit next to the sales director and discuss the situation. During the holiday season, your customer always stops using the regular supplies you deliver to them, and they switch to using supplies printed with the theme of that year's holiday season. That is the

---

3 Your company has learned that a team composed of both analytics and sales types can deliver awesome results if they learn how to play together and get creative. This is similar to the way mission teams in online games (World of Warcraft for example) are composed - they are always a mix of people with the right blend of skills called for to succeed on the mission.

start of a high anxiety time of year for your company. Your customer depends on the holiday themed products as part of their public image. Your company moves the supplies from your regional warehouses to the cutsomer's stores, and those stores use a lot of supplies, so you have to make deliveries every two or three days to every store. If any of your warehouses run out of holiday supplies and have to deliver regular supplies to the stores instead, that gets you into big trouble. Nobody wants that to happen.

In years past, there has been a group of inventory planners at the customer's headquarters who monitored their sales data and watched inventory levels in their regions and stores around the country. They would also monitor our store deliveries and try to track holiday inventory on hand in our regional warehouses. As the season progressed, they made decisions about when to move holiday inventory from one region to another and communicated with a person at your headquarters who then sent instructions out to your regional warehouses.

There are problems with this process. The customer's systems track inventory differently than your systems, so the numbers often don't agree. Another problem is that you can't see your customer's store sales data or the holiday promotions planned by different regions, so you have no way to anticipate when inventory shortages might occur in one region or see when excess inventory is building up in another.

Communication is mostly just one-way, top-down communications from the customer to you and from your headquarters out to your business operating units. As a season gets underway, it always happens that actual use of holiday inventory is different than what was planned for, and there are increasingly heated phone calls and emails from the customer to you and from headquarters to your business units. The customer sends sudden instructions to move inventory from one region to another, and in order to meet short deadlines, you use air freight instead of rail or trucks. Every time you air freight inventory, you loose money, which leads to people saying unkind things and feeling increasingly cranky—and it is reciprocated by the customer. Whew.

Everyone feels this is an information problem and figures a new computer system is needed to solve the problem. And since you are the CIO, it is therefore a good idea for you to do something. You check with the customer's IT group and their analysis of the situation leads to estimates that they need about a million dollars and about a year to build the required system. You have nowhere near that kind of money and only 90 days. So you decide to take a different approach—*You make it into a game.*

Multiplayer Online Game about Supply Chain Management

As defined in Chapter 1, the four traits of a game are a goal, rules, feedback systems, and voluntary participation. You know the goal of this game—move holiday supplies around the country as efficiently as possible so no stores run out of holiday supplies, and also prevent excess inventory from building up that will have to be written off at the end of the season. You already know the rules of this game; they were spelled out in the service contract you have with the customer. You can't order anybody to participate; all you can do is show people a process for working together and what the benefits might be. People can decide to do something else (like more of the traditional hollering and hand-waving) if they don't like what you show them.

The cause of the problem in the past was not just a lack of information. It was the lack of a good feedback system (timely information made available to everyone). Because of that lack, people who did have information spent a lot of time telling people who didn't have information what to do. And since there were only a few who had information and a lot who did not, those few who had information spent a lot of time telling everybody else what to do. They often didn't have enough time to do other things like better analyze the data and update their plans as things changed. In other words, the feedback loops were really slow and didn't work well. And because the situation you were trying to manage changed quickly, nobody could keep up with the pace of change. Nobody had fun.

The trick for you is to show people something that can be put in place within 90 days (and won't cost too much to build) and will give people hope of meeting the goal set by the customer. If you do this, then people will probably buy into the idea. This is clearly a multiplayer game, so you need everybody to buy in—not just your company, but also the customer and the different manufacturers of all the holiday supplies.

Since better feedback systems are what you need to make this game come alive, your main focus for designing this game is to figure out how to quickly let people in different companies around the country all see continuously updated end-to-end supply chain data. Because you are the distribution company, you are the guys in the middle who can see what both the customer and the manufacturers are doing, so your systems have the most complete and timely information. You make the pitch that the numbers in your system are the best approximation of reality.

After some discussion, everybody agrees to use your numbers as the single best version of the truth.

Then you arrange for the manufacturers to send you their inventory data via electronic data interchange (EDI) or a simple text file transfer process (FTP). Your business operating units can send in data the same way and so can the customer when it is necessary to update inventory data that your system didn't have.

Inventory data gets extracted from your system and loaded into a central database, and your programmers write some programs to pull data from that database and populate a spreadsheet. On the spreadsheet, there are tabs for each manufacturer, for each of your business units, and for each of the customer regions. Each manufacturer's tab shows item inventory amounts on hand and on order from your company at each of their facilities. Each of your business unit tabs shows amounts on hand, amounts delivered to stores, and amounts on order from the customer stores they serve. Each regional tab for the customer shows the stores in the region and inventory amounts on hand and on order. You write some macros in the spreadsheet to do simple demand forecasting and produce line graphs and bar charts. It's simple but functional.

When people from the manufacturers or the customer or your business units go to your website and log in, their PCs are set to automatically open up a copy of this spreadsheet in their browsers. They can then save and analyze the spreadsheet locally if they want or just view it online. The data is updated every night, so everybody gets an accurate daily view of the whole supply chain that moves inventory from the factories through your distribution centers out to the customer's stores.

You have this system in place quickly. The resulting transparency creates a much more responsive feedback system than what was previously used. You begin doing conference calls every few days to review status and make decisions. When you want to tweak the forecasting algorithms, it is easy to change a few macros in the spreadsheet, and everybody can see the new projections. Very quickly, the tone of communications on the calls goes from demanding and defensive to collaborative and creative.

Maybe you won't call this system a game because you don't want people to get hung up on all the misconceptions that the word "game" stirs up in a business context. You call it the Inventory Visibility System or IVS for short (but a game by any other name is still a game).

The IVS System provides people with the widespread, relatively real-time transparency needed to set up an effective feedback loop to guide their actions. When everybody in all the different companies involved in the supply chain can see what is happening day by day, you can all figure out what to do without waiting to be told by a small group of experts. You can collaborate, reach consensus, and take action.

As shown in Figure 2-1 at the start of this chapter, the feedback system you have created is guided by the goal of this game (keep stores supplied and prevent buildup of excess inventory) and you accomplish this goal within the rules defined by your service contracts. This game generates enthusiastic participation from players at the different companies and your performance gets better and better. Work (almost) becomes fun.

At the end of the holiday season, your customer is pleased. By their own calculations, excess holiday inventory is reduced by more than 50 percent and the process is so effective they want to use your system year-round to coordinate distribution of products beyond just the holiday items. The effect of this little game you have put in motion is starting to grow beyond the initial reason you put it in place. That's good. It means people are enthusiastically participating and thinking up new ideas and uses that this can be put to.

The traditional response to the kind of challenge that is presented in this thought experiment is to do what the IT department at the customer figured they would have to do - spend a million dollars and a year analyzing, designing and developing and installing complex and costly systems and technology. By choosing to take a different approach you are able to successfully rise to the immediate challenge, and you also set in motion a chain of events that can open up further opportunities with your customer and other customers who have similar needs.

There are three game mechanics at play in this situation. The IVS system provides the near real-time data transparency mechanism which is the spark that brings the game to life. The second mechanism is the distributed authority to act that was then possible for all the players. Without transparency that would not have been possible. The third mechanism was that everybody has a stake in the outcome; a reason to care and a reason to keep learning and improving their performance over time.

It turns out that when everybody can see the numbers and look at the forecasts, people can quickly reach consensus about what has to be done and people can see problems developing much earlier than before. When there are lots of different people looking at the data, you don't need complicated systems to spot trends. And because people see trends and problems earlier, your company can move inventory by train or truck instead of air freight and hold down costs. People can also prevent stock-outs of supplies and buildup of excess inventory because the data transparency provided by the IVS System enables everyone to better collaborate and coordinate our operations.

As events unfold over the next couple of years, the initial system you created can be enhanced with new features to provide more and better feedback to help people improve their skills and achieve better and better results. Dashboards of key performance indicator (KPI) score-cards can monitor real-time transactions and display performance as measured by standard supply chain indicators such as those illustrated in Figure 2-2.

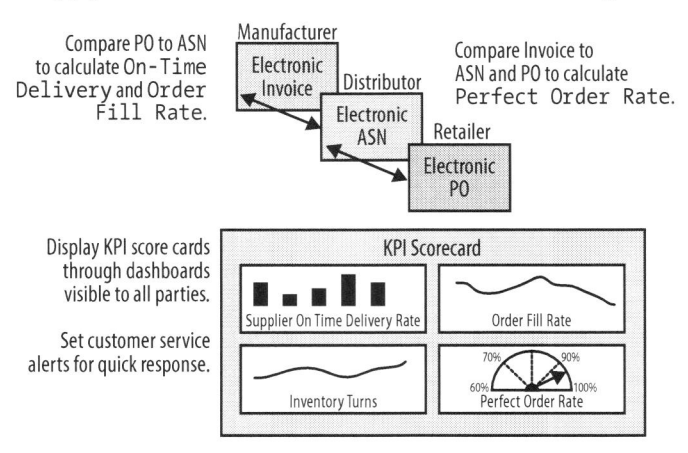

Figure 2-2. Performance visible to all

This is what agility is all about. Put the first version of an application system in place quickly using components you have readily available. Don't overdesign your application. There is a saying that describes this approach, "Think big; start small; and deliver quickly." As you do so, keep in mind the three game mechanics and keep thinking about how you can encourage and enhance their operations to meet situations that arise. One good idea will lead to another

FEEDBACK IN THE REAL-TIME ECONOMY (WHY GAMES MATTER)

As you reflect on the results of the recent holiday season, you realize that the applications and the game mechanics they support now enable your company to play a very competitive game of supply chain management in fast-paced and unpredictable environments. That is a capability that your company can use to stand out in a crowd and go after other companies that need the same kind of service. The training your people get and the skills they develop from using the IVS Systems (playing the game of supply chain management) makes your company an attractive business partner for other customers - and you won't always have to be the lowest price bidder to win new business.

This is how to grow your company and make money.

3

Feedback Systems Drive Business Agility

A GAME IS A powerful way to produce the collaborative problem-solving behavior needed to handle a challenge like the case study described in Chapter 2. Situations where collaboration and coordination between different people or organizations is needed can benefit from the introduction of a well-designed game. Such a game can produce results that exceed anything that can be achieved from using traditional top-down command and control methods where a few people at the top of an organization try to tell everyone else what to do.

In many business settings, the first two traits of a game (a goal and rules) already exist, so the next thing to do to bring a game into being is to create an effective feedback system. There are three necessary mechanisms for creating effective business feedback systems: (1) real-time transpar-ency of relevant data; (2) authority to act delegated to each player; and (3) a stake in the outcome for all players. This is illustrated in Figure 3-1.

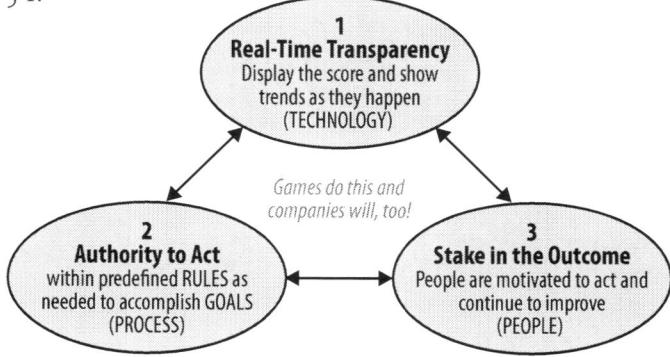

1 Real-Time Transparency
Display the score and show trends as they happen
(TECHNOLOGY)

Games do this and companies will, too!

2 Authority to Act
within predefined RULES as needed to accomplish GOALS
(PROCESS)

3 Stake in the Outcome
People are motivated to act and continue to improve
(PEOPLE)

Engaging feedback systems emerge when these three conditions are present.

Figure 3-1. Feedback systems create participation

When people are given real-time or near real-time data that provides adequate insight into the area of their concern, then everybody is able to see for themselves what is happening and they can self-organize and respond quickly without having to wait around to be told what to do. In many situations, when only a small group of managers or supervisors know what is going on, there isn't enough time available to do all the needed thinking. So the orders these people give to everybody else often produce results that are less than desired. It's better to let everybody share in the thinking by letting everyone see the data.

If people have local authority to act on what they see, then they don't have to ask permission and wait to get confirmation before they act. They can act quickly, and because they act in a timely manner, their actions are likely to produce the results people desire. Organize people into autonomous operating units and give them authority to act as long as their actions fall within predefined ranges (as defined by the goal and rules of the game).

When people have a stake in the outcome their actions produce, they are motivated to act and are motivated to learn from their actions and keep getting better. This stake in the outcome can and should be a variety of elements from increased prestige and reputation to more interesting work and money rewards as well. People are motivated by various combinations of these elements depending on the situation.

These three conditions can be introduced readily enough when senior managers wish to do so, and when that happens, a feedback system will come into being—just as fire happens when you introduce fuel, oxygen, and a spark. Once called into being, a feedback system, like fire, is a powerful creation. The trick is then to guide it toward useful ends.

Guide feedback systems by providing them with goals that they will try to accomplish. And guide them by providing rules that define what they can and can't do. If the goal is clear enough and the rules are coherent enough, they will be accepted and influence the behavior of people in the feedback system. People will continuously steer the feedback system toward accomplishing its goal and they will use behavior that is allowed by the rules. Now you have harnessed a most powerful form of organizational energy.

Creating and harnessing feedback systems to perform useful activities is perhaps the most powerful way of organizing work since the introduction of the assembly line. Feedback systems and the games they bring to life are constantly adjusting their behavior to respond effectively as situations change. As companies get good at applying feedback systems to the way they operate, they will see the results show up in the form of consistently outperforming their more traditionally run competitors who are not as quick and responsive.

The easiest way to provide goals and rules to guide internal company behaviors is to use bonus programs. Everyone understands the concept of a bonus program. Start by defining a goal that is clear enough and which people believe they can accomplish if they work hard and smart. Then lay out whatever rules and guidelines you think are needed. Keep the rules simple and clear. Try not to overregulate; too many rules will cripple the operation of the feedback system.

Start with a simple bonus plan, and then over time, fine-tune and modify the plan as you learn from experience. The challenge we have to overcome with bonus plans is that they already have a long and hallowed tradition of being fuzzy creations where well-meaning companies try to do good things, but get off on the wrong foot and never recover (and then can't understand why their plans fail to motivate people or motivate them to do the wrong things).

When creating their bonus plans, companies need to consider more than just monetary rewards. Daniel Pink, in his book *Drive*,[1] defines what he calls the three elements of motivation. The first element is autonomy—our desire to be self-directed. The second element is mastery—our desire to make progress and get better at what we do. And the last element is purpose—our desire to be part of something larger than ourselves.

These elements of motivation are quite similar to the four essential human cravings that Jane McGonigal defined (satisfying work, hope of success, social connection, and meaning through being part of something larger). So companies need to remember to create work that speaks to Pink's three elements of motivation and McGonigal's four cravings.

If a company does not use its bonus plan to clearly lay out what employees are supposed to accomplish on a yearly or quarterly basis or give them reasons to care whether they accomplish those things, then they have missed the best reason for having a bonus plan. The bonus plan is the best place to define company goals and get people's buy-in and enthusiastic

---

[1] Daniel Pink, *Drive: The Surprising Truth About What Motivates Us* (New York: Riverhead Books, 2009), 10. Watch a video of a short talk he gave titled "The Surprising Science of Motivation" at *http://www.ted.com/talks/dan_pink_on_motivation.html*.

commitment to accomplish those goals. This is how to start up and guide the great game you want your company to play.

Let's take a look at the tactics and techniques related to creating effective bonus plans. To do this, we'll review two bonus plans and see where one fails and where the other succeeds. The first plan is representative of traditional bonus plans that many companies have in place. Traditional bonus plans don't work. They typically ignore any motivators beyond the use of money to reward and punish certain behaviors or outcomes. And they often pit individuals within the same company against each other by specifying conflicting individual performance goals.

The second bonus plan is one used by Mike Chakos, who over the years has learned ways to motivate and guide people to play the great game of business in the companies he has started and managed. This plan is simple. There are no individual bonus objectives, only company-wide bonus objectives. The plan pulls people together and focuses them on a few important objectives that are central to company success.

Traditional Bonus Plans Fail to Provide Clear Goals and Rules

There is a hallowed tradition in business where toward the end of each year, senior managers convene for planning meetings, and VPs and directors discuss possible goals for the coming year, and objectives or performance targets that might need to be achieved if those goals were to be accomposhed. Ideas are discussed, but often no consensus is reached.

The new year starts and time goes by. At some point senior managers recieve their bonus plans which are meant to incentivise them and focus their actions. Often these are individual bonus plans that inevitably pit different executives and their groups against other groups in the company. For instance the sales people are often assigned challenging revenue objectives but inevitably other departments whose support is needed to make the sales effort successful are given objectives for big cuts in the amount of money they spend to support sales or anything else. Often people have no say in setting these objectives, and often don't know what they are until some time into the year. And often annual bonus payouts wind up being a predictable percentage of base salaries regardless of what happens from one year to the next. So people just don't pay that much attention.

This behavior can seem puzzeling to those who spent so much time crafting and writing up and distribuiting those bonus plans. Often CEOs and their finance staff spend considerable time creating these plans and the formulas and criteria they devise for measuring the achievement of various bonus objectives reflect much though and hard work. The problem though, is that all the thought and hard work was done by a small group of people without much input from the people who are then expected to operate under these plans. Also the fact that these plans are indeed complex and hard to understand make them even less interesting. People are busy these days and the world is complex enough already. There is often not much time available in people's schedules to read through complex bonus plans and understand what they mean or what they might require to accomplish them. And each person is on their own to follow their own plans. Even if doing so leads them into conflict with other managers in the company that they have to work with on a daily basis.

CEOs and finance people can become frustrated by the lack of attention paid to these type of traditional bonus plans. Other company managers are just smiling and nodding and trying to get on about their jobs as best they can.

A common problem with such plans is that they lack credibility because, after all is said and done, bonus payout amounts are still governed by calculations and other factors that nobody except a few really understand or are privy to. Company goals are often fuzzy and objectives are hard to actually pin down. Time spent contemplating such bonus plans is not productive. It only creates confusion and irritation. How can people take plans like this seriously?

Due to standard company privacy policies and other requirements many company do not provide clear feedback on progress toward bonus objectives. People don't get regular reports on their progress, or on company operating results from one week to the next. When the information is available it is often in the form of quarterly reports that are deliberately vague or complex and require much effort to decypher and understand. So people just don't pay that much attention.

Attempting to play a game like this where the rules and the scoring process is so hard to understand is like the scene out of *Alice in Wonderland* in which Alice is trying to play croquet with the Queen of Hearts but the croquet mallets are flamingoes that keep flying away and the Queen keeps changing her mind about what the rules are and then punishing players for breaking the rules.

People are always glad to get whatever bonus payouts they eventually get, but there is no buy-in from them. They had no meaningful say in setting their bonus objectives or in tracking their progress or calculating their bonus amounts. These kind of bonus plans do not lay out clear measures or stir up much enthusiasm. People are not committed; they are just along for the ride.

And this is the kind of bonus plan that passes for normal at lots of companies. What a missed opportunity. Such plans fail to define coherent goals, they fail to define consistent rules to play by, and they do not generate enthusiastic participation. And, because there is no regular feedback and not enough data transparency, the feedback systems that are created are not very effective and do not provide the guidance needed. The game people play at many companies is (as so well described in movies and popular TV sitcoms) frustrating.

Effective Bonus Plans Create Trust and Participation in the Game

One reason Mike Chakos has been so successful in starting and growing his newest company during the tough business climate of the last several years is that the company bonus plan aligns with and reinforces their game-like operating model. Their bonus plan lays out a clear business goal and provides a set of rules everyone can understand. And people are given the financial and operating data they need to track for themselves how they are doing (effective feedback systems). People can see what they need to do and take action without waiting to be told what to do.

The bonus plan at North American Coatings is focused on the overall performance of the company and the regional operating units. There are no individual objectives, so people are not caught in conflicts between their personal bonus objectives and the good of the company overall.

The basic model of the bonus plan over the years has been that 25 percent of pretax earnings are set aside to fund the bonus pool. Monthly financial reports provide transparency so people can see the dollar amount that is accumulating in the bonus pool. People know the bonus pool will then be divided up between regions and teams based on the amount of profit that they delivered during the year.

When I look at Mike's company, I see a company that from the start had the three conditions needed to bring about effective feedback systems: (1) data transparency; (2) a local authority to act; and (3) employees with a stake in the outcome.

They created and then harnessed the power of self-adjusting feedback systems to succeed at the game of business as defined in the bonus plan. This is the essence of their operating model. Because it is a game-like operating model, it gets buy-in and active participation from everyone. That is how the company can consistently outperform competitors.

They outperform their competitors because when everyone knows how to make money and everyone knows what the score is, then people can self-organize and respond quickly as events unfold and unexpected things happen. People do not have to wait around to be told what to do. A coherent goal, clear rules, and good feedback systems motivate people to act every day, every week, every month to save money here and make money there—and it all adds up. This is how companies generate that higher gross profit margin I call the "agility dividend."

The bonus plan is clear and short. It has evolved over the last several years so that everybody participating in the plan can quickly understand it. The plan focuses on a handful of most important things that need to get done and shows people how they will share in the company's success.

Everybody participating in the bonus plan gets monthly financial reports that allow them to track the numbers for their offices, regions, and for the whole company. There are no surprises as to company profitability and the total bonus amount. And people get simple weekly reports showing them their operating performance on their jobs. They can track number of hours planned for a job versus number of hours actually spent to date; they can track cost of materials planned versus actual costs to date. People know where they stand and know what they need to do to be successful.

There are some subjective decisions made by senior management as to the final allocation of the total bonus amount. But the decisions are made in public for reasons that everyone can debate and, as CEO Mike Chakos explains, "the discussions that ensue improve the health of our company immeasurably."

Although individual bonus amounts are different, everyone can see the total bonus amount paid for each region and they know what part of that they received, and they can decide for themselves if they are being treated fairly based on their contributions and duties in the company. This is what creates the trust and commitment that motivates and focuses everyone in the company to achieve their goals.

The bonus plan aligns people with company goals and gets everyone pulling hard in the same direction. That is what drives the consistently high operating performance of the company and its above market profitability (their agility dividend of 2 to 6 percent) even in these tough times.

"These people are achieving not only for the company, but also for themselves. They no longer feel like they are being left out or without the opportunity to achieve great things." Mike reports that the 75 percent of income (after bonuses) remaining with the owners is more than 100 percent of the income that owners of other companies without this program are experiencing.

Game Dynamics Promote Business Agility

When companies organize the way they work so that the three conditions necessary for real-time feedback systems are present (data transparency, local authority to act, and stake in the outcome), they attract talented people because those are conditions that talented people like. They are conditions that most people like to work under.

These three conditions get the voluntary participation of talented people and enable feedback systems to emerge. Effective bonus plans provide goals and rules to guide these feedback systems. And when this happens, the four traits of a game are present. Now, an organization has the potential to put game mechanics to use and excel at the great game of business. Figure 3-2 shows how companies can implement the four game traits and the effect that they will have on peoples' behavior.

GAME TRAITS	BUSINESS IMPLEMENTATION METHODS	EFFECT ON PEOPLE'S BEHAVIOR
GOALS	- Bonus Plan - Business Plan	Focused on Goal
RULES	- Bonus Plan - Service Contract	Guided by Rules
FEEDBACK SYSTEMS	- Data Transparency - Local Authority - Stake in Outcome	Highly Responsive
VOLUNTARY PARTICIPATION	- Data Transparency - Local Authority - Stake in Outcome	Deeply Committed

} BUSINESS AGILITY

Figure 3-2. Using games for business agility

The result for the company when its people demonstrate the behaviors shown in Figure 3-2 is that it benefits from the company-wide, real-time coordination that happens. Employees are engaged moment to moment in company operations and they can act autonomously (within predefined rules) to achieve company goals. And because people have a stake in the outcome of their actions, they are motivated to act and motivated to keep getting better. This is what leads to that much talked about capability known as "business agility."

The benefit for a company of achieving business agility is the ability to consistently earn slightly higher gross profit margins than other companies in its industry. A company is able to earn these higher margins because it is able to make a hundred small adjustments as conditions change. These continuous and timely adjustments result in earning a bit more money here and saving a bit more money there, and it all adds up much like the effect of compound interest over time. Agility also allows a company to pounce on great opportunities that may come along every now and then, and earn a lot of money in the process. That is how an agile company earns the agility dividend.

The agility dividend is gross profits that are consistently 2 to 4 percent (and sometimes more) above relevant industry averages. The ability to earn the agility dividend is the financial reason to go through the effort of becoming agile. Earning the agility dividend is what tells you if your company is doing well at playing its great game of business.

There is a strong correlation between learning to play a game well and learning to be agile. We know good athletes are agile; they have to be agile in order to compete and win in contests with other athletes. The same holds true for companies. The following case study explores how game mechanics can promote business agility.

A Multiplayer Online Game of Agile Supply Chain Management

Let's investigate a high-level conceptual design for applying game mechanics to coordinate the actions of a network of separate companies that all do business together. These companies are manufacturers, logistics providers, distributors, and retailers, and they are all members of a common supply chain.

We'll start by imagining a company called Fantastic Corporation. They make a fantastic home entertainment system. It's got wide-screen HDTV with surround sound, broadband Internet connection, and a built in high-performance PC with enhanced graphics capabilities. There are modular plug-ins for other devices such as DVD players, video cameras, even turntables to play vinyl records. It's a great piece of gear for a great price and everybody wants one. Sales have been ramping up nicely.

Their product and its success has also attracted the attention of competitors. If Fantastic can't keep up with customer demand, then competitors will certainly step in with similar products to meet demand. So the game right now for Fantastic is to coordinate with its supply chain of suppliers and retailers to increase production to meet demand at existing stores and introduce the product into new stores to expand market share.

The consumer electronics industry is one where product life cycles are measured in months (not years) and where prices and demand forecasts fluctuate from week to week. Nobody wants to get locked into long-term contracts because of the risks involved with this market uncertainty. Most products use similar combinations of electrical components so component manufacturers can sell their output to whichever product company shows the greatest demand and best prices. Nobody anywhere in the supply chain from manufacturers to distributors and retailers wants to get stuck with excess inventory because the short product life cycles cause excess inventory to rapidly lose its value. This means close cooperation between all parties in the supply chain to accurately forecast demand and make and move products effectively to meet demand (this is a more complex form of the holiday supplies case study described in the previous chapter).

Fantastic needs voluntary participation and enthusiastic cooperation from the players in its supply chain if it is going to increase its sales and expand market share. If Fantastic can bring these manufacturers, distributors, and retailers into a collaborative game, then it has a chance to move a lot of product and make a lot of money. And that chance is what the other players are looking for as well. So the challenge for Fantastic is to show its supply chain partners that they can all make good money if they all work together.

The folks at Fantastic organize an event to kick off their campaign. People attend online or in person at Fantastic's corporate office. As the meeting starts, everyone logs on to the Internet and accesses a collaboration system called SCM Globe.[2] It provides a map of the world that is projected on the large screen at the front of the conference room for those

---

2 The SCM Globe system (*http://scmglobe.com/*) is a supply chain design and simulation application. At present, SCM Globe is used in university courses and supply chain training programs as a learning tool for people to design and simulate the operation of different supply chain configurations. As further functionality is added, it will be available for companies to use as a supply chain collaboration platform to work with supply chain partners and monitor and manage actual supply chain operations. I am the lead designer and producer of this game-like application.

present at Fantastic, and people online see this on their screens. All participants can follow along and talk to each other using voice, video, and chat links. The map starts out showing the global reach of the Fantastic supply chain. The facilities of all the companies and routes between them are shown. By clicking on facilities, people can see relevant information; by clicking on routes, it shows the vehicles that travel on those routes and other relevant information. Figure 3-3 shows a global view of Fantastic's supply chain.

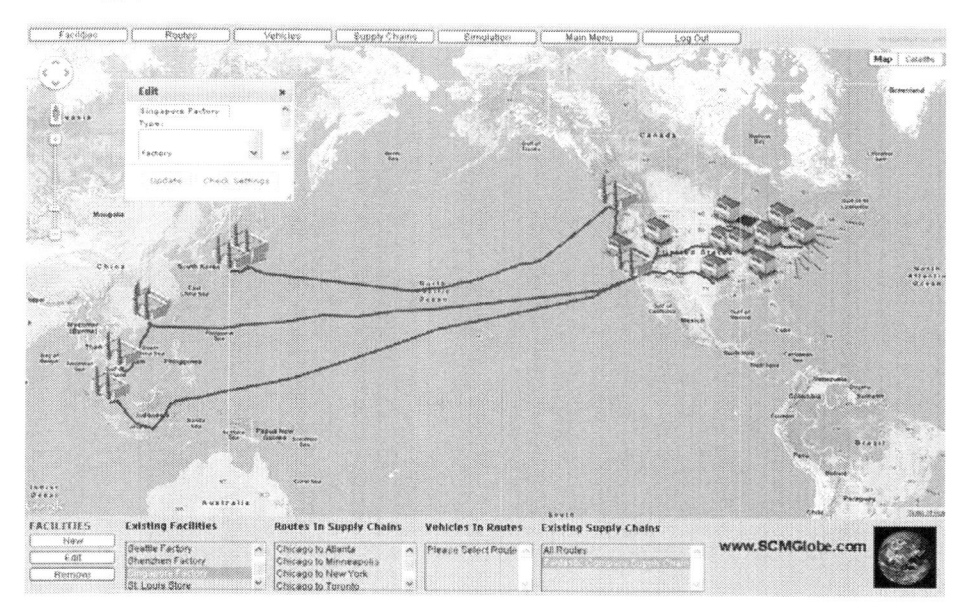

Figure 3-3. Global view of the Fantastic Corporation supply chain

Participants at the Fantastic office sit in comfortable chairs and have tablet computers or laptops that show a smaller version of the same display on the big screen. Changes people make on their displays at Fantastic or online elsewhere are seen by everyone. People use touch-screen controls to call up information and draw in new facilities or routes. By tapping on countries or cities, they can access specific market data. The map displays current sales by product category and sales trend lines over the last several months or years can also be shown with a further tap of the finger.

As the session gets under way, all participants are able to communicate with each other via phone or text messages, and they can direct their communications to other individual participants, to the whole group, or to a subgroup. There is a master of ceremonies from Fantastic who is acting as the leader, but that mostly means facilitating a free flow of ideas and keeping people focused on tasks at hand.

People from three of the manufacturers draw in additional factories their companies are building that could deliver components for the Fantastic home entertainment product. Then a guy from the logistics company that supports stores on the East Coast adds in a new distribution center they are opening up and shows on the map how they could support additional store deliveries of the Fantastic product (this is illustrated in Figure 3-4). Then some retailers said they were opening additional stores and if they started stocking the Fantastic product, their demand forecasts would go up and they entered higher demand numbers at a bunch of their stores. As the meeting progresses, the visibility and interaction makes it possible to get a good consensus on amounts of product that can be sold and the amounts of component parts and distribution services needed to support this sales growth.

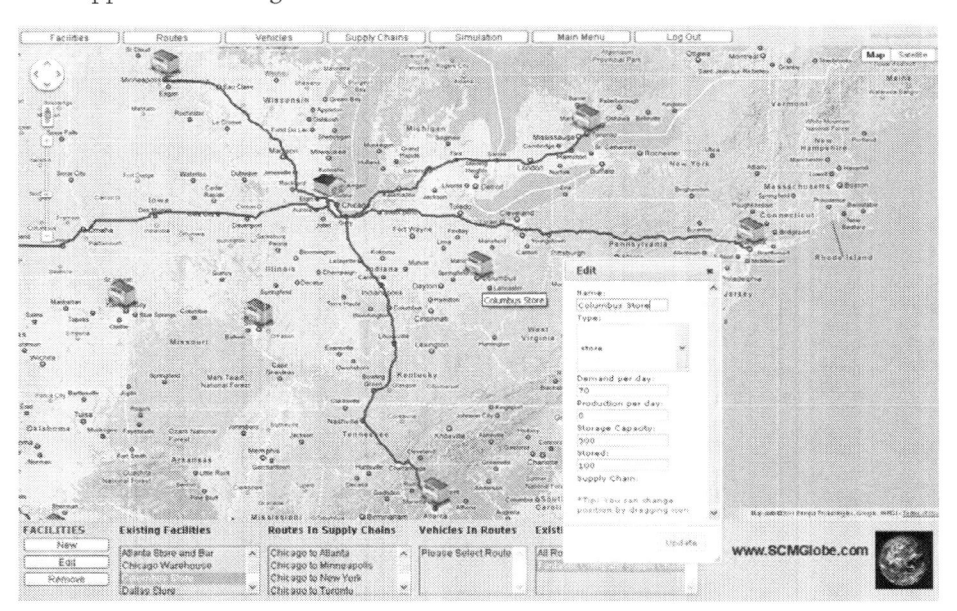

Figure 3-4. New distribution center supports additional stores

Then people run simulations on the supply chain configuration they have designed to see if it can handle the volumes required to meet sales forecasts. The system runs the simulation before everyone's eyes and shows where problems will crop up. Figure 3-5 shows results from one of the simulation runs. It shows the inventory delivered to each of the stores and then shows a red circle over the New York store indicating that this store has run out of inventory by the end of the second day.

People respond as these problems crop up in the simulation and make changes to the design and rerun the simulation. After several iterations and some spirited discussions, a supply chain configuration is arrived at that delivers needed performance levels at an operating cost that is acceptable.

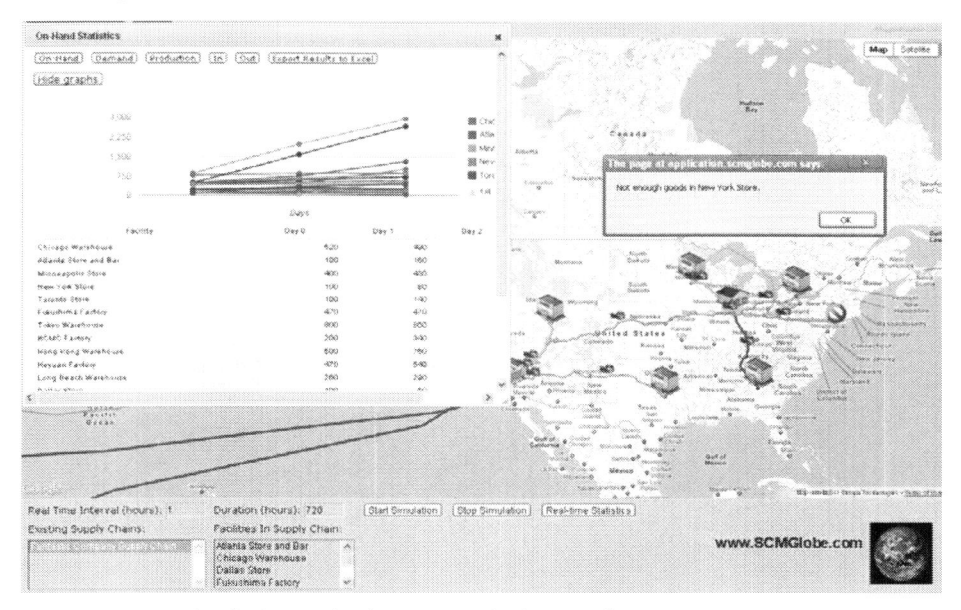

Figure 3-5. Simulation results showing supply chain performance

This session harnessed a notion from gaming called "crowd sourcing" to arrive at the supply chain design. Fantastic Company invited its supply chain partners to an open exchange of ideas and simulations to test the goodness of forecasts and designs. The group arrived at a good solution and that solution also has the active support of the relevant parties. So it is likely to be successful.

Everyone participated in setting the goals that need to be met, and the roles and rules for each company are set forth in their contracts with Fantastic. People at each company feel good about what they accomplished and each party in this multiparty online game sees how they can make money and even have some fun doing so. As people go back to their offices, they are all committed to accomplishing the goals that were agreed on. This is business—all people want to make a profit, and they understand how much money their companies can make if they accomplish their goals.

This conference lasted for a day; two sessions of two hours each with a break in the middle of the day for lunch and individual conversations. Substantive work was done, and everyone was expected to be following along and contributing. During the conference, the feedback people got from the simulations and from interacting with each other drew them in and focused their attention on the challenge at hand. It brought out their collective creativity and they worked out good solutions for a range of complex issues. They experienced that state of mind that gamers call "flow." We all know what flow is; it's what happens when you lose your self-consciousness and time gets distorted and you are engrossed in an experience that provides pleasure and satisfaction in its own right. Good work is produced when flow happens.

Everything people need to continue working together is there online in the collaboration system, and information will be updated in real time or near real time as people start carrying out the activities they agreed to. This collaboration system is an upgraded version of the IVS System presented in Chapter 2. And it is not just for planning; it will be used every day (as the IVS System was) by all parties in the supply chain to monitor operations and resolve issues as they arise.

This event would never be confused with that bane of corporate existence known as a meeting. This event was what gamers would call a massively multiplayer online role-playing game (MMORPG or MMO). MMOs are a type of game that closely resembles business activities such as those described here. In the next chapter, we'll go into more detail on MMOs and other kind of games relevant to business operations.

Games and gamers have pushed the technology to do things like what is described here as a regular matter of course. Players in MMOs do everything described here and a lot more. Because of games and gamers, the technology has arrived. It does what we need and it does it in real time and at a price point that is affordable. This kind of technology used to be the exclusive domain of big governments and wealthy corporations, but not any more.

What will happen when we take game technology and its close cousin, social technology, and apply these technologies to the way we do business? What new things will it allow us to do and what things will we have to do differently to get the full benefits of using this technology?

4

New Paradigms and Operating Principles

WE CAN FEEL THE pace of change in business accelerating. It's being driven by the convergence of a handful of key factors. The first of that handful of key factors is demanding economic times. A demanding economy speeds up change because it increases the urgency to find new ways of operating. People often change only when they have to, and demanding times make change mandatory.

Combined with tough times, there is a wave of rapidly evolving new technology in the form of mobile consumer IT devices like smartphones and tablet computers that is spreading throughout the world. Hand in hand with the spread of consumer IT is the growing use of social media such as Facebook, Twitter, and YouTube. And underpinning the spread of consumer IT and social media is the rise of cloud computing. Cloud computing makes social media and consumer IT possible by delivering computing power and data storage and retrieval to billions of people almost anywhere in the world through high-speed wireless connections to the Internet. As mentioned earlier, we'll refer to this combination of consumer IT, social media, and cloud computing as social technology.

Demanding times and the spread of social technology are pushing companies to change how they organize and carry out work. And as companies apply this new technology, we are learning more and more about the operating models that make the best use of its strengths.

Consider what happened in the early decades of the last century when companies combined the technology of the assembly line with the industrial model of doing work. This combination produced the sustained increase in economic productivity that gave birth to the consumer economy we have today.

The industrial model of organizing work is a model where activities are broken down into repeatable sequences of tasks and then those sequences are carefully organized and repeated over and over, hour after hour, day after day. This model of work was well supported by the industrial technology of the assembly line. So the combination of these two produced the explosion of productivity that ushered in the mass consumer economy that first took hold in the West and then spread around the world during the twentieth century.

Now, social technology can be applied to amplify the four game traits in companies that start using a game-like operating model. This amplification of the four game traits produced by social technology will in turn further engage people (customers, employees, and partners) and further enhance and strengthen company operating results. Companies that figure out how to apply social technology effectively to empower game-like operating models will see an increase in their productivity and profits that sets the pace for others in their industries to follow.

Social technology at present is used mostly in people's personal lives, so there is a tendency for companies to feel that it either has no place in business or that it is trivial or mostly a distraction to be paid lip service to. Those who feel this way should also consider that when the assembly line was first introduced into manufacturing companies at the turn of the last century, there were many who did not understand the potential of the assembly line and rejected that technology as not being relevant or important to their businesses' operating models.

At present, companies use social media like Facebook, Twitter, and YouTube mostly to deliver advertising messages, but that misses their real potential. The real potential is to combine social media with relevant in-house systems like order entry, customer service, purchasing, and business intelligence. When that happens, real-time two-way connections are created between companies and their wider value chains—the business ecosystems in which they operate. Companies are suddenly able to sense and respond to a range of feedback that enables them to coevolve with their markets and their customers.

NEW PARADIGMS AND OPERATING PRINCIPLES | 39

Let's look at a hypothetical example of how a company could combine social media with their in-house systems to enable a game-like operating model for communicating with and responding to customers and business partners. Begin the example by imagining that a wholesale distributor called Super-Duper Company invites the companies (not the individual people) it does business with to friend it on Facebook. Its supplier and customer companies use their Facebook accounts to friend Super-Duper and then they all use Facebook to create a multimedia real-time collaboration platform. It would cost almost nothing to set this up and operate it.

All of the people in all these companies can now communicate with each other and share text, pictures, and video to plan and coordinate new sales campaigns, educate customers on new products, or handle any number of customer service activities. Figure 4-1 shows how Super-Duper Company can use a social media platform like Facebook to create its own business-to-business network and real-time feedback system.

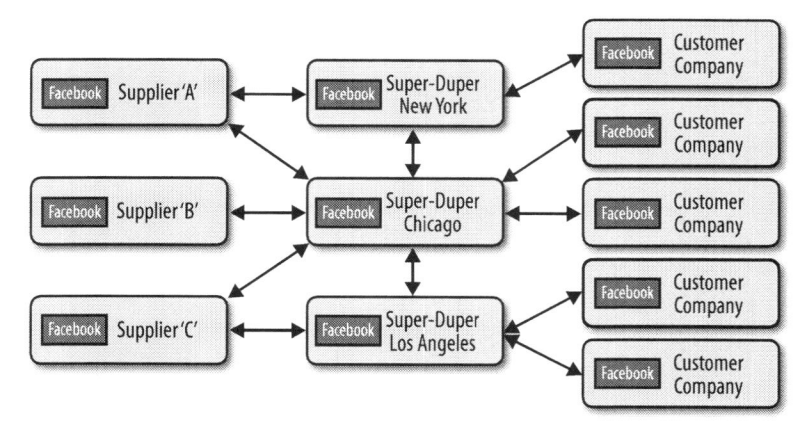

Use social media for *business friends* (not personal friends) to create business collaboration networks

Figure 4-1. Business to business (B2B) social media networks

Once the Super-Duper Company has created a business network like that shown in Figure 4-1, then the next step is to connect selected social media platforms with relevant internal systems in the company. This is illustrated in Figure 4-2.

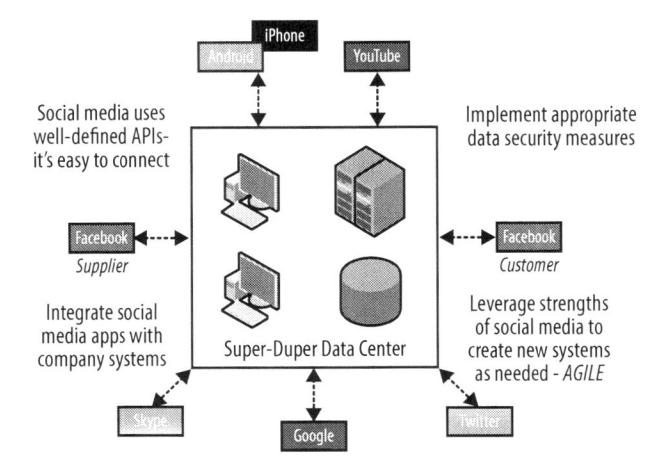

Figure 4-2. Social business connections

If all these people were engaging with each other in the context of a game-like model of operations, if these people were not just chatting with each other to while away the time, but if in fact they were enthusiastically engaged with each other to collaborate on a daily basis to accomplish specific goals that were important to them and their companies, then this use of social technology is clearly a big part of how the new game of business will be played and how success will be achieved.[1]

This social business network offers big benefits. People already know the user interface for these social media platforms, so the learning curve is not steep. And the new systems will run on all sorts of mobile devices like iPhone, Android, and iPad, and will stay current as new devices come out because the social media vendors (Facebook, Skype, Twitter, etc.) do that job for us. Social media has well-defined application program interfaces (APIs), so it is a straightforward task to connect them to relevant in-house systems and to company websites. And because the data sent to and received from these social media applications is well defined, companies can apply appropriate security screening to the data as it moves back and forth.

Use of social technology in this way is how your company can connect with the broader social technology web that has spread around the globe in

---

1 Two companies that already offer social business software similar to this are Jive and Yammer. Jive (*http://www.jivesoftware.com/*) describes itself as "the world's #1 social business platform." Yammer (*https://www.yammer.com/*) describes itself as "a private social business network for your company."

the last decade. Now your company can become a player in this emerging MMO that is the new incarnation of the great game of business in this century. It's already happening as you read these words.

If your company implements the four game traits (a goal, rules, a feedback system, and voluntary participation) in its operating model, and if you and others in your company use these game traits to self-organize and focus on accomplishing goals, then the application of social technology as described can unleash a surge of energy and coordination.

Research being done by McKinsey and Company on the application of social technology to company operations indicates that the effective use of social technology will make your company more agile and responsive to changing situations, enabling your company to earn the agility dividend of an extra 2 to 4 percent gross profit (and sometimes more) above the market averages in your line of business.[2]

Games, Gamers, and New Business Strategies

In 2009, the *National Gamers Survey* reported[3] that 83 percent of the US population played video games during the year, and that includes 72 percent of men and women over the age of 50. According to the Entertainment Software Association, from data collected in 2011, the average gamer age is 37.[4] About 40 percent of gamers are women; 25 percent of gamers are over 50; the average gamer has been playing for 12 years; and most gamers expect to keep playing for the rest of their lives.[5]

Currently, the National Gamers Survey reports that for populations aged 10 to 65 worldwide who have Internet access, Germany has the highest proportion of active gamers, where 66 percent of the population are active players. Next is Mexico with 57 percent, Russia with 53 percent, the United Kingdom with 52 percent, Brazil with 47 percent, and the United

---

2 Jacques Bughin, Angela Hung Byers, and Michael Chui, "How Social Technologies Are Extending the Organization," *McKinsey Quarterly* (November, 2011). On page 5 is a reference to "self-reported operating-margin improvements, correlated positively with the reported percentage of employees whose use of social technologies was integrated into their day-to-day work." Here is a link to this report (*http://www.mckinseyquarterly.com/How_social_technologies_are_extending_the_organization_2888*).

3 Download a PDF of the 2009 United States National Gamers Survey at *http://www.tnsglobal.com/_assets/files/Factsheets_US.pdf*.

4 Entertainment Software Association, "Game Player Data," *http://www.theesa.com/facts/gameplayer.asp*.

5 Jane McGonigal, *Reality is Broken: Why Games Make Us Better and How They Can Change the World* (New York: The Penguin Press, 2011), 48.

States with 42 percent. China now has more gamers than the United States, but because their population is so large, the percentage of gamers is still relatively small.

People on social networks like Facebook spend a lot of time playing games such as "FarmVille" and "Words With Friends." Yes, these games are trivial. But they are just the start. Games respond to our essential cravings, and skillful combinations of the four traits of a game enable us to create powerful engagement engines. Thousands, millions, even billions of people can participate. Games, as they evolve, will be the medium that enables us to learn and keep learning at a scale, level, and depth of popular participation that we have never seen before.

All new media are subject to the same criticisms when they first appear, and that new media we presently call "video games" is going through this traditional criticism. New media are always said to encourage time wasting and laziness. It seems incredible now, but when print media and the mass circulation of books began in Europe in the mid-1400s, that too was criticized for these same reasons. It was said to make people lazy because they no longer had to memorize long lists of facts and complicated historical narratives. They could just write them down and read them instead.

On reflecting on the insights they gained from their research, the authors of *Total Engagement* had this to say regarding the future of work: "We are more confident that games will change work than we are that they'll change work for the better."[6] Games are a set of practices backed by a set of technologies.[7] They can be used for good or evil because we humans are capable of doing both.

We stand just at the beginning of a development that is rapidly becoming one of the central themes of our real-time, networked, planetary culture and economy.

---

6 Byron Reeves and J. Leighton Read, *Total Engagement: Using Games and Virtual Worlds to Change the Way People Work and Businesses Compete* (Boston: Harvard Business Press, 2009), 6.

7 Kevin Hoffman (*http://www.linkedin.com/in/kevinmhoffman*), digital strategist and facilitator in game and user interface design, recommends two books for broadening perspectives on the capabilities of games. The first is *What Videogames Have to Teach Us About Learning and Literacy* by James Paul Gee (Palgrave Macmillian, 2nd Edition, 2007), an excellent informative source on how games teach, but from a much more academic and theoretical perspective. The second one is *Beyond Fun: Serious Games and Media*, Drew Davidson, ed. (Lulu.com, 2010), which is a good collection of chapters from some of the best in the field, but suffers from being piecemeal and uneven in places.

All the World's a Game

The use of game-like operating models is actually not that big of a change for many business operations. A lot of activities within companies already operate much like games. When there is an effective feedback system already in place, there is likely to be a process for doing work that has the four traits of a game.

One of the most important activities in any company is sales and sales operations, which have a lot in common with games because there is usually a feedback system that shows sales targets and tracks peoples' progress toward those targets. Some years ago, I was hired by a company to develop a new sales system to support the company's growth and enable their expansion into new markets.

The application of game techniques to design and develop this new system demonstrates the power of using games to organize work. Game concepts proved useful in understanding the existing sales operations and in designing the new operations and the new system that would support the company's growth.

I started the project by doing what any good game designer would do. I immersed myself in the subject matter. I spent time traveling to different sales offices and talking with company salespeople to develop an understanding of how they did their work. One day, at one of the company's regional headquarters, I was sitting with an inside salesperson talking to him about his job and how he did his work. As we talked, I could see the sales VP for that region watching me from his office.

After about 15 minutes, the sales VP came out of his office and walked up to the cubicle where we sat. He greeted us both, then turned to me and said, "You want to know what it's like to use the systems we have now?" He looked over at the sales guy Steve, and said, "Steve, move over. Let Mike take your calls and see for himself what it's like." I looked up at the vice president and I knew he could see the fear in my eyes. I tried to stammer out some excuse but he wouldn't have any of it. He responded, "Don't worry if you screw things up; that's how you learn. We make mistakes too."

If I was to go any further with this project it was clear I had to take his dare. So I sat down in Steve's chair and started taking incoming calls. They were mostly from building contractors who needed something in a hurry and wanted to know if I had it in stock. My goal was to sell them what I had at the highest profit I could get by figuring out how to add on extra items or services they needed and truly be helpful and make people feel like they got a good deal.

It was sink or swim time. I had to engage callers on the phone and understand what they wanted. Often, they were busy and talked fast. I had to remember how to use the existing sales system to look up products people were asking about and see if it was in stock, and if it wasn't in stock, find something else that would fit their needs. And while this was going on, I was also deciding on the price I would quote based on looking at prices other salespeople had gotten for these items and factoring in variables such as the quantity the customer wanted and whether he would come to pick it up or if we would deliver it.

Sometimes I quoted too high a price and people said they'd get back to me later, and of course they never did. Other times I was intimidated into quoting a price that didn't have much profit in it at all. But I kept getting calls, and I kept getting better at figuring out what they needed and engaging people in conversations that allowed me to add a few more items to their order and suggest other things we could do, like assemble some of the items or arrange for delivery or whatever. And I kept getting better at quoting prices with a good profit margin but not so high that I didn't get the order.

At the end of the day, the system printed out my daily sales activity report, calculated the average profit margin on my sales, and showed the total amount of profit I had brought in that day. I delivered it in person to the vice president. He looked at it for a moment and then looked at me and asked if I now understood what the job was like and what a new sales system could do to make his people more productive. I said I did.

During the day, as I cycled through the activities involved in the job, I began to see them as a game. That gave me a framework to understand the big picture. The goal of the game was to sell as much as possible at as good a profit margin as possible. And to achieve this goal, there were rules that defined skills to develop, resources to use, and actions to take. In this game people got instant feedback from the responses of customers and prospects they were talking to on the phone, and the results of their actions were tracked and reported so other salespeople and managers could see how their performance compared with that of other salespeople.

In this company, each salesperson ran their own desk as if it was their own business, and in many ways it was. As they learned the business, they were able to specialize in certain kinds of customers and products and their total compensation was determined by the amount and profitability of their individual sales. This provided a way to advance in the game that drew people more deeply into the game and was a source of continuous growth in the company's sales.

I also saw this was not a game each player played alone. It was a multiplayer game that changed over time as business conditions changed. When I went to look at product quantities ordered and prices paid by other customers, I could call up almost real-time data based on what salespeople in my office and other offices in the region were doing. This gave me a feel for whether prices were trending up or down and what kinds of customers were buying what kinds of products.

Because the outcomes of my actions were being recorded, I was building up a reputation. The sales manager in my office could see my activity as well as managers in other offices and at headquarters. So after that afternoon, people at other sales offices knew who I was even though I had only been with the company for a short time. People opened up to me. They wanted me to know about ideas they had for this or that new system feature. Often their ideas fit nicely into the emerging design for the new sales support system.

As the project went on, the game analogy helped us all imagine more and more ideas for what the new sales system would be. It enabled two very different groups of people, sales and IT, who often see the world quite differently, to use game concepts and game mechanics to create a common vision that got the needed buy-in and support from a wide group of stakeholders. And we were then able to turn that common vision into a new system that was rolled out around the world and has driven the company's continued growth and profitability ever since. We did this by *making the project into a game*. The game analogy became the common language we all spoke and it was central to our success.

We'll return to the story of how game mechanics were used to design this new sales support system in Chapter 8. But before we do this, it will be useful to explore some key concepts and practices of games and see how they can apply to business.

The understanding we develop in doing this is the foundation for a deeper discussion of how to combine games and business operations.

5

Gamification

You may have heard people use the term "gamification." It is a word that seems slightly awkward, yet is presently in common use. Over time, new terms will probably arise to take its place, but for now, it is the name given to the first widespread application of video game techniques to specific business activities such as advertising, marketing, public relations, sales, and customer service.

Gamification is a practice that stirs up strong pro and con sentiments in the game designer community.[1] Some people point to the fact that gamification practices embody a field tested and proven set of techniques that companies can put to use right away. Others point to the fact that current gamification practices often fail to connect with the full depth and power that games can call forth, and in so doing, they trivialize peoples' perception of games.

Here are some current definitions:

> "Gamification is the use of game design techniques, game thinking and game mechanics to enhance non-game contexts. Typically gamification applies to non-game applications and processes, in order to encourage people to adopt them, or to influence how they are used. Gamification works by making technology more engaging, by encouraging users

---

[1] Gamification taps into the way humans are wired, says James Macanufo (*http://www.amazon.com/James-Macanufo/e/B003UV32BK*), coauthor of the book *Gamestorming* (O'Reilly Media, 2010) and a director in the visual thinking practice at XPLANE. "We are wired to have 'fun' with things, and they steer our behaviors and motivations as individuals and as groups." Yet Macanufo admits some practices of gamification make him "cringe." He feels background works on the nature of play itself are relevant for helping to get perspective and recommends the book *Man, Play and Games* by Roger Caillois (University of Illinois Press, 2001).

to engage in desired behaviors, by showing a path to mastery and autonomy, by helping to solve problems and not being a distraction, and by taking advantage of humans' psychological predisposition to engage in gaming."[2]

"Gamification is the concept of applying game-design thinking to non-game applications to make them more fun and engaging."[3]

"The integration of the mechanics that make games fun and absorbing into non-game platforms and experiences in order to improve engagement and participation."[4]

"Integrating game dynamics into your site, service, community, content or campaign, in order to drive participation."[5]

Why Gamification?

The trend called gamification has come about due to the confluence of trends in technology and demographics. On the technology side, the widespread use of social media such as Facebook and Twitter and the rapidly expanding use of mobile consumer IT devices such as smartphones, netbooks, and tablet computers has created a new avenue to reach and interact with customers that did not exist before. The number of people who can be reached through social media and mobile consumer IT devices is orders of magnitude larger than the people who could be reached through websites and desktop PCs. And the connection with people through social media and mobile devices is continuous because people carry their smartphones with them and they are always on.

On the demographics side, the number of people who play video games is large and is growing quickly as shown in the statistics quoted in Chapter 4. One of the most popular activities that people engage in on social media platforms like Facebook is playing games such as *FarmVille*. A significant portion of today's teenagers and twenty-somethings have grown up playing video games. And now, social games are bringing game

---

[2] Wikipedia, "Gamification," *http://en.wikipedia.org/wiki/Gamification*.

[3] *The Gamification Wiki*, "Gamification," *www.gamification.org*.

[4] Kyle Findlay and Kirsty Alberts, "Gamification: How Effective Is It?" *http://www.slideshare.net/ervler/gamification-how-effective-is-it*, (accessed September 26, 2011). Video.

[5] Bunchball Inc., "Gamification 101: An Introduction to the use of Game Dynamics to Influence Behavior," *http://www.bunchball.com/sites/default/files/downloads/gamification101.pdf*, (accessed 2010).

play to large numbers of people in their 40s and beyond. Because so many people are already familiar with and enjoy playing games, it means conditions are ripe to extend game techniques beyond traditional boundaries and employ them in other activities that people perform online.

Gamification software companies such as BadgeVille, Bunchball, Gamify, and other companies such as Achievers and Igloo Software[6] that apply game elements to business systems are able to provide case studies from their work over the last several years that show companies can reap significant benefits from the use of gamification. They have customers who report that gamification has helped them to increase product awareness, increase sales volumes, grow their base of customers, and increase customer satisfaction with their products and services.

Market research firm Gartner says that more than 70 percent of global 2000 companies will have at least one gamified application by 2014.[7] And market analyst firm M2 Research projects that revenue from gamification-related projects will grow from $100 million in 2011 to $2.8 billion by 2016.[8] They estimate gamification projects will account for 23 percent of social media marketing budgets by 2015.

Concepts and Techniques of Gamification

People in advertising and marketing have traditionally had to use one-way technologies ranging from the printed page to radio, TV, and movies to communicate with people. Now, two-way technologies enabled by social media and mobile consumer IT are available, and the challenge is to make use of these two-way capabilities to better attract and engage prospects and customers. This creates an opportunity to employ what game designers have learned from years of designing video games. Video game techniques can be used to motivate people to take actions and participate more actively in relationships with companies, campaigns, and products.

Gamification can be understood in terms of the four defining traits of a game (goals, rules, feedback systems, and voluntary participation). The

---

6 Websites for these companies are BadgeVille (*http://badgeville.com/*), Bunchball (*http://www.bunchball.com/*), Gamify (*http://gamify.com/*), Achievers (*http://www.achievers.com/*), Igloo Software (*http://www.igloosoftware.com/*).

7 Gartner makes these predictions in a press release titled "Gartner Predicts over 70 Percent of Global 2000 Organizations will have at Least One Gamified Application by 2014" (*http://www.gartner.com/it/page.jsp?id=1844115*), 9 Nov 2011.

8 M2 Research, "Gamification in 2012" (*http://www.m2research.com/gamification-2012.htm*), 2012.

goal is typically to get people interested and engaged with a company product or promotional campaign. The rules are typically designed to reward people the more they participate, as defined by website visits, comments, or purchases of products. Feedback systems are where current gamification applications focus most of their attention.

Through the use of techniques such as points, leaderboards, badges, and levels, gamification creates a feedback system that responds to peoples' actions and encourages them to further actions.[9] When people perform a desired action, they are awarded points or badges. These rewards are designed to encourage more activity. Leaderboards are used to highlight people with the most points and badges and to let them see how they compare with others. This is designed to bring out peoples' competitive instincts and keep them involved. And as people acquire points and badges, they are promoted to higher and higher levels. This is designed to appeal to peoples' desire to gain prestige. This is illustrated in Figure 5-1.

The next four sections are examples of how individual companies have applied gamification to attract new customers and increase their levels of participation. As you read through these examples, refer to Figure 5-1 and see how these companies have addressed the four game traits in their gamification applications.

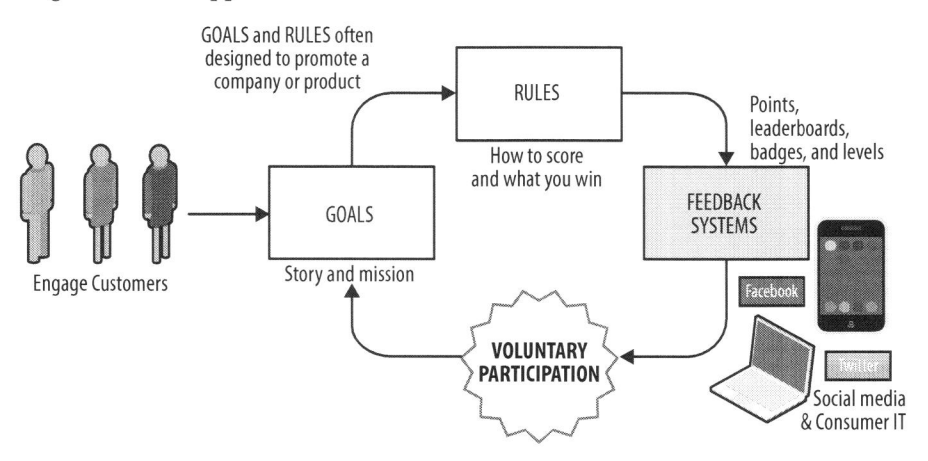

Figure 5-1. Gamification focuses on feedback

---

9 Concepts of points and badges are not unique to video games or gamification. They have been used for hundreds of years by military organizations that award medals for bravery or by the Boy Scouts and Girl Scouts that award merit badges for demonstrating certain skills. People in all of these organizations wear their medals and badges on their uniforms to show others their achievements; they become their own leaderboards in effect. And, of course, people in these organizations get promoted to higher levels as they accumulate points, medals, and badges.

foursquare

In any discussion of gamification, a good example to start with is provided by the social media company foursquare.[10] foursquare was founded in 2009 and has pioneered the application of popular gamification techniques. The company is known for its creative use of badges and how those badges are awarded to people using this application.

Foursquare defines its goal as:

MAKE THE REAL WORLD EASIER TO USE
- Keep up with friends
- Discover what's nearby
- Save money and unlock rewards

The foursquare application runs on mobile consumer IT devices such as smartphones, and the GPS feature in the device tells foursquare the user's location. It enables users to find restaurants, museums, and entertainment events that are in their vicinity. When they enter a query, it displays a map and text that helps people choose what they want to do and where to go to find that activity.

Then, as people arrive at locations that interest them, they check in through foursquare and they get points for doing this. After checking in a certain number of times at certain locations, people are awarded badges that recognize their actions. They are also able to see if there are other foursquare users in that location. When they check in, people can qualify for specials being offered by these locations, such as special prices for meals at restaurants or reduced ticket prices at entertainment events. This is illustrated in Figure 5-2.

---

10 foursquare (*https://foursquare.com/*).

52 | ENTERPRISE GAMES

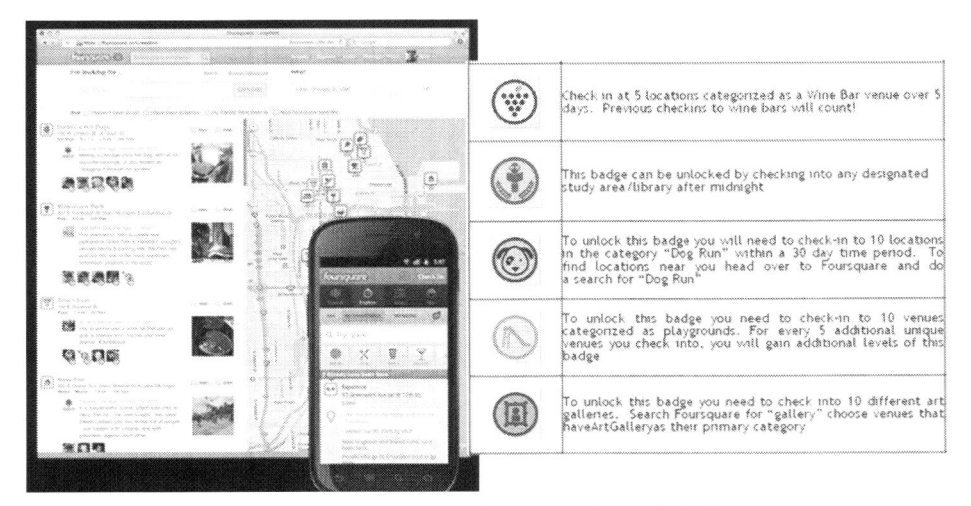

Figure 5-2. foursquare displays locations of interest and awards badges courtesy of foursquare

Playboy

Playboy's goal for their gamification application was to "find new ways to engage users with the Playboy brand and attract a younger demographic." To do this, they created a Facebook application called "Miss Social," which was described as "Playboy's only non-nude model search using social media to find fresh new faces."[11] A screenshot from the application is shown in Figure 5-3.

Any woman who desires to be in Playboy can submit her photos to the application and try to win more votes on any given day than other participants. At the end of each month, the woman who has won the most votes is crowned Miss Social for a month and stands a chance of starring in a pictorial on Playboy.com. The rules also allow contestants to use Facebook to encourage their friends and followers to vote for them.

Playboy reports that this application has helped them to attract the younger male demographic that they had not been able to attract before, and they report that the application has generated a high rate of repeat engagement with this new demographic. They also report that the application has delivered significant monthly increases in revenue. Playboy

---

11 Playboy's Miss Social app on Facebook (*http://www.facebook.com/PlayboyMissSocial*).

partnered with gamification software vendor Bunchball and used their Nitro software platform to create this application.

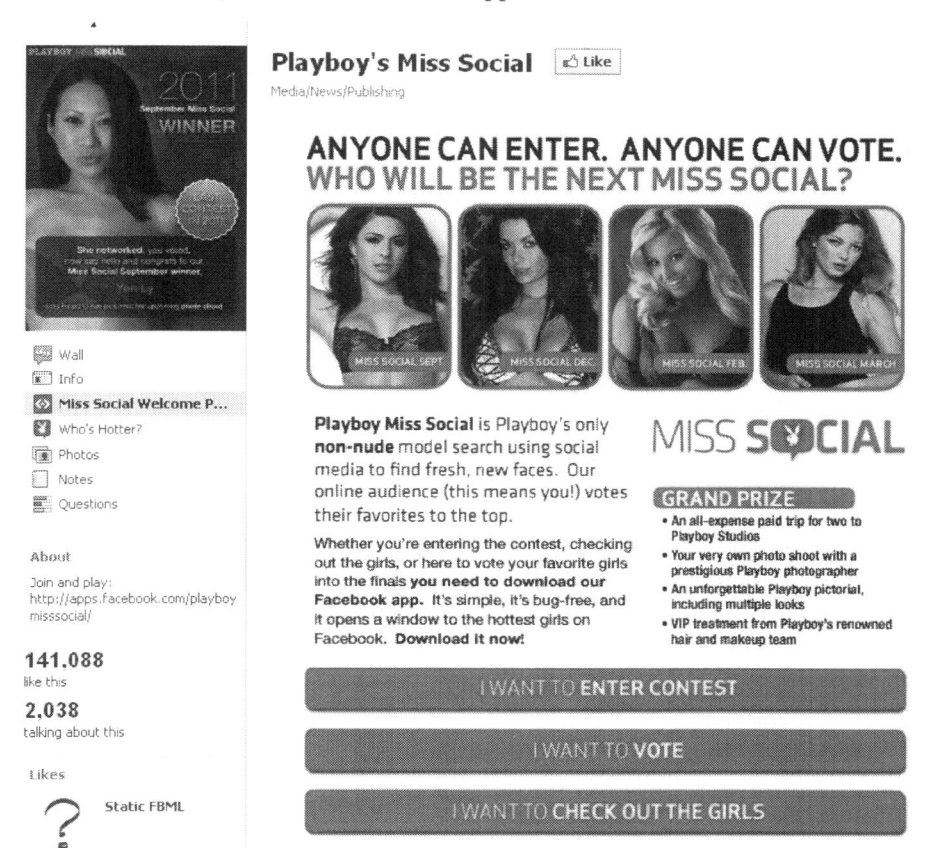

Figure 5-3. Playboy's "Miss Social" gamification application, courtesy of Playboy

Samsung Electronics

Samsung's goal for this project was to recognize and empower the online community of people using Samsung products and motivate them to review their favorite products and spread the word to their friends. To accomplish this goal, Samsung integrated leaderboards, badges, and points throughout its US corporate website.[12]

---

12 Gamified Samsung Nation website (*http://www.samsung.com/us/#latest-home*).

Kris Narayanan, Samsung VP of Digital Marketing explained: "We created Samsung Nation as another way to demonstrate to these enthusiasts that we appreciate their loyalty and interest." The use of gamification is designed to recognize and reward Samsung customers who visit the site often and post comments and reviews of Samsung products. The gamification features are also designed to provide real-time analytics to Samsung staff that show what people are doing on the site, and that enables Samsung staff to respond in the moment with specific rewards and offers to customers. Figure 5-4 shows a portion of the gamification that is built into the home page of Samsung.com. Samsung partnered with gamification software vendor Badgeville and used their Social Fabric platform to provide the gamification features and the real-time analytics.

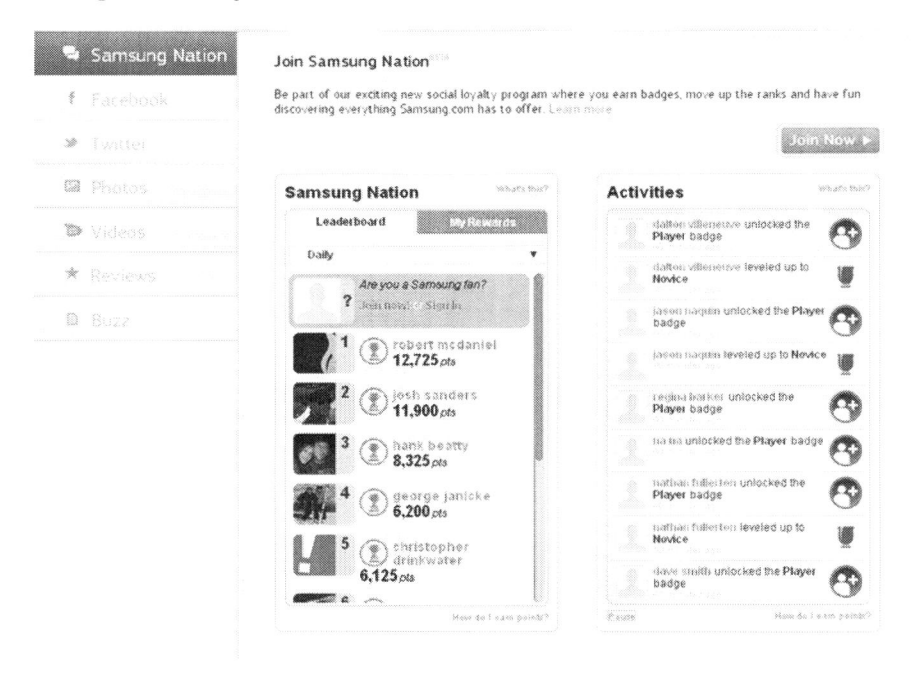

Figure 5-4. Gamification features on Samsung.com, courtesy of Samsung

Salesforce.com

The goal for the gamification of the Salesforce application is to integrate widely used motivational techniques for salespeople into the online environment provided by Salesforce.[13] It allows sales managers to set up sales campaigns and competitions, and it tracks the progress being made by each salesperson and displays this progress to the sales manager and all of the salespeople working under that manager.

A sales manager uses an administrative console to set up their campaigns and to assign points to certain activities and define new levels and rewards that their salespeople can attain when they accumulate enough points. These points, levels, and rewards are then visible to all of the salespeople working under that manager, and it serves as a continuous reminder to keep them focused on the campaign.

The application also provides analytics that track individual salespeople and show their progress and activity. This sets up a feedback system that can be used by the sales manager and the salespeople to assess where they are making good progress and where they need to improve performance or try different approaches. Salesforce.com partnered with gamification software vendor Bunchball and used the Bunchball Nitro platform to create this application. A sample screenshot from this application is shown in Figure 5-5.

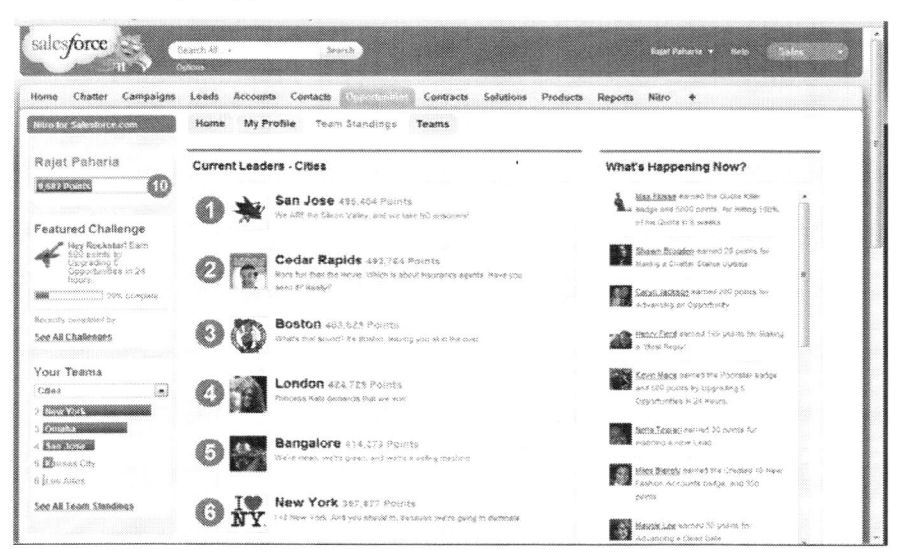

Figure 5-5. Sample of Salesforce gamification application, courtesy of Salesforce

---

13 "Salesforce.com's Chief Scientist on Why Gamification is the Future of Work" (*http://www.readwriteweb.com/enterprise/2011/06/gamification-future-of-work-salesforce-rangswami.php*), 17 June 2011.

Gamification Is a Controversial Practice

Rajat Paharia is CEO of Bunchball, a company founded in 2005, whose original business mission was working with clients to incorporate social gaming dynamics into their websites to increase engagement with their target audiences. As the company evolved, Bunchball started to zero in on a set of services and software that it began describing with the word "gamification" starting in the year 2010.[14] Since then, the word has been adopted in the press and media generally. But the word does not sit well with many game designers and others who have thought deeply about the impact games can have in business and society. They feel the word trivializes and obscures the true potential of games to transform the world and the way people work.

Many game designers see the focus on the use of points, badges, and leaderboards as a distortion of what games are about. They feel these game features have been copied and taken out of context when applied to commercial websites and applications, the main purpose of which is to promote a product or company or to sell merchandise online. They are concerned that the more powerful features of games will be ignored.

Games are an art form, just like movies or novels. Games can tell stories that inspire players to embark on quests to learn new skills and find out more about the story the game tells. To see this art form reduced to telling shallow or manipulative stories aimed at obvious commercial ends is deeply disappointing to people who see a larger calling for games.

Ian Bogost, a prominent game designer and professor at Georgia Tech, published an articulate statement of this disappointment with the word gamification and the practices that it has employed in an article titled "Gamification is Bullshit."[15] He makes the case that the word gamification is being used as a vaguely defined catchphrase designed to hide the ignorance of those who use the word to sell products or services. He expresses the distaste that many gamers and game designers have when they see game techniques employed for obvious commercial ends when he states:

> More specifically, gamification is marketing bullshit, invented by consultants as a means to capture the wild, coveted beast that is videogames

---

14 Rajat Paharia made this statement in a telephone interview with the author on January 17, 2012.

15 Ian Bogost, "Gamification is Bullshit," *http://www.bogost.com/blog/gamification_is_bullshit.shtml*, August 8, 2011.

and to domesticate it for use in the grey, hopeless wasteland of big business, where bullshit already reigns anyway.

He points out that in many cases, gamification is a word and a practice meant to reassure corporate vice presidents and brand managers who are under pressure to meet sales quotas. It tells them that they can increase sales by adding game features such as points, badges, and leaderboards to their websites. It tells them they can reengage existing customers and attract new customers and win their loyalty by doing superficial and repetitive things. Bogost says gamification has become an attempt to create a "Viagra for engagement dysfunction."[16]

He finishes this article with the observation that mediocrity is easy. And because the superficial practices he has labeled as gamification are mediocre, they are attractive to corporate executives with no broader vision. Yet he also points to a more transformative future for games in business. He states that, "those of you who would consider that games can offer something different and greater than an affirmation of existing corporate practices, the business world has another name for you: they call you 'leaders.'"[17]

Beyond Gamification

Companies are starting to employ game mechanics that go beyond just the use of points, badges, and leaderboards to create feedback loops. Simple feedback loops like this can lose their appeal if they are not backed up by more substantial game features. In particular, successful games often communicate stories and missions that the players can identify with and will want to learn more about.

Games can create goals that are more than just getting the highest point score. Games can present situations and challenges and can invite people to explore these situations. The challenges can require players to attain knowledge and skills to respond successfully to those challenges.

Some companies have created games that present situations that relate to their areas of expertise. These games then engage players in

---

16 Ibid.
17 Ian Bogost's article stirred up lively debate and rebuttals. An example of the rebuttals to his article is a blog post by Mario Herger titled "Gamification is Bullshit? The Academic Tea-Party-Blog of Gamification," which can be viewed at *http://enterprise-gamification .com/index.php/en/blog/4-blog/18-gamification-is-bullshit-the-academic-tea-party-blog-of-gamification*.

learning more about the situation and about the products and services the company offers that can be used to address challenges posed by the game. Two examples of this kind of game application are shown in the following sections.

CityOne by IBM

IBM launched a game called *CityOne*,[18] which simulates the workings of a city and allows people to try different actions to address the challenges faced by this city. Players have to address problems and opportunities in four different areas of city operations—power, water, retail, and banking. The trick is to find ways to address problems in these four areas so that improvements in one area also lead to improvements in the other three areas. As they play the game, players get advice on possible courses of action from IBM consultants.

The game presents more than 100 real-world scenarios where players must respond to a crisis and transform their city through initiatives such as alternative energy, traffic management, water management, banking, and retail supply chains. In all of these missions, players have to determine the best way to balance the city's financial, environmental, and sociological interests.

They make decisions and work under the constraints of a limited budget to improve the city by accomplishing revenue and profit goals, increasing customers' and citizens' satisfaction, and making the environment greener. In the process of doing this, players learn about IBM products and services such as business process management, service reuse, cloud computing, and collaborative technologies, and they see how these offerings can make a city work more effectively. A sample screenshot from the game is shown in Figure 5-6.

---

18 The lead game designer of *CityOne* (*http://www-01.ibm.com/software/solutions/soa/innov8/cityone/*) was Phaedra Boinodiris (*http://www.linkedin.com/in/phaedra*) at IBM. I had the good fortune to meet and work with her during the time she was engaged in developing *CityOne*. In the Level-Up section of the game, there are inspiring quotes and insights from people such as Albert Einstein and the Dalai Lama. Phaedra flattered me by including some quotes of mine on the subjects of agility, transparency, and responsiveness.

Figure 5-6. Screenshot from CityOne, *courtesy of IBM*

Plantville by Siemens

Plantville[19] is a realistic game that allows players to assume the role of a plant manager and take on the challenge of improving the productivity, efficiency, and sustainability of a simulated factory. The game presents players with three different kinds of factories that each have different characteristics. Players can select to run a bottling plant, a vitamin production plant, or a train assembly plant.

Players need to find ways to improve the plant safety record, its quality levels, and its ability to deliver products on time. In doing this, they have to take actions that do things such as optimize energy usage or boost employee satisfaction. In the process of taking these actions, they learn about Siemens products such as energy-saving servo motors, automation systems, and sprinkler systems.

There is a fourth kind of plant, a "Factory of the Year," which is managed by an expert plant manager named Pete who gives players an introduction to the game. During the game, Pete appears and gives players

---

19 Plantville (*http://www.facebook.com/plantville*) can be accessed on Facebook.

helpful tips by using short films, puzzles, and online chats in the *Plantville* café. Real-life plant experts are presented who focus on subjects ranging from energy efficiency to optimizing the use of different kinds of machines. The game also has a social component that lets players share their experiences on Facebook, LinkedIn, and Twitter. Figure 5-7 shows a sample screenshot from the game.

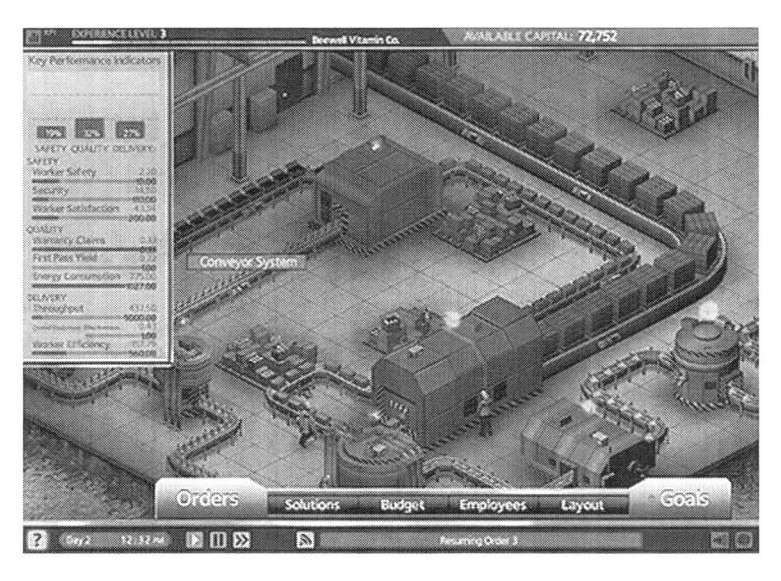

Figure 5-7. Sample screenshot from Plantville, *courtesy of Siemens*

Gamification Is Just the Start

The techniques and practices currently known as gamification are clearly just the beginning of what can be done when companies apply game dynamics to business operations. The examples in this chapter show what is being done already; as these ideas spread through companies, and as companies learn from their experiences and from the examples of other companies, they will apply game mechanics in even more creative and substantial ways.

Both IBM and Siemens report that the use of these games has helped customers and prospects to learn more about their products and services. These games have proven to be effective ways to engage with customers, to educate them about company offerings, and to increase sales.

The learning games from IBM and Siemens employ game mechanics, such as simulation modeling and avatars, and they take their structure from a class of games known as "serious games." In the following chapter, we will review a continuum of functionality that games present, which can be used in business.

Points, badges, and leaderboards are a start, and with the additional capabilities that games offer, games will be employed in business on an increasing scale.

6

A Continuum of Functionality: Simulations to Serious Games

THE GAMIFICATION EXAMPLES IN the previous chapter make use of a range of game techniques and mechanics that have evolved over the years. To get a deeper sense of what these are, let's take a look at the functionality offered by different kinds of games and how that functionality has evolved. We will explore three areas where there is a strong overlap between games and business: simulation modeling, serious games, and real-time collaboration. These three areas use technology and functionality that build on each other, and they are all evolving rapidly now. Their evolution is driven by constant demands for higher levels of performance in our increasingly unpredictable world.

The borders between these three areas are blurry and they blend with each other at the edges, but a useful framework for discussion can be identified. We will use the framework presented in Figure 6-1 to structure our conversation in this chapter and the next. Each of the three areas has its main features and uses, and the first two areas have developed technologies that serve as a transition to the next one. These features, uses, and transition technologies will be explored in some depth.

```
    1              Flight        2        Massively          3
                 Simulators            Multi-player
 Simulation                ──▶  Serious  Online Games   Real-Time
  Modeling                       Games       ──▶       Collaboration

  ANALYTICS                     TRAINING                 OPERATIONS
- Prediction                - Develop Skills          - Observe Events
- Optimization              - Best Practices          - Send Alerts
- Linear Programming        - Pilots, Soldiers, and   - Explore Options
- Spreadsheets                Surgeons                - Take Action
                            - Strategy Games
```

Figure 6-1. Framework for discussing gaming technology in business

A Continuum of Functionality in Game Capabilities

Simulation modeling is used to research a given situation and to find optimal solutions to problems in that situation. For instance, we can build models of things such as a financial portfolio or a bridge across a river valley. Then we can use techniques like linear programming to find an optimal solution given our expectations for the situation we are simulating. We can find the best allocation of money in a financial portfolio given our expectations about financial conditions, and we can find the best design for a bridge given our expectations for cost of construction and the load that will be placed on the bridge. Over the years, simulations have become central to many video games. They show us what happens when we take certain actions in certain situations.

The first computer simulations ran on expensive hardware and were out of reach for all but the largest companies and government organizations. Then came the personal computer and that amazing invention called the spreadsheet. Dan Bricklin and Bob Frankston created the first electronic spreadsheet called VisiCalc, which ran on the Apple II, the IBM PC, and other personal computers.[1] The spreadsheet is a simulation modeling tool that was so useful it stimulated the first big surge in PC sales in the late 1970s and early 1980s. The spreadsheet became the first "killer app" of the computer age. It changed microcomputers from being machines for hobbyists into being general purpose business machines.

About the same time that Dan Bricklin and Bob Frankston were developing their VisiCalc spreadsheet, another inventor was working on a program to simulate and continually display the results of flying an airplane. In 1980, Bruce Artwick released a program called *Flight Simulator* for the Apple II.[2] Where spreadsheets displayed their results as columns of numbers or static diagrams such as line graphs or pie charts, *Flight Simulator* brought moving graphics to the screen and allowed users to respond in real time to what they saw. As they responded, the moving graphic display

---

1   Dan Bricklin was a first year student at Harvard University when he came up with the idea of a spreadsheet (*http://news.harvard.edu/gazette/story/2012/03/a-vision-of-the-computing-future/*). Read a short history and overview of VisiCalc at *http://www.bricklin.com/visicalc.htm*.

2   The Wikipedia article on Bruce Artwick is can be read at *http://en.wikipedia.org/wiki/Bruce_Artwick* and you can watch a YouTube video of an interview with him at *http://www.youtube.com/watch?v=FUCT0MobR6E*.

immediately showed the results. An engaging cause and effect feedback loop was created between the computer and the human being.

Flight Simulator and other real-time simulations like it turned simulation into a game by providing a real-time visual feedback loop linking action and result.[3] The four traits of a game came into existence. The goal was to fly your airplane from one spot to another and learn to pilot it though maneuvers such as climbing and diving, flying loops, and barrel rolls. The rules were the flight characteristics of the plane that were programmed into *Flight Simulator*, and the feedback system was the moving graphics on the computer screen that showed the plane's instrument panel, the scenery moving past, and the plane itself as it flew.

As successive versions of the program were released and PCs became more powerful, the simulations became more realistic and the interactions between human and computer became more life-like, which attracted a growing number of users. Figure 6-2 shows a screenshot from an early version of *Flight Simulator* on the bottom, and screenshots on top show how the program graphics became more realistic over time.

Serious games arise from simulation systems where feedback from the simulation influences player behavior, and the ongoing cycle of action and results is used to train players in the best responses to different kinds of situations. Simulations using interactive 3-D graphics go beyond traditional classroom training and become interactive experiences for the trainee. This involvement makes knowledge transfer better and builds skills faster. There is an old saying in the training world that goes like this: "Tell me and I'll forget; show me and I'll remember; involve me and I'll learn."

---

3 For the latest version of Microsoft Flight Simulator, visit *http://www.microsoft.com/games/flightsimulatorx/.*

Flight Simulator, created by Bruce Artwick and licensed by Microsoft in the early 1980s, has continually improved graphics and realism of simulations and will become a multiplayer simulator through the Microsoft Live network.

Figure 6-2. Real-time interactive graphics turned Flight Simulator *into a game, courtesy of Microsoft and Wikipedia Commons*

Pilots, Soldiers, and Surgeons Play Serious Games

What do pilots, soldiers, and surgeons all have in common? Answer: They all work in professions where the cost of failure can be severe. The situations they deal with are unpredictable and they cannot always employ routine responses. As situations unfold, they have to think fast and do the right thing. That takes lots of practice and lots of learning from failures to see what works and what does not work. And because of this, these three professions presently make the most intensive use of interactive simulations and serious games.

It seems like these three professions get better and better all the time. I wonder if there are examples here that other organizations could apply to their own situations.

Tom Chatfield, in his book *Fun Inc.*, points out that a game can "turn just about any complex and potentially overwhelming system of variables into a manageable simulation that can be played, refined and analyzed as many times as you want."[4] This is a capability that offers tremendous value for the money. Failing in simulation situations is obviously a better and less costly way to learn. In many cases, it is the only way for people to survive their mistakes long enough to learn what they need to know to do their jobs well.

Because these simulations used by pilots, soldiers, and surgeons involve real-time feedback systems, they are games. But they are not to be confused with entertainment games or games played just to pass the time. So a term for these kind of training games has been created: "serious games."

Even though the name is relatively new, the idea of such games is not. Military officers around the world have been using war games to develop strategic skills and to try out new tactics for a long time. One early example of a serious game is a nineteenth century Prussian military training game called *Kriegsspiel* (the German name for war game).[5] Now, with the use of computer technology, these simulations are fast paced and visually realistic. Players identify with what is going on almost as if they are in real situations. A player's heartbeat rises, concentration sharpens, and players get to try one thing after another until they find out what works. And then these serious games allow people to practice what works and to get better and better at it.

This is how airline pilots learn to fly new airliners. It is how they learn to fly their planes out of difficult situations before they have to do it in real life. Soldiers training on new weapons systems use simulations to learn the skills to operate the weapon and how to use the weapon to get the results they want. Surgeons learning to use minimally invasive robotic surgery tools learn by doing operations first in simulation, and only graduate to real human beings when they score high enough in their training simulations.

---

4 Tom Chatfield, *Fun Inc.: Why Gaming Will Dominate the Twenty-First Century* (New York: Pegasus Books, 2010), 193. His website is *http://tomchatfield.net/* and you can watch a video of a talk he gave titled "7 Ways Games Reward the Brain" at *http://www.ted.com/talks/tom_chatfield_7_ways_games_reward_the_brain.html.*

5 You can go to a website devoted to a video game version of the game of Kriegsspiel at *http://chingfordgames1.homestead.com/kriegspiel.html.*

Serious Games for Pilot Training

Have you ever wondered how pilots learn to do those difficult things they do, like fly their airplane out of a thunderstorm when the engine on the left wing suddenly conks out or how they land their aircraft on an icy runway while contending with a serious crosswind that could blow their plane off the runway or even tip it over? They have to learn these skills in a safer place than the real world because otherwise they might not survive the mistakes they make while learning.

When manufacturers roll out a new airplane, they also roll out a flight simulator to go along with it. This is especially true for commercial airliners and military aircraft. Pilots log literally hundreds of hours learning to fly these planes in simulators before they ever enter the real plane and take it up for a spin. And when they do take the real plane up, they already know how to operate it in a wide range of conditions and how to fly it out of difficult situations. Figure 6-3 shows pilots training in the flight simulator for the Boeing 787 Dreamliner airline.[6]

Figure 6-3. Pilots training in simulator for Boeing 787, courtesy of Boeing

The training seen in this figure is similar for pilots flying any make of airliner. Pilots train on both a PC-based flat panel training simulator and also on a full-flight simulator like the one shown here. The full-flight simulator goes beyond visual realism to provide real sensations of rising and falling and feeling the airplane vibrate. The instructor sitting behind the two pilots can trigger all sorts of unexpected events that the simulator

---

6   Watch a YouTube video with raw footage from a training session inside the Boeing 787 flight simulator at *http://www.youtube.com/watch?v=jqOV6aOw544*. It illustrates the immersive real-time experience that simulators can deliver.

will enact and the pilots learn how to respond effectively and develop the reflexes they need. Airplane manufacturers deliver full training curriculums with their new aircraft because that is how their customers who buy the airplanes will develop the qualified and competent crews to operate these aircraft.

Serious Soldier Games

The military simulation and virtual training market has experienced rapid growth in the last several years and it is expected to continue growing.[7] At a time when weapons technology is changing so fast, armed forces around the world are turning to military simulation and virtual training tools as a way to deliver increased training and reduce the costs associated with live training that uses real vehicles and ammunition in the real world.[8]

Figure 6-4 shows a soldier and instructor using a simulator to train in the use of a new anti-tank missile system used by the US Army. The scene on the left shows what the soldier sees; it is a night vision view of desert terrain with an enemy tank shown off in the distance. The instructor can introduce a range of different terrains and targets, and the soldier can practice using the weapon to acquire and destroy the targets.

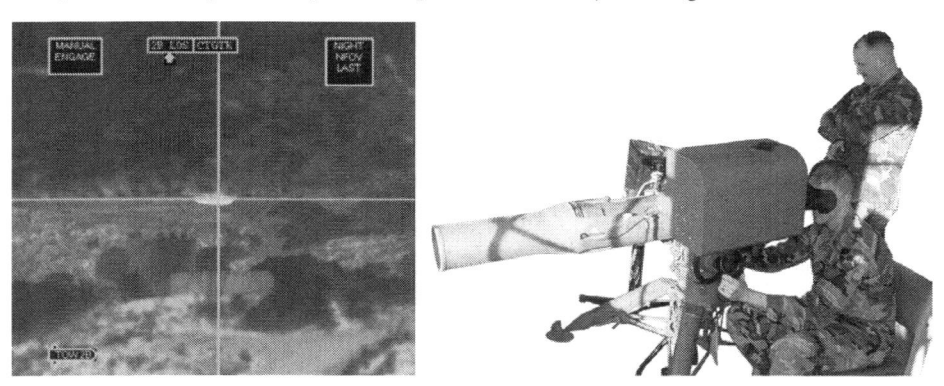

Figure 6-4. Soldier and instructor using weapon simulator for training, courtesy of US Army

---

7 Visiongain, *The Military Simulation and Virtual Training Market 2010–2020* (Vashi, Navi Mumbai, India: Bharat Book Bureau, 2010).

8 Watch a YouTube video showing a combat simulation and training system called Virtual Interactive Combat Environment that was developed using video game technology at http://www.youtube.com/watch?feature=endscreen&NR=1&v=CwQOEZISDT4.

Surgery Is a Serious Game

Advances in medical technology and techniques have produced a growing body of procedures for minimally invasive surgeries to respond to a wide range of medical conditions. Minimally invasive surgery is both less expensive and also less traumatic for the patient, so its use is growing rapidly. And along with the new technologies and techniques, there needs to be appropriate training methods for the surgeons who will use them.

The new advanced surgical simulation devices used to provide training for surgeons are based on jet pilot flight simulation, and they provide trainees with appropriate levels of challenge and instruction.[9] Shown in Figure 6-5 is an example of a new surgical simulation device. It is the RoSS™ Robotic Surgical Simulator and it features training for complete surgical procedures. Its hands-on surgical training modules use virtual reality to guide the trainee through the actions of a master surgeon.[10]

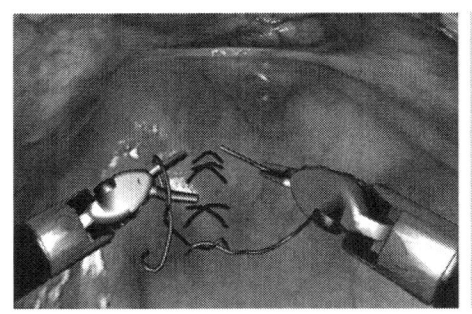

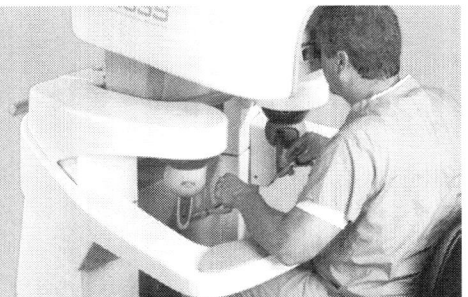

Figure 6-5. Surgical simulators are used to train surgeons in minimally invasive techniques, courtesy of Simulated Surgical Systems

---

9 M. P. Fried , B. Sandoughi, M. J. Gibber, et al., "From Virtual Reality to the Operating Room: The Endoscopic Sinus Surgery Simulator Experiment," *Otorhinolaryngology-Head and Neck Surgery*, 142 (2010): 202-7.

10 Simulated Surgical Systems, Williamsville, NY (*http://www.simulatedsurgicals.com/*). Watch a YouTube video of a simulation exercise for training surgeons in use of ROSS at *http://www.youtube.com/watch?v=bICtjMCeXmQ*.

Simulations and Serious Games Merge with the Real World

The merging of games and reality was anticipated and described in detail in the award-winning science fiction book *Ender's Game*.[11] In the book, Earth has been attacked twice by aliens and the human race is almost destroyed. So, Earth's government begins training for the next war by using games. The book's hero, Ender Wiggin, excels at war games and is selected to lead teams in increasingly sophisticated and realistic games where he battles fleets of alien spaceships. At some point, the border between games and reality simply fades away and Ender winds up defeating a real alien invasion fleet while playing what he was told was only a game.

In the world today, it can become impossible to tell the difference between a training scenario, taking place using a virtual drone within a game-generated environment, and an actual mission as relayed by the cameras and sensors attached to a real drone aircraft. In 2011, the Air Force trained more drone pilots than fighter and bomber pilots combined.[12] Holloman Air Force Base in New Mexico is where the US Air Force is developing this new breed of pilots who fly unmanned aerial vehicles, or drones.

Students at Holloman begin their training in simulator bays packed with computer processors and monitors (see the picture on the left in Figure 6-6). At their workstations, the student pilot sits on the left, the sensor operator—the person who monitors the aircraft and weapons systems—sits on the right. Then, an instructor loads in images of a mission they will train for.[13]

---

11 Orson Scott Card, *Ender's Game* (New York: Tor Books, Tom Doherty Associates Inc., 1985). To see a YouTube video of Orson Scott Card discussing the "Ender's Game" movie go to *http://www.youtube.com/watch?v=hik-3WWanvs*. Also, watch a fan made movie trailer for what Ender's Game could look like at *http://www.youtube.com/watch?v=hik-3WWanvs*.

12 Rachel Martin, "Drone Pilots: The Future of Aerial Warfare," *http://www.npr.org/2011/11/29/142858358/drone-pilots-the-future-of-aerial-warfare*.

13 You can see a YouTube video showing drone controller technology in action at *http://www.youtube.com/watch?v=p3HuSdauvZc*. It's clear how this has evolved from video game technology and flight simulator software.

Figure 6-6. Students using simulators to learn to fly pilotless drones, courtesy of US Air Force

The mission might be to fly a drone over Afghanistan and provide an escort for a convoy making its way through a mountain valley in dangerous territory. The simulation that is loaded will provide highly accurate visuals and other information about the route the convoy is traveling, and the students can then fly around and investigate the simulation space and see if there are any threats to that convoy. This is almost identical to what they will be doing when they begin actually flying real drones.

Just as drones are free-roaming aerial robots, free-roaming robots of all kinds are proliferating to do jobs on land and at sea. All of these free-roaming robots are controlled by technology similar to that used by drones, and people who operate these robots are trained in similar ways. Figure 6-7 shows the controls for and an example of a rapidly growing kind of free-roaming robot used for bomb disposal. Training starts out in simulation and progresses on to the real world. The border between simulation and reality is blurring.[14]

---

14 As drones blur the boundary between simulation and reality, they also raise questions about legality and the conduct of war. You can watch a short video where Professor of Law Mary Ellen O'Connell at the University of Notre Dame comments on some of these issues from the perspective of the Catholic Church's Just War Doctrine at *http://www.youtube.com/watch?v=-C_4UuDLVQw*.

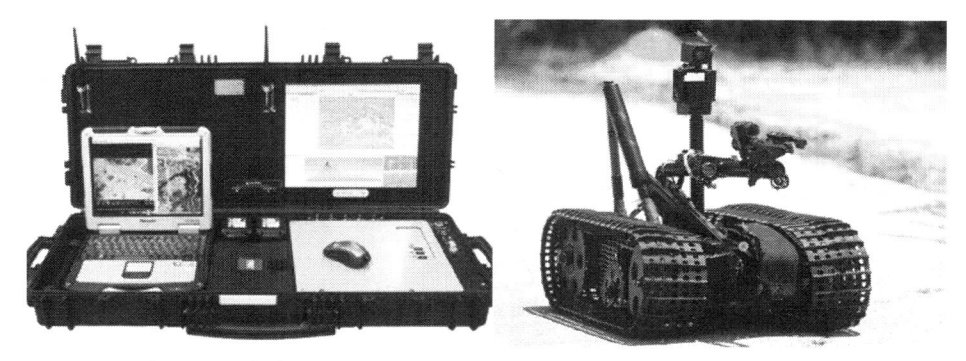

Figure 6-7. Controls for and example of a bomb disposal robot, picture of controls from UAV Factory and robot from US Navy

Use of Serious Games Is Growing Quickly

The US military alone now spends about $6 billion a year on various kinds of virtual and simulated training programs.[15] Military use of simulations and serious games is increasing as countries move to reduce defense spending in the face of economic pressure. The United States is a big user of military simulation and virtual training and now it is being joined by countries in Europe, such as the United Kingdom and France, as well as countries in the Middle East, such as Saudi Arabia and countries in Asia, such as China and India.[16]

Video games are now able to simulate reality so well that many military organizations are building serious games for training, from technology developed for the popular entertainment industry.[17] Video game production companies are incorporating their game engines into serious game development packages and using them to develop games and simulations for military and government use. These packages have extra features that go beyond what is available to the general public.

An example of this is a gaming environment called *Virtual Battlespace 2 (VBS2)*. *VBS2* is a more sophisticated version of *Operation Flashpoint*, a popular video game produced by Bohemia Interactive. The British Army

---

15 Tom Chatfield, *Fun Inc.*, 188.
16 Rachel Martin, "Drone Pilots."
17 To see a short YouTube video that introduces the US Army's new virtual simulation training system go to *http://www.youtube.com/watch?v=rHA81e8LNW8*.

is using *VBS2* to create serious games for training and for exploring the results of using certain strategies and tactics.[18]

Using this game development package, the British Army can add topographical databases and new equipment can be quickly and inexpensively programmed. The package allows people to manage what Bohemia Interactive calls the four features of a serious game: (1) creating the geography and setting for training; (2) defining the objects and players involved; (3) running the scenarios to train players and test the effectiveness of different tactics; and (4) reviewing the scenario results to measure skills and outcomes. This is shown in Figure 6-8.

America's Army Game

In 2002, the US Army launched an online PC game called *America's Army*. It uses another popular game engine, the Unreal Engine developed by Epic Games,[19] and was designed as a learning game and recruitment tool. By 2007, it had more than 8.5 million user accounts, and players had participated in over 200 million hours of game play. There were players registered in 60 countries with over 40 million game downloads. The game grew from an online PC game to encompass game console and cell phone games as well. "*America's Army* game brand has had an incredible impact around the world placing Soldiering front and center within popular culture and showcasing the high-tech, team-oriented and values-driven nature of the Army," said Colonel Casey Wardynski, originator of the *America's Army* game.[20]

America's Army exposes players to a virtual experience within which to explore entry-level through advanced training, as well as operating in small units.[21] It has virtually taken players through boot camp, Ranger and

---

[18] Bob Sherwood, "War-gaming... with the FT," *The Financial Times*, March 4, 2012, (*http://www.ft.com/cms/s/2/d9e733a8-4536-11e0-80e7-00144feab49a .html#ixzz1k1shBUmm*). A short video of VBS2 in action can be viewed at *http://www .youtube.com/watch?v=KgVU8WljP1k&feature=player_embedded*.

[19] Epic Games (*http://epicgames.com/*) was founded in 1991 and is headquartered in Cary, North Carolina. They have design and production facilities in Europe, North America, and Asia and are the creators of best-selling games such as the *Gears of War* series and *Infinity Blade*.

[20] Phoenix, US Army, "*America's Army* Five Year Anniversary," *http://login.aa3 .americasarmy.com/press/news.php?t=42*.

[21] To see a YouTube video showing sequences from actual game play which illustrates how it is used to train soldiers in small unit tactics go to *http://www.youtube.com/ watch?v=DjIqkmWF4-U*.

Airborne training, and introduced them to the Army's elite Special Forces. Players have learned about rules of engagement, battlefield first aid, laws of war, and the set of US Army values known as the warrior ethos.

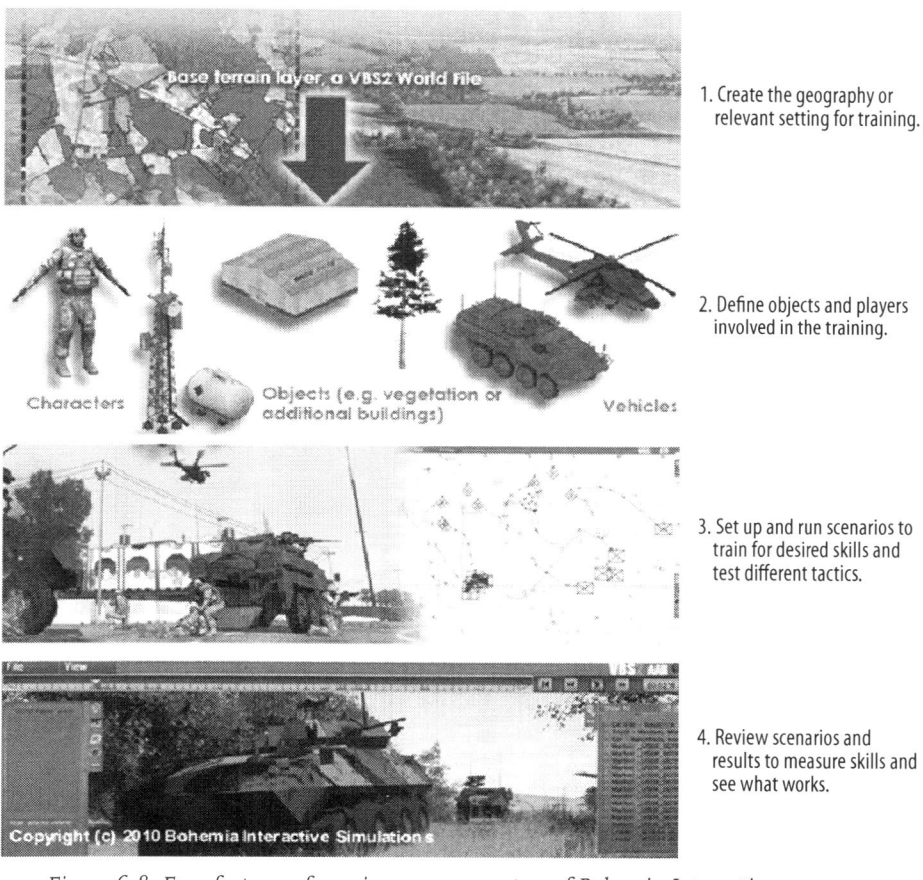

1. Create the geography or relevant setting for training.

2. Define objects and players involved in the training.

3. Set up and run scenarios to train for desired skills and test different tactics.

4. Review scenarios and results to measure skills and see what works.

Figure 6-8. Four features of a serious game, courtesy of Bohemia Interactive Simulations

A nonpublic version of *America's Army* is a serious game used extensively inside the US Army to teach soldiers and officers theory and techniques in areas such as convoy survivability, adaptive thinking, and leadership. Figure 6-9 shows the game website homepage and a screenshot from the game.

Figure 6-9. America's Army *website and a screenshot from the game, courtesy of the US Army*

The nonpublic version of the game is used as a simulation environment for many of the new weapons and vehicles that the Army plans to introduce to its soldiers. It gives soldiers training on the new gear, and it is a source of feedback in the form of comments from soldiers that designers and engineers can use to continue improving the new weapons and vehicles. An example of this is described in the projects section of the *America's Army* website:

> The *America's Army* teams have implemented the XM25 Air Burst Weapon System into *America's Army* environments. The XM25 scenario was developed for PM Individual Weapons as a virtual prototyping project for weapons concepts. Through virtual prototyping, the system can be implanted in the game environment and given to Soldiers throughout the world to try out. Soldiers can give feedback to the weapons developers. This process will help developers to build a weapon that the Soldiers want and need while saving time and money. A version of the XM25 may also appear in future versions of the public *America's Army* game.[22]

Chinese People's Liberation Army Game

On May 13, 2011, the *China Daily USA* reported on the development and upcoming release of a game quite similar to *America's Army*:

---

22 US Army, *America's Army* website, projects section, *http://info.americasarmy.com/projects.php?id=11.*

Chinese People's Liberation Army (PLA) officers and soldiers will soon have the chance to play the army's first self-developed military game, as it finishes the main development and is in the debugging process. The video game, *Mission of Honor*, was co-developed by the PLA's Nanjing command and the Wuxi Giant Interactive Group Inc. two years ago, the PLA Daily reported Friday.[23]

The game is set in a soldier's life at a military camp, and the final mission is to complete a large-scale military drill code named "Mission of Honor." Its three modules—basic training, individual mission, and team combat—provide players with the sense of growing from a rookie into an experienced veteran. Figure 6-10 shows two video frame grabs from an official promotional video.[24]

Figure 6-10. Screenshots from the game Chinese People's Liberation Army *courtesy of China People's Liberation Army*

According to PLA sources, the initial release of the game allows a maximum of 32 online players. It is the PLA's first large-scale local area network (LAN) video game for use in training Chinese soldiers. Xinhua reported that the design of the characters, weapons, and vehicles in the *Glorious Mission* game reflected real PLA equipment.[25] The PLA says the game has been distributed within the PLA and, so far, it is not available for

---

23 Zhang Jiawei, *China Daily USA*, May 13, 2011, *http://usa.chinadaily.com.cn/china/2011-05/13/content_12507419.htm.*
24 YouTube video showing official promo video for China's PLA Game, "PLA first person shooter: Glorious Mission (Mission of Honor)," *http://www.youtube.com/watch?v=QCOu4e8luF8.*
25 Xinhua News Global Edition, "PLA to Distribute Video Game for Military Training," June 29, 2011, *http://news.xinhuanet.com/english2010/china/2011-06/29/c_13956979.htm.*

ordinary game users. Reports earlier said the PLA will launch a "civilian" version of the game in 2012.

The Rise of Multiplayer Online Games

The heart of these games and others like them is in their team-based multiplayer battles. These battles are not just individual players engaging in chaotic running and shooting. Instead, there are game rules that guide players toward the idea of working together in disciplined units where each player has a specific role to play and must play it well in order to succeed and in order for the larger unit to succeed.

These kind of multiplayer online games represent one of the fastest growing game categories. The cooperative player interaction required by these games is very attractive and engaging to a growing body of players. Like flight simulators before them, these games are a transition from one category of games to a new category of games.

We will discuss these multiplayer online games and the new category of games they create in the next chapter.

7

Massively Multiplayer Online Games and Real-Time Collaboration

ONE OF THE FASTEST growing features of game play is the feature where multiple players in a game play together. Most players are not as interested in competing one on one with other players as they are in forming groups and cooperating with others in their group to accomplish common goals. This pursuit of goals certainly involves competing with other groups of players or with game-generated characters, but the competition is in the context of achieving the group's goals. This cooperative game play reflects our human instincts to form groups (or tribes or guilds or corporations) and cooperate to build something bigger than ourselves.

As games enable larger and larger groups of simultaneous players to cooperate and compete with each other in real time, they become what are known as massively multiplayer online role-playing games (abbreviated as MMORPGs or just MMOs). Wikipedia gives this definition of MMOs:

> Players assume the role of a character (often in a fantasy world) and take control over many of that character's actions. MMORPGs are distinguished from single-player or small multi-player RPGs [role playing games] by the number of players, and by the game's persistent world (usually hosted by the game's publisher), which continues to exist and evolve while the player is offline and away from the game.[1]

Players in MMOs take on a role and they create an avatar to represent the character they play in the game. This character has to learn certain skills to succeed and reach higher levels in the game. Through their avatars, players interact with other players and build their reputations in the game.

---

1 Wikipedia, "Massively Multiplayer Online Role-Playing Game," *http://en.wikipedia.org/wiki/Massively_multiplayer_online_role-playing_game*.

Reputations are composed of the players' skill levels as reported by the game, and their histories in the game of participating in the raids and missions of the groups they belong to. Players with higher skill levels who have a history of success in the missions and groups they belong to are sought out by other players and are always in demand to become members of groups.

One of the most popular MMOs is *World of Warcraft*; the publishers of this game report that by the end of 2011, they had more than 12 million registered players.[2] *World of Warcraft* is based on a *Lord of the Rings*–style fantasy theme. Another popular MMO is *EVE Online*, which is based on a *Star Wars*–style science fiction theme. There are many other popular MMOs based on themes ranging from military combat to automobile racing.

Within the game worlds of these MMOs, players collaborate and compete with each other in real time in highly detailed and visually rich 3-D virtual worlds. In his research into the applicability of games to business, professor Byron Reeves at the Stanford Graduate School of Business has this to say about MMOs:

> MMOs require extraordinary teamwork, elaborate data analysis and strategy, recruitment, evaluation and retention of top players in guilds and corporations of people who have complementary skills and roles who must work together.[3]

He goes on to report that many of the people he interviewed for his research reported that their experience as group leaders in MMOs improved their real-world leadership capabilities. In effect, MMOs are serious games for leadership training. People can develop leadership skills and learn by doing in these simulated game worlds without all the risks that come from practicing and failing in the real world.

---

2 Blizzard Entertainment press release, "World of Warcraft: Cataclysm One-Month Sales Top 4.7 Million," January 10, 2011, *http://us.blizzard.com/en-us/company/press/pressreleases.html?id=2847887.*

3 Byron Reeves and J. Leighton Read, *Total Engagement: Using Games and Virtual Worlds to Change the Way People Work and Businesses Compete* (Boston: Harvard Business Press, 2009), 5.

When Serious Games Become Massively Multiplayer Online Games

One of the popular MMOs that is also closely attuned with actual business practices is *EVE Online*. For that reason, it makes a good case study for how MMO technology and practices can be applied to solve problems in the business world. In this chapter, we'll take a deeper look at *EVE* and note how a business application system using features from an MMO like *EVE* could be created to provide companies with a real-time collaboration system to address problems in our real-time global economy.

The world of *EVE* is highly realistic in that it accurately models the laws of physics (such as gravity, mass, and motion) and the laws of economics (such as supply and demand). Within the constraints of these laws, players are free to do whatever they wish and interact with other players as they see fit. Players take on the roles of miners, traders, pilots, engineers, and business executives. Situations in the game evolve as a result of the combined actions of all the players; nothing is prescribed by the game. Just like the real world, this world is an "unscripted, emergent experience" that comes about through the actions of the players and the workings of the laws of physics, economics, and cultures. Figure 7-1 shows the login screen for *EVE*.[4]

Note the three bold titles at the bottom of the screen: Career Options, Working with Others, and Massive Community. How is this different than what you would see on the home page of any global corporation today? These three titles appeal to what Jane McGonigal has described as the essential human cravings: satisfying work, the hope of success, social connection, and the chance to be part of something larger than ourselves.

Players must first spend time learning to fly and equip spaceships and learning the skills of their chosen roles. Then they join corporations and go on missions for exploration and acquiring raw materials to earn money and build their reputations. Only when they have mastered these skills and built their reputations can they graduate into the higher levels of the game and participate in the political and economic maneuvering and intrigue that takes place between and among vast and shifting alliances of players. Figure 7-2 shows some sample player avatars, the awards they can

---

4   The URL for EVE Online is *http://www.eveonline.com/*. Their short promotional video titled "EVE Online: The Butterfly Effect" illustrates how the game evolves and can be viewed at *http://www.youtube.com/watch?v=08hmqyejCYU*.

earn, and the alliances they can join. The large picture is a screenshot of spaceships from the game.

Figure 7-1. Login screen for EVE Online *courtesy of* EVE Online

Figure 7-2. Avatars, awards, alliances, spaceships, and 3-D worlds, courtesy of EVE Online

MASSIVELY MULTIPLAYER ONLINE GAMES AND REAL-TIME COLLABORATION | 83

The game dynamics of *EVE* start with the constraints imposed by the limited availability of raw materials, which are mined in the asteroid fields scattered throughout the *EVE* universe. The big money in the game comes from controlling the sources of raw materials, protecting the transport ships, and building and operating processing and manufacturing facilities. The picture on the left in Figure 7-3 shows an engineer in a manufacturing facility designing a spaceship, and the other picture shows a warship escorting a convoy of transport ships.

Almost 95 percent of all items, from clothing to spaceships to processing plants, in *EVE* are made by the players from scratch and sold through *EVE*'s economic market system. Players form corporations to mine and transport natural resources and to design, build, and sell products. Corporations form alliances with other corporations to compete for economic and military success. At any given time, there are tens of thousands and sometimes hundreds of thousands of players simultaneously playing the game online. As players interact, other dynamics of the real world—dynamics like psychology, sociology, politics, and culture—are manifested in this virtual world. This is very much like the real world.

Figure 7-3. An engineer at work and a convoy of transport ships, courtesy of EVE Online

In *EVE*, as in many MMOs, the action that occurs when players compete is almost as realistic and fast paced as the battle sequences in the serious games used by military organizations. Battles in *EVE* are often the clash of large fleets of warships of different sizes and capabilities. Players operating the different spaceships must coordinate with other players in their fleet and use battle tactics that combine capabilities of the available ships to win against the opposing forces.

Perhaps business software has something to learn from games and from MMOs in particular. Many of the MMOs use well-designed heads-up data displays (known as HUDs) that combine data analysis with group collaboration capabilities. This is illustrated in Figure 7-4, which shows two of the heads-up displays used by players flying spaceships in a battle. Note how the game uses moving 3-D displays to present information from real-time data feeds provided by the game.

Unlike mere columns of numbers or static data charts, these moving 3-D game displays provide a rich context that we humans are already equipped to understand. We see and respond to our world based on 3-D visual displays and audio signals brought to us by our senses of sight and sound. The context provided by moving 3-D data displays enables us to quickly orient ourselves, understand what is happening, and make decisions about how best to respond. This could be the basis for designing powerful and effective business intelligence systems.

In addition to the moving 3-D displays in the center of the screens, notice the other information shown around the edges of the screens. There are dials and readouts with relevant data, and thumbnail displays showing current status and the actions of other players people are collaborating with. To supplement these visual displays, players also communicate with each other moment to moment using text messages via chat features and Internet-based voice messages that can be directed to individual players or the entire group through headphones and microphones. This moves collaboration far beyond the current corporate collaboration systems that provide for document sharing and video conferencing.

Process dynamics from MMOs such as *EVE Online* are creative examples that companies can use to support and energize their own operations. This short discussion of *EVE* shows ways that companies could provide business goals and rules and a feedback system to engage their people by using rich data displays and player communication in real time. These ideas are the next step for companies as they move beyond the use of points, badges, and leaderboards currently used in many gamification applications.

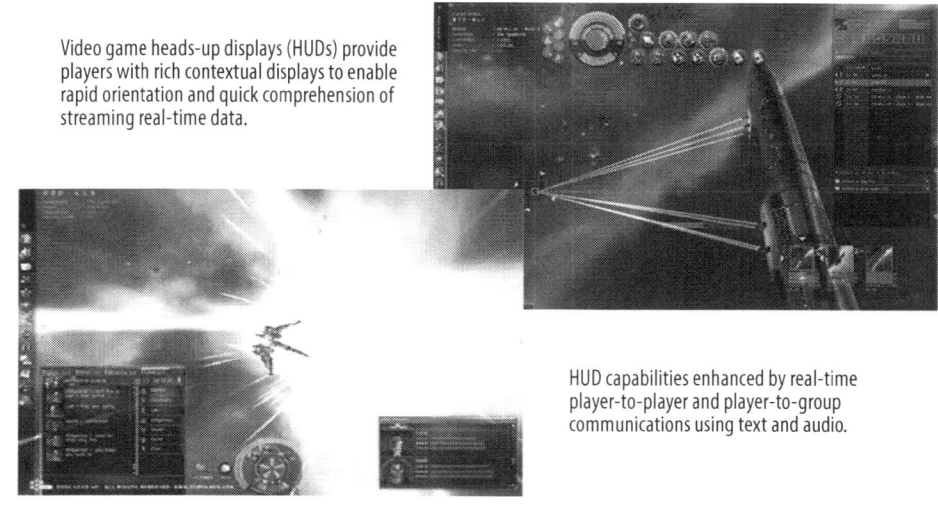

Video game heads-up displays (HUDs) provide players with rich contextual displays to enable rapid orientation and quick comprehension of streaming real-time data.

HUD capabilities enhanced by real-time player-to-player and player-to-group communications using text and audio.

Figure 7-4. EVE player heads-up displays courtesy of EVE Online

Game Ingredients and Building Blocks

In this and previous chapters, we have investigated a range of different kinds of games and looked at the techniques they use and how games work. It will be useful to summarize this information to help us as we start applying these game examples to the design of business systems. In the following sections, we'll take a look at the work of Byron Reeves and Aaron Dignan, who have each written about the application of games to business. In his book *Total Engagement*, Reeves puts forth 10 game ingredients, and in *Game Frame*, Dignan identifies 10 building blocks for games.

GAME INGREDIENTS

From their research, professor Byron Reeves and his coauthor J. Leighton Read present what they call 10 game ingredients to guide real work.[5] These ingredients are:

---

5 Reeves, Byron and J. Leighton Read. *Total Engagement: Using Games and Virtual Worlds to Change the Way People Word and Businesses Compete* (Boston: Harvard Business School Press, 2009), 61–89.

Self-representation with avatars
> Avatars in games take advantage of highly evolved human talents for communication through the use of facial gestures and body movements. When we create customized avatars to represent us in games, research shows that we identify with them and it increases our involvement in the game.

Three-dimensional environments
> Virtual space works like real space; no instruction is necessary for us to start operating and finding our way around in 3-D environments, and we can learn as we go because that's how we work in the real world. Virtual 3-D space gives us a physical sense of where things are, and the environment itself communicates qualities that can motivate and inspire us.

Narrative context
> Stories are how humans communicate and make sense of situations; good stories present important facts in a way that gives people ways to engage with the facts and personally relate to the situation described. Narratives tell people what is happening and suggest possible courses of action.

Feedback
> Feedback changes our behavior because it tells us if we are getting closer to or further away from some desired goal, and we can then use this to guide our actions. The best feedback takes forms that engage all our senses—visual, auditory, tactile, and so on.

Reputations, ranks, and levels
> Your reputation takes a long time to build, and as it does, it becomes more and more valuable. Most MMOs wouldn't work if their players didn't care about their reputations, because improving their reputations is a large part of what motivates them to learn new skills and get better at playing the game.

Marketplaces and economies
> Game economies enable scorekeeping and they motivate players to play well and strive to improve in order to get higher scores and win. Marketplaces and economies help people understand what they need to do to score.

Competition under explicit and enforced rules
>Most people play to win and rules are what make competition work; they allow people to trust the game and believe that they will be rewarded fairly for their actions. With ambiguous or poorly enforced rules, however, some players will cheat to win, and that causes other players to lose their motivation to participate.

Teams
>Team identification is wired into our genetic makeup; we like to work together with other people to achieve common objectives. Teams provide a sense of belonging and purpose to what we do.

Parallel communication systems that can be easily reconfigured
>Teams in action need to constantly communicate with each other as events unfold in order to stay together and respond effectively. Communications include visuals, audio, and text, and people need to easily switch from talking to people outside their group to people inside their group or to single individuals.

Time pressure
>People need to feel the urgency of situations and act in a timely manner. If there is no urgency, then there is no action. People learn best by combining study with action; as they see what happens, they keep trying new approaches until they find the ones that work.

GAME BUILDING BLOCKS

Through work at his digital strategy firm Undercurrents, Aaron Dignan has identified what he calls the 10 building blocks that make up a behavioral game. In his book *Game Frame*, he shows how these 10 building blocks create a game design framework that people can use to guide their work in creating games.[6] Those building blocks are:

Activity
>The real-world endeavor that the game is built upon. The endeavor can be anything from cooking to brainstorming to selling products.

---
6 Aaron Dignan, *Game Frame: Using Games as a Strategy for Success* (New York: Free Press, 2011), 87 - 96. You can view a video of a talk he gave titled "Why the Future of Work is Play" at *http://vimeo.com/23167866*.

Player profiles
> Descriptions of the drivers that motivate the players in a game. Different players are motivated by different desires, such as self-interest or group-interest. Profiles also contain a description of the abilities and skill levels of the players.

Objectives to achieve
> Clearly define the game objectives toward which players will direct their efforts and strive to achieve.

Skills to develop
> The specialized abilities that players need to learn and will use in the game.

Resistance
> The force of opposition that creates tension in the game and makes it interesting. Two common forms of resistance are competition and chance.

Resources for use
> The spaces and supplies that players can acquire and use in the game to achieve their objectives.

Actions
> Define the moves that are available to the players and when, where, and how these moves can be made.

Feedback
> This is the game response to a player's actions. Feedback is what allows players to judge the effectiveness of their actions and make decisions about what to do next.

Black box
> This is the set of rules that gives structure to the game and guides players' actions. It can consist of a set of written instructions or a collection of computer programs.

Outcomes
> These are the results that occur as players take action in pursuit of their objectives. Outcomes can be positive or negative and are reflected in ways such as scoring points and moving up a level or losing a resource and having to start over again.

MASSIVELY MULTIPLAYER ONLINE GAMES AND REAL-TIME COLLABORATION | 89

Note that there is a fair amount of overlap between these ingredients and building blocks, but they are not identical. They can also be seen as a further elaboration of the four traits of a game as defined by Jane McGonigal. This kind of commonality and overlap is a good thing because it provides different views of the same thing as seen from a variety of perspectives. It gives depth and clarity to that thing we call a game.

If we combine these ingredients and building blocks in a table, we can see where the overlap is. And from the overlap we see that game ingredients can be used to create game building blocks. This is useful insight for the task of creating games. It can influence the way we work and the way companies operate. Figure 7-5 shows what this combination looks like.

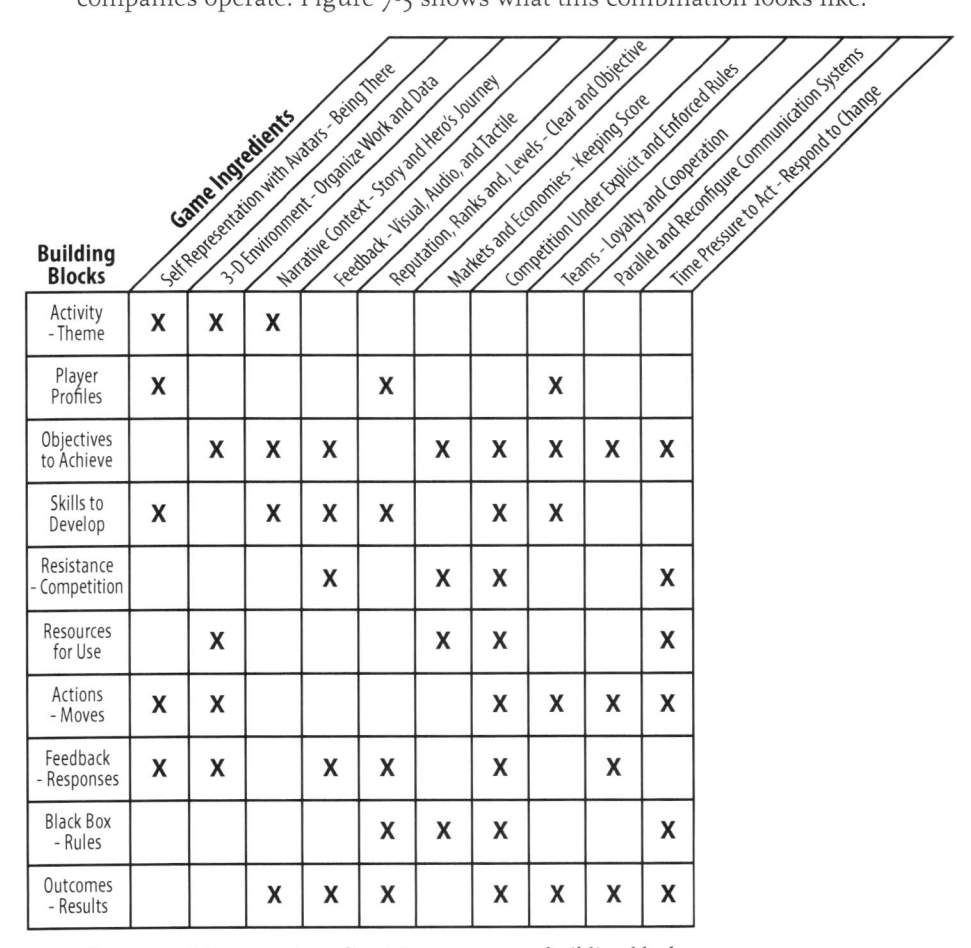

Building Blocks	Self Representation with Avatars - Being There	3-D Environment - Organize Work and Data	Narrative Context - Story and Hero's Journey	Feedback - Visual, Audio, and Tactile	Reputation, Ranks and, Levels - Clear and Objective	Markets and Economies - Keeping Score	Competition Under Explicit and Enforced Rules	Teams - Loyalty and Cooperation	Parallel and Reconfigure Communication Systems	Time Pressure to Act - Respond to Change
Activity - Theme	X	X	X							
Player Profiles	X			X		X				
Objectives to Achieve		X	X	X		X	X	X	X	X
Skills to Develop	X		X	X	X		X	X		
Resistance - Competition				X		X	X			X
Resources for Use		X				X	X			X
Actions - Moves	X	X				X	X	X	X	
Feedback - Responses	X	X		X	X		X		X	
Black Box - Rules					X	X	X			X
Outcomes - Results			X	X	X		X	X	X	X

Figure 7-5. Use game ingredients to create game building blocks

Professor Reeves makes the case that game ingredients can be used in small batches or even one at a time. Companies don't have to use them all or create an entire game to get value from game ingredients. This is already shown by current gamification applications where the emphasis is mainly on using simple feedback systems and building player reputations though the use of points, badges, and leaderboards.

What if companies were to start creating MMOs that modeled the real world instead of fictional worlds? And what if the players worked for real companies and those real companies competed and collaborated with each other in global industries such as finance, retail, manufacturing, and supply chains? What ideas can be gotten from games like *EVE* for creating game ingredients that put game building blocks in place?

The situation companies face in the real-time economy of this century is much different from the slower and more predictable economy of the last century. And the responses needed to thrive in this economy are different than the traditional responses companies learned from the last century. Figure 7-6 illustrates these differences.

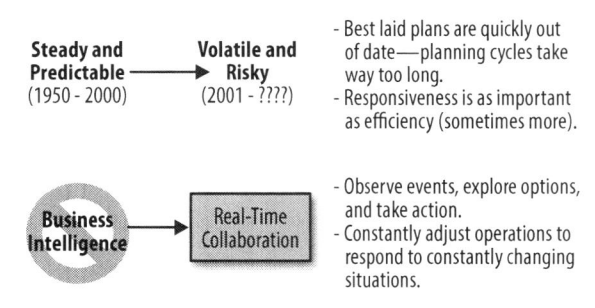

Figure 7-6. Business challenges in the real-time economy

Real-time collaboration platforms combining the functions of social media with the dynamics of MMOs are a model for how companies can structure and manage their internal operations and also for how they can structure and manage their interactions with other companies.

Massively Multiplayer Online Supply Chain Games

Let's examine an example of using MMO game concepts and techniques to design a real-time business collaboration system. We'll discuss a collaboration system designed for use by different companies that need to work together and coordinate their actions day to day as situations change. Supply chains are, by definition, multiplayer games. They are not just one company; they are a network of companies stretching from raw material providers to manufacturers, distributors, and retailers, and ultimately, to the end use customers. Supply chains that were in many cases put in place during the 1990s need to be redesigned to better respond to the pace of change and level of uncertainty we live with now.

The opportunity exists to create an MMO that provides a content-rich data display environment where data is continuously updated and is presented in a context that allows people to quickly understand the data and see themselves in relationship to the other companies in their supply chains.

We saw an example of what a system like this would look like in Chapter 3 in the scenario where Fantastic Corporation convenes an onsite and online conference with its supply chain partners to kick off a new sales campaign. Like any MMO, this supply chain collaboration system provides a highly visual real-time environment that players use to work together.

People draw supply chain designs (facilities, routes, vehicles) on global maps that are visible to all. They define different demand, supply, and cost scenarios and then simulate supply chain performance. Map displays provide instant feedback on how well these supply chains work under different conditions. People select and implement the supply chain designs that demonstrate the best performance characteristics for the expected conditions.

This system (the MMO) then collects real-world, real-time performance data from actual supply chain operations of the facilities and vehicles involved. It receives data from RFID chips, GPS devices, store POS systems, and ERP systems. The system monitors actual performance variables and sends alerts when they start to drift outside of predefined ranges.

When alerts are sent out, people convene online as needed to assess situations, try different responses, and reach consensus on the most effective actions. People use this game to collaborate and continuously adjust and improve supply chain designs and performance in a continuously changing world.

Many supply chains in business now need this kind of close collaboration between different parties. In the example shown in Figure 7-7, we show a supply chain set up to support clinical trials for a new drug. The drug is made in the United States and is being tested for approval in Europe. Without a responsive and effective supply chain, this activity and other activities like it cannot succeed.

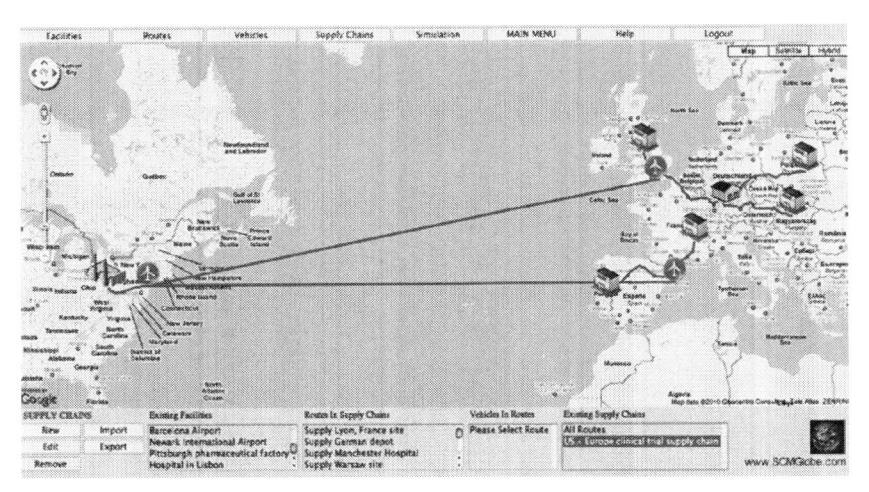

Figure 7-7. Collaboration platform for responsive and timely supply chains

We can assess how close an application like this is to a game such as an MMO by using the table of game ingredients and building blocks shown in Figure 7-5. All the game ingredients except self-representation with avatars and a 3-D virtual environment are present in this application. Future versions of this application can migrate from using Google Maps as the visual organizing environment to instead using Google Earth, which is a very detailed 3-D virtual environment that shows the real world.[7]

As technology and real-time graphics already developed by the video game industry are applied to systems like this, the result will be to deliver real-time collaboration systems that will move business operations to a new level of agility and responsiveness.

Companies that make effective use of technology like this can reap significant competitive and collaborative advantages.

---

7 This system is already available as a learning application called SCM Globe (*http://scmglobe.com/*). A short video overview of the application can be viewed at *http://www.youtube.com/watch?v=aN6BWAHUXy0*. It can be used alone or as a companion to my book on supply chains, which is used in business schools and training programs around the world. The book is *Essentials of Supply Chain Management*, 3rd Edition (Hoboken, NJ: John Wiley & Sons, 2011).

8

Driving the Great Game of Sales

IN THIS CHAPTER, WE take a more detailed look at techniques for applying game mechanics to motivate and educate the inside sales force of a multibillion dollar corporation. These game mechanics were combined to create a sales support system used successfully for more than 15 years by a global supplier of communications and security products and electrical wire and cable. We continue the story begun in Chapter 4 in the section titled "All the World's a Game." Since its creation, this game-inspired sales support system has been central to the company's ability to expand its sales force around the world and grow from just over $1 billion when the system was first introduced to more than $6 billion in annual revenue today. This system is both a serious game for training and a game that the company's sales force uses moment to moment every day to help them understand customer needs and sell more products at better profit margins.[1]

In many companies, the sales process already has in place the four traits of a game (goals, rules, feedback system, and voluntary participation). So, the challenge for the game designer in this situation is to clarify and focus those traits in such a way that two things happen. The first is that the resulting game is fun to play and it gets voluntary participation from salespeople. And the second is that by playing the game, salespeople learn, earn, and continue to get better at what they do.

---

[1] The company referenced here is Anixter International. In the early 1990s, I was the manager of systems design at Anixter and I worked with the sales group to design a game-based sales support system called SALE. I led the project team that developed and rolled out the system worldwide. The system has been updated and enhanced many times since then, but its core functionality remains the same and it is in use by over a thousand Anixter inside salespeople all day, every day around the world.

At this company, Anixter International,[2] each inside salesperson ran their sales desk as if it were their own business (they got monthly profit and loss reports, etc.) and people were compensated based on how well they ran their businesses. Real-time systems tracked sales and gross profits for each office and for the salespeople in those offices. This information was available at appropriate levels of detail to everyone from individual salespeople to branch managers and regional vice presidents. The company was and still is a sales-oriented company, and that culture creates a strong narrative context. Sales is indeed a hero's journey in this company.

Sales and training people at the company responded positively when introduced to the notion of a game as the organizing metaphor for designing the new sales system. So we ran with it. We broke up the activities at a typical sales office into what we called "the moves in the game" and we designed a system to fit smoothly with those moves and empower salespeople to improve their performance in these moves. We built in system features that helped them find products and also educated them at the same time. And as they got more knowledgeable about certain families of products, they could do better problem solving with their customers and they could sell more.

A design team of people from sales, training, and IT was put together to work under my guidance to build the new system. The company was expanding into new product markets and new countries. It needed to increase the pace of hiring in the sales force, find ways to quickly train new people in the products the company sold, and help these people sell at good profit margins.

The New Sales System Design

We focused on designing and building a working version of the system as quickly as we could. In that process of getting the first version built, we were lucky to attract some early supporters from the sales force. These early supporters saw the benefits of the new system and were enthusiastic in communicating these benefits to other salespeople. We focused on designing clear and intuitive user interfaces and screens that brought

---

2 Anixter International is a publicly traded corporation (NYSE: AXE) headquartered in Glenview, IL, with offices around the world. Here is a link to their 2011 annual report (*http://marcom.anixter.com/annual_reports/2011/index.html*).

together relevant real-time data that salespeople could use in those critical moments when they were on the phone with customers talking about products the customers wanted.

Figure 8-1 shows the pattern of activities that the design team created for the new sales process. We redesigned and streamlined the earlier sales workflow. We automated routine tasks and provided new capabilities for salespeople to call up relevant data as they talked with customers. The design goal was to empower salespeople to make better decisions and sell more items at better profit margins.

In redesigning the sales office workflow, we coined the term "elegant simplicity" as a guiding principle. The new workflow had to be simple and it could not lock people into a rigid sequence. It had to be flexible to change as individual sales situations changed. And the system we designed had to fit this new workflow smoothly. We used the phrase "intuitively obvious" to describe what was needed. We did not want long learning curves or heavy training requirements for people starting up with the new system.

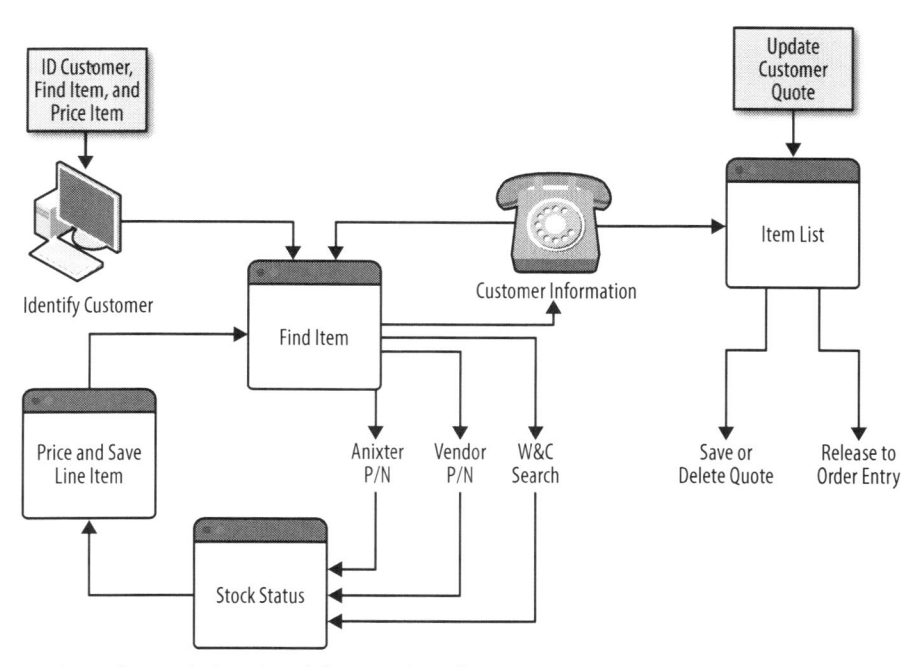

Figure 8-1. Redesigned workflow at sales offices

We defined our three design objectives as (1) design and build a system that reinforces sales training and stimulates development of strong sales skills; (2) provide critical information via a central point of focus screen during the crucial one- to two-minute period when the customer is on the phone; and (3) help the salesperson continuously learn and master "the skills of the game" through using this system.

We designed the new system to coexist with the old system that experienced salespeople were used to using. Figure 8-2 shows how the new system fit in front of the old one. It also shows how the functional components of the new system supported the new sales workflow illustrated in Figure 8-1. Salespeople were more willing to learn a new way to do their job if they knew they could always switch back to the old system if they needed to. Over time, as people got comfortable with the new system, use of the old system just withered away and it was eventually turned off.

The new system was named SALE. The name was meant to signify that the new system was built to help people increase their sales.

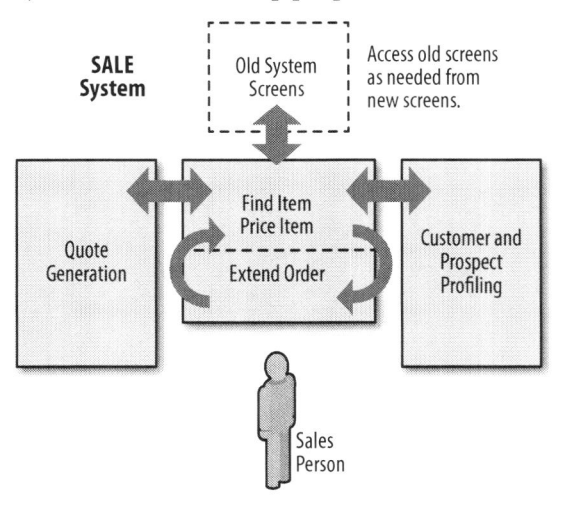

Figure 8-2. SALE system conceptual design

As shown in Figures 8-1 and 8-2, the heart of the inside sales process was to find the item the customer was asking for and quote a price that had a decent profit margin but was competitive enough so customers would buy and not go to a competitor to try to get a lower price. The system showed salespeople the standard costs for items and suggested sell prices depending on factors such as purchase quantity and recent sales prices for that item at offices in the region. But individual salespeople were free to quote whatever price they felt was appropriate as long as it was not below the standard cost.

Salespeople's bonuses were tied to how much a person sold and how much gross profit they earned on their sales. That turned the pricing decision into the moment of truth that required the most skill and attention from salespeople. We designed the new system to deliver as much information and support as possible during this point in the sales process.

For the design of this particular "moment of truth" part of the new system, we adopted the example of the heads-up display (HUD) used by jet fighter pilots. In designing that screen to support the item pricing decision, we literally used the example of a heads-up display from a popular video game at the time. This game was a fighter jet flight simulator game called *F-15 Strike Eagle*,[3] and it had a very cool user interface for the time and the technology that was available (circa 1991).

Figure 8-3 shows the heads-up display from the game and below it is the item pricing screen. We were restricted to a character-based screen because the first version of the new system was built to run entirely on the company's mainframe computer. But the power of a good idea is that it can be implemented in many different environments. We used design techniques involving screen layout and color to maximize available user interface capabilities for the presentation of critical information. Since that first version went into production, the system has been upgraded with a graphical user interface and new features have been added over the years, yet its mainframe core is still there.

---

3   *F-15 Strike Eagle* [http://en.wikipedia.org/wiki/F-15_Strike_Eagle_(video_game)] was a PC video game first released by MicroProse in 1985 and subsequently enhanced in following releases over the next seven years. It won the "Action Game of the Year" award in *Computer Gaming World*'s 1985 reader poll, and sold over 1.5 million copies.

98 | ENTERPRISE GAMES

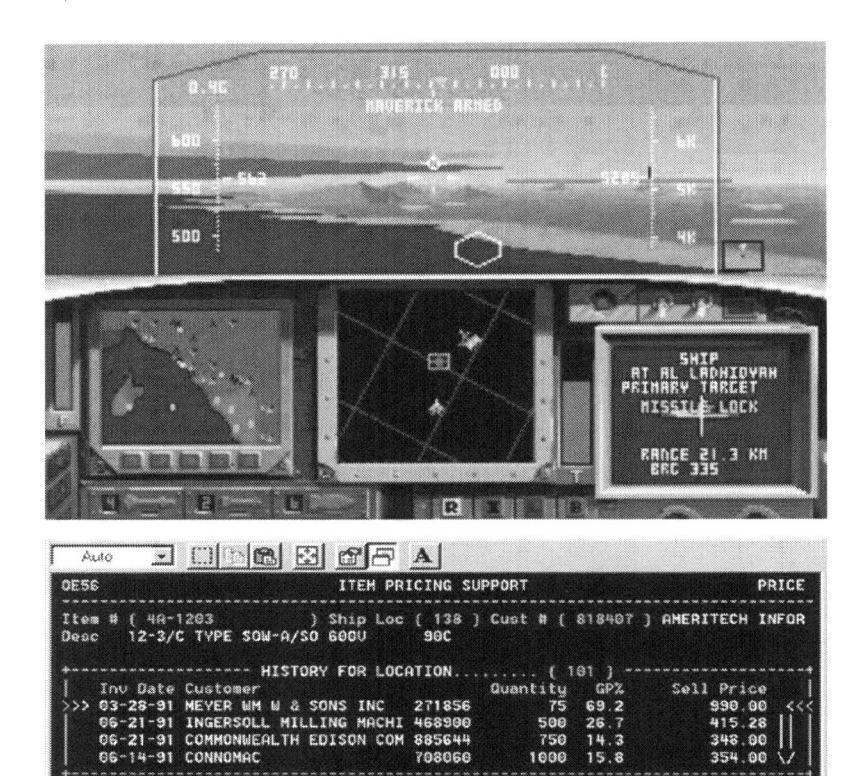

Figure 8-3. Heads-up display from F-15 Strike Eagle game influenced design of item pricing screen from SALE system

Once a salesperson found and priced an item the customer asked for, the challenge was to extend the order by asking about additional items the customer might need along with the original item. The complete order was defined as an order in which the salesperson didn't just sell the first item the customer asked for. As Figure 8-4 shows, every wire and cable item needed to be supported, spliced, protected, terminated, and tested. So we designed a set of screens that would give salespeople the confidence they needed to start up conversations with customers to ask about their need for additional items in those categories.

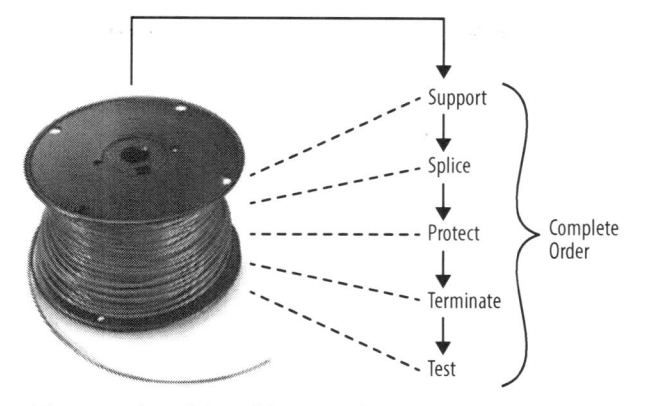

```
                           ┌──────────────┐
                           ▼
                        Support  ⎫
                           ▼     ⎪
                        Splice   ⎪
                           ▼     ⎬ Complete
                        Protect  ⎪  Order
                           ▼     ⎪
                        Terminate⎪
                           ▼     ⎭
                        Test
```

- Ask customer about all the stuff that goes with initially requested item.
- Provide sales person with information to work through this process.

Figure 8-4. The complete order process extends the order

The idea was to present information in a way that would educate salespeople on products while helping them sell. We did not want to put in artificial intelligence that simply prompted salespeople through computer-generated lists of questions. Treating people like trained monkeys would do little to motivate and educate them. So, instead, we presented a series of decision trees where they could look and decide for themselves which branches of the decision trees were relevant to the conversations they were having with customers on the phone.

Like a well-designed game, this enabled the salespeople to improve their knowledge the more often they played. The more they used the system to find new products to sell to customers, the more they would also be learning about those products. And that enabled people to specialize and build reputations in product areas that they were particularly interested in. These were key game mechanics deliberately applied to drive this sales force learning and improvement cycle.

Again, we were constrained to work with the capabilities of a character-based user interface. But constraints are part of any problem, and when you embrace constraints, they help guide the design process. Note how the use of decision trees enabled us to employ a clear graphic design to display complex data even on a character-based screen. Figure 8-5 shows a screen that helps a salesperson start up the complete order conversation. The labels across the top of the screen identify the complete order item categories; the screen shows Support, Splice, and Protect. The arrow at the lower-right corner of the screen shows that there is another screen showing the options for Terminate and Test.

After looking at these screens, think about how they might be designed to work with a graphical user interface (GUI) on a PC. Also think about how they might be designed to work on a mobile device like a tablet computer (such as the iPad) or even on a smartphone. How would you redesign them to take advantage of new user interface features available on these devices?

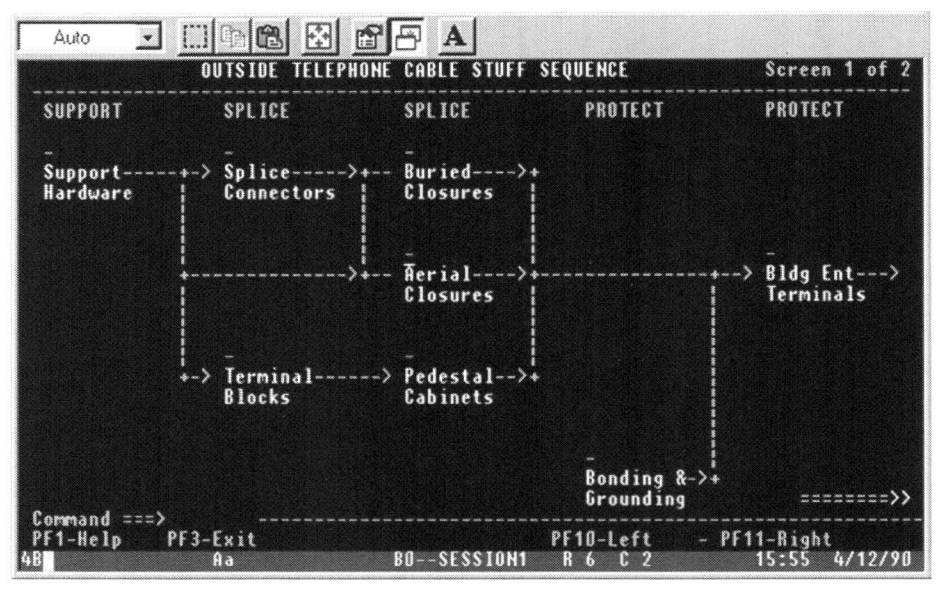

```
 Auto                OUTSIDE TELEPHONE CABLE STUFF SEQUENCE          Screen 1 of 2
 ---------------------------------------------------------------------------------
 SUPPORT             SPLICE            SPLICE           PROTECT         PROTECT

 Support------+-> Splice----->+-- Buried----->+
 Hardware     |   Connectors  |   Closures   |
              |               |              |
              |          +----|-->+-- Aerial---->+----------------+-> Bldg Ent--->
              |          |    |   Closures       |                |   Terminals
              |          |    |                  |
              +-> Terminal----> Pedestal-->+
                  Blocks       Cabinets

                                                  Bonding &->+
                                                  Grounding                =======>>
 Command ===>                                 --------------------------------------
 PF1-Help    PF3-Exit                         PF10-Left    - PF11-Right
 4B                    Aa              BO--SESSION1   R 6  C 2          15:55  4/12/90
```

Figure 8-5. Product decision trees guide salespeople in customer conversations

In this example, the item the customer just bought is shown at the top of the screen as outside telephone cable. A salesperson can then ask the customer what they will use to support, splice, and protect the cable they just bought. Suppose the customer says they do need to splice the telephone cable they just bought. Under the Splice category, it shows five possible kinds of stuff the customer might need for splicing: Splice Connectors, Terminal Blocks, Buried Closures, Aerial Closures, and Pedestal Cabinets. Looking at this screen, a salesperson gets enough information to start up and sustain a conversation with the customer. They can ask questions that are focused and helpful. They can build rapport with the customer and increase the order size.

Suppose the customer says that aerial closures are what they need. Figure 8-6 shows the screen that comes up when the salesperson clicks on Aerial Closures. This screen shows a decision tree to guide the salesperson through a conversation about the kind of aerial closures the customer might need. The salesperson sees they can ask questions about the number of pairs to close, pairs per close diameter (DIA), gauge, and splice type.

This design ensures they are not just powerless order takers. When salespeople work through a decision tree to the end of the relevant branch and click on the end of that branch, the system takes them back to the heads-up display screen to help them price the item.

And round and round the process goes as the salesperson engages the customer in a relevant and helpful conversation about all the stuff they need to do the job for which they originally ordered the first product. This design had the effect of inducing that state of confidence and willingness to tackle new challenges that gamers call "flow." In the past, salespeople had been hesitant to start up a conversation to extend the order because they didn't want to risk talking about items they didn't know much about and wind up looking stupid in front of the customer. So they just took the order the customer gave them. Now they had the support to be much more adventurous, and sell more stuff, and make more money. Salespeople liked that; they said it was fun.

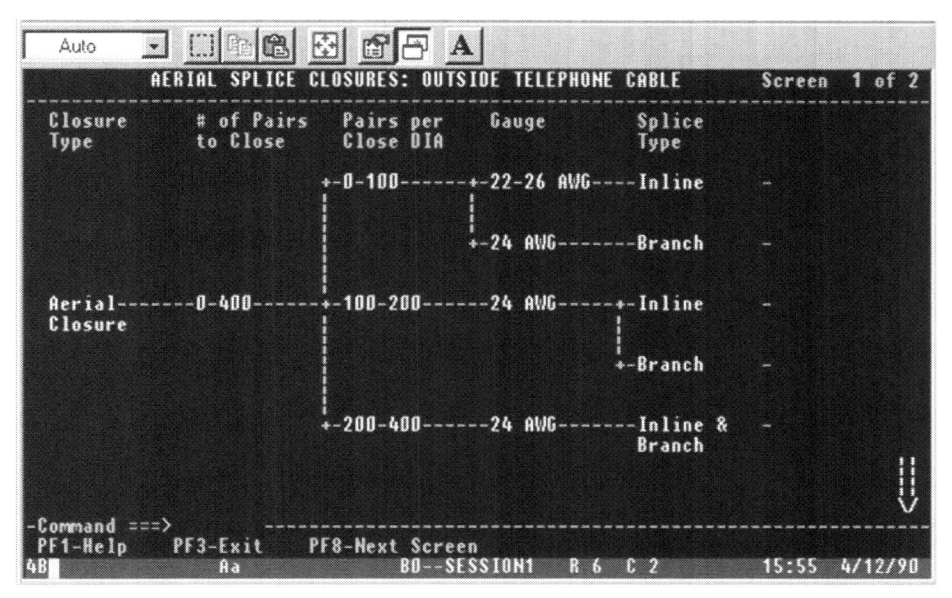

Figure 8-6. Salespeople zero in on specific items

Game Metaphor Extends Through to System Rollout

We rolled out the first version of the system and lavished attention on the first few sales offices that began using it. Those few sales offices started to show slight but noticeable increases in daily sales and gross profits. This induced one of the four regional vice presidents to publicly commit to switching over all the offices in his region to the new system.

Over the following months, we worked closely with the sales offices in that VP's region and continued to add new features, fix bugs, and smooth out rough edges as we got feedback from those sales offices. In those months, the region using the new system clearly outperformed the other regions. And that information was available online for everyone to see in the form of daily, weekly, and monthly sales reports.

This created a welcome bandwagon effect. We made the rollout of the new system into a game itself. We worked with the bigger offices in each region and they would in turn train the smaller offices. A team of training and IT people would show up in person and spend a day and a half with the salespeople in those bigger offices.

We would start usually on a Tuesday afternoon at 5:30, after normal business hours (Mondays were not good, they never are). In a well-rehearsed 90-minute session, we walked people through a system overview, helped them to log in to the new system, and as a group we worked through some common tasks. They saw how the system made it easier to look up products and how it gave them better information for pricing decisions. We showed how the system helped them engage customers in conversations to find out more about their projects and to suggest other products that would be useful. We pointed out that there was a pattern to these activities and showed how we had designed the system to accommodate that pattern.

As with the launch of any new system (or game), it was often met initially with skepticism or indifference. Any new system (even one that people say they want) involves a lot of change in the way work gets done. And convincing people who are already busy to make those changes and take the time to learn new things is a huge challenge.

After the system demo, we would take the salespeople out to a white-tablecloth restaurant—the kind of place they would take one of their best customers. The social environment that created was a great opportunity for system developers and salespeople to talk one on one and to form personal relationships. The next day, we would spend the whole day sitting with different salespeople—watching, listening, and giving help when asked. The developers wore headsets and plugged into a phone jack in each salesperson's cubicle so that they could listen as the salesperson talked with customers and used the new system.

The developers also played a game within the broader game of rolling out the system. The game was for every developer to take notes while they sat with different salespeople and find 10 ways to make the system better. They could be big or small; it didn't matter. The point was to keep improving the system and keep involving new system users by incorporating their ideas. People who saw their ideas incorporated into the system would in turn become active promoters of the system to their fellow salespeople.

We would release new system fixes and enhancements every couple of weeks and the salesperson who had thought of a new feature would get a personal call from the developer that implemented the feature. This produced a relationship between formerly estranged groups in the company that no one had thought possible. These two groups at first seemed to exhibit almost opposite behaviors and personality types. Yet the game format that we used for the project brought out a powerful collaboration dynamic that focused people on working together on tasks that had to be accomplished for the mission to succeed.

This is an example of the enduring nature of a system that engages and teaches its users as they actually do real work. The design of the system transcends the technology used to build it, and the design has been able to accommodate the addition of new technology and new features over time.

These days, when technology and user interface designs are changing so quickly, it is important to start with an elegantly simple and intuitively obvious system design and then use available technology to implement the design as best as possible. When people become distracted by and overly fixated on a particular technology or style of user interface, the design that results can be clever and visually impressive, but often it is not an enduring design because it is not easy to use and cannot evolve as technology and needs change. Designs like that are similar to movies that have little plot or character development and are composed mostly of special effects—they are dazzling on first view but have no power to engage people over time.

In the following chapter, we'll take a look at some game-based systems that use the latest technology and user interfaces (circa 2012). They mesh well with the workflows they are designed to support, and they too have the potential to endure and evolve over time.

9

Game Mechanics in Products, Services, and User Interfaces

MUCH OF THE USE of games in business in the last few years has focused on public relations, sales, and loyalty programs. We saw examples of this in Chapter 5 when we explored the gamification concepts and techniques used by companies like foursquare, Playboy, Samsung, and Salesforce. These applications are a start, and there is great potential to apply game mechanics to an even wider range of business activities. In this chapter, we'll look at three examples of other areas where companies are using game mechanics to influence peoples' behavior and improve performance.

The first example shows how one company is improving the productivity and accuracy of work done in accounts payable departments. They are using game mechanics to turn what is often a deadly dull and boring activity into something much more interesting. The second example is from a healthcare and wellness company, and it shows how they are using games to encourage people to change their lifestyles and engage in more healthful behavior. And the last example is from the automobile industry; it shows how some automobile companies are using game mechanics to change driving habits and show people how to get better mileage from their cars.

The Game of Accounts Payable

This is an example of game mechanics applied to the design and operation of a software product. The goal is to make that product more engaging and effective for the people who use it to do their jobs.

The job of manual data entry can be one of the most boring tasks in business today. Increasingly, the data entry task is being automated by capturing the data electronically at its source, but there are still many situations where, at least for now, there is no other way except to have people type in data from paper documents that are delivered through the mail.

Accounts payable is a case in point. In most companies, this function still involves enormous amounts of manual data entry.

In the summer of 2011, the software company SAP held a Gamification Cup challenge at its Palo Alto, California, office. SAP invited three prominent experts in the game design field: Amy Jo Kim, an influential game designer and teacher; Stanford University professor Bryon Reeves, who is a leading expert on the psychology of interactive media and coauthor of the book *Total Engagement*; and Gabe Zichermann, an entrepreneur, author, and gamification thought leader.[1] At the end of the challenge, each team presented their designs, and a panel of judges selected the winning design. The design created by the accounts payable team was chosen as the winner.

Mario Herger, SAP technology strategist and community manager, described what they learned from this.[2] He started by saying that the accounts payable design was appealing because it emphasized collaboration more than competition. Competition is often a central element of games, but research shows most people are not as motivated by individual competition as they are by group collaboration. Mario described how the competition in the accounts payable game is not between individuals; it is instead between accounts payable teams in different offices and different regions.

People win "karma points" by collaborating with each other to answer questions and requests posted by others in accounts payable. These range from questions about how to book a certain kind of invoice to requests for help in researching a payment problem. This collaboration leverages the expertise of the most experienced people and raises the education and skill level of everyone else in the process of doing their job. The design combines the SAP accounts payable software with the SAP collaboration platform called Streamworks.

---

1 Gabe Zichermann is the chair of the Gamification Summit and Workshops, and is coauthor of the book *Game-Based Marketing* (Wiley, 2010), in which he makes a compelling case for the use of games and game mechanics in everyday life, the Web, and business. Gabe is also coauthor of the book *Gamification by Design* (O'Reilly, 2011) and a board member of *StartOut.org* and facilitator for the NYC chapter of the *Founder Institute*. A native of Canada and resident of NYC, Gabe frequently muses about games and the world at *http://Gamification.Co*.

2 Phone interview between author and Mario Herger, January 2012.

People within SAP used a prototype of this gamified accounts payable system and their experience with it is providing data that shows the system improves the accuracy and reduces mistakes made in accounts payable as well as increases the amount of data being entered each month. SAP is investigating how to make this software available to interested customers. Sample screens from this application are shown in Figures 9-1, 9-2, and 9-3.

Mario also said that with the spread of cloud computing and software as a service (SaaS) applications, SAP and other software vendors are moving into a new type of market. In the traditional market, customers paid up front for software packages and then installed and operated them in-house. This created a certain amount of lock-in for customers once they had paid for and installed a given software package.

The new market that SAP and other application software companies are entering is a pay-as-you-go market. Customers do not make big up-front payments; instead, they work on a per person monthly fee. Applications are delivered over the Internet as software as SaaS apps. It is much easier for customers to switch from one SaaS app to another if they become unhappy. SAP believes game mechanics applied to their applications have the potential to better engage customers and keep them from leaving.

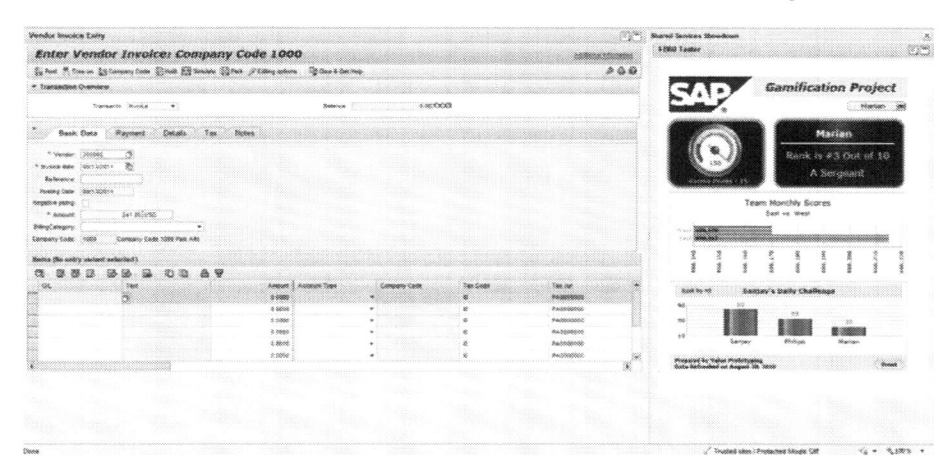

Figure 9-1. Sample screen showing status of teams and players at start of day, courtesy of SAP

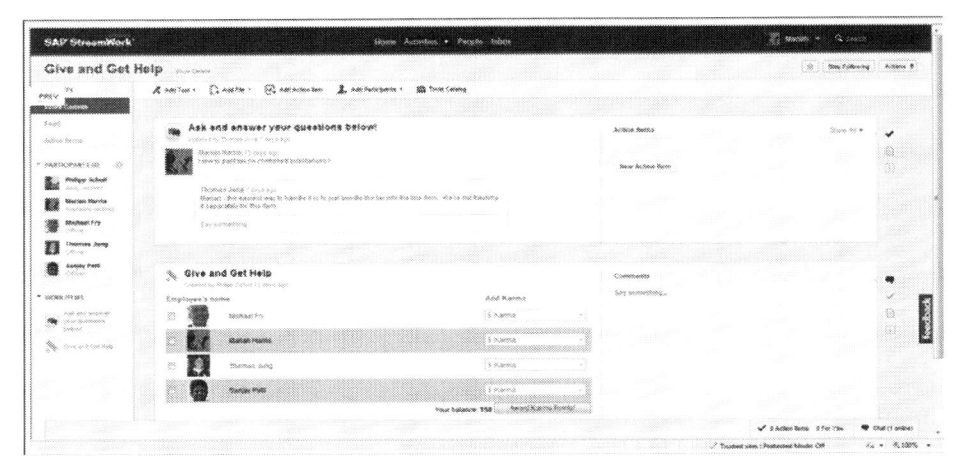

Figure 9-2. Collaboration screen showing people working together, courtesy of SAP

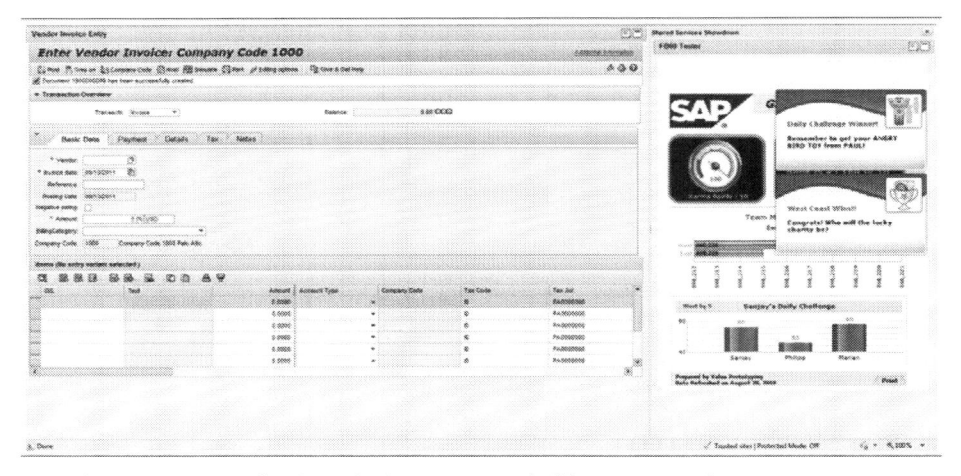

Figure 9-3. Screen showing winning team at end of day, courtesy of SAP

Health and Wellness Benefits from Games

Health and wellness is more about helping people develop and maintain healthy habits than it is about the use of drugs and medical procedures. Here is an example of applying game mechanics to an online subscription service that helps people get more involved in developing new habits that promote their health. MeYou Health uses game mechanics to deliver wellness services. Companies sign up with them and then their employees are able to participate in MeYou Health games and challenges. The games are fun so as to attract voluntary participation and people learn and change their behaviors in the process of participating in the games.

Trapper Markelz, director of Product Development at MeYou Health, explained the company's approach to using game techniques: "Gamification's value is not so much in turning something into a game, but it is a framework for how we can interact. It makes interaction predictable and comfortable."[3] He gave the example of a man sitting on a park bench. People probably wouldn't stop and talk to him because they wouldn't know what to expect if they did. But if you put a table and a checkerboard in front of him that provides a context and structure for interaction, people would be much more comfortable about communicating with him because it would be in the context of playing checkers or chess.

Markelz went on to explain that sharing badges is powerful because it creates scenarios where we can predictably interact with each other and share our progress with others in the game. It creates a context that makes it easy to have conversations about well-being because it's expected, so it's comfortable. Games are good at creating context and comfort to talk about otherwise awkward subjects.

At MeYou Health, an insightful distinction between products and games is drawn. "I'm drawn to the idea of how games focus on journeys where products focus on outcome," said Markelz. He said the whole point of a game is about playing the game to see what happens—emergent outcomes. It's not about creating a process and getting people out the other side as efficiently as possible. Instead, it's about sustaining and playing the game as long as possible—endless gaming. "We're not trying to create a mastery process in which you win, but to create an endless process in which you can sustain yourself."

In its gamification designs, MeYou Health uses three game components that Markelz learned from to Amy Jo Kim:[4]

---

3 Phone conversation between author and Trapper Markelz at MeYou Health (*http://www.meyouhealth.com/*), February 2012.

4 Amy Jo Kim (*http://www.shufflebrain.com/*) is a social game designer who has worked on Rock Band, eBay, There.com, MetroGirl, Photograb, and Netflix. She wrote *Community Building on the Web*, a design handbook for networked communities that's available in seven languages (English, Spanish, German, Italian, Japanese, Korean, and Chinese) and is required reading in game design studios and universities worldwide. She holds a PhD in behavioral neuroscience from the University of Washington and a BS in Experimental Psychology from The University of California San Diego.

- Dynamics that let you know when and where
- Mechanics that let you know where you've been and where you're going
- Aesthetics that are fulfilling as a reward for the journey

The combination of these three—mechanics, dynamics, and aesthetics[5]—is how a process is gamified. Here's how it is used in the design of the Daily Challenge: The process starts with an appointment dynamic—people expect to receive a Daily Challenge email promptly at 7:00 every morning. Then they use a mechanic called a countdown—everybody has 24 hours to complete the Daily Challenge, and if they do, they receive points for doing so. And the aesthetic is the feeling people get and how they share that feeling when they click the big green "Done" button in the Daily Challenge email, signaling they have accomplished their challenge.

As people complete challenges, they get tokens, and when they collect 15 tokens, they can use them to unlock categories of challenges that are most interesting to them. The challenge categories are influenced by what employers want, but people playing the game are free to select the categories they find most interesting.

The Daily Challenges create awareness and mindfulness about the choices people make and the results those choices bring. It leverages social aspects such as sharing comments and achievements with others. Well-being is as much about creating networks of people who influence the choices and opinions of each other as it is about individual accomplishments. Figures 9-4, 9-5, and 9-6 show sample screens from MeYou Health.

---

5   The concept of mechanics, dynamics, and aesthetics is generally known as the MDA Framework and is attributed to Huncke, LeBlanc, and Zubek, as noted in their paper cited at *http://en.wikipedia.org/wiki/MDA_framework*.

GAME MECHANICS IN PRODUCTS, SERVICES, AND USER INTERFACES | 111

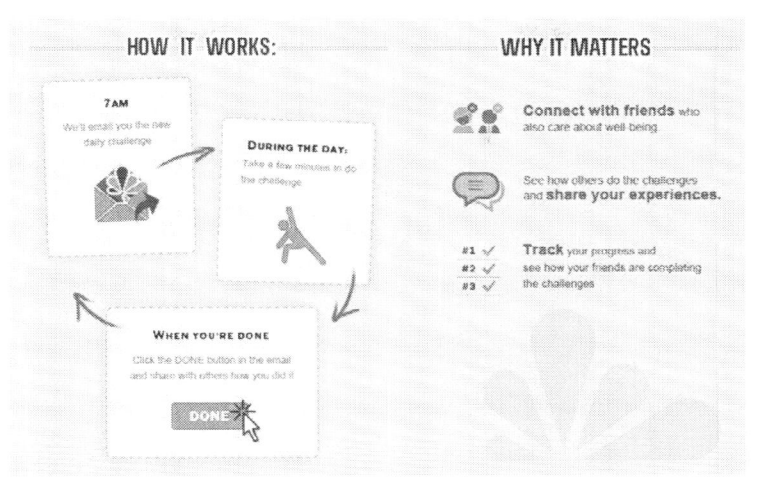

Figure 9-4. How the Daily Challenge works, courtesy of MeYou Health

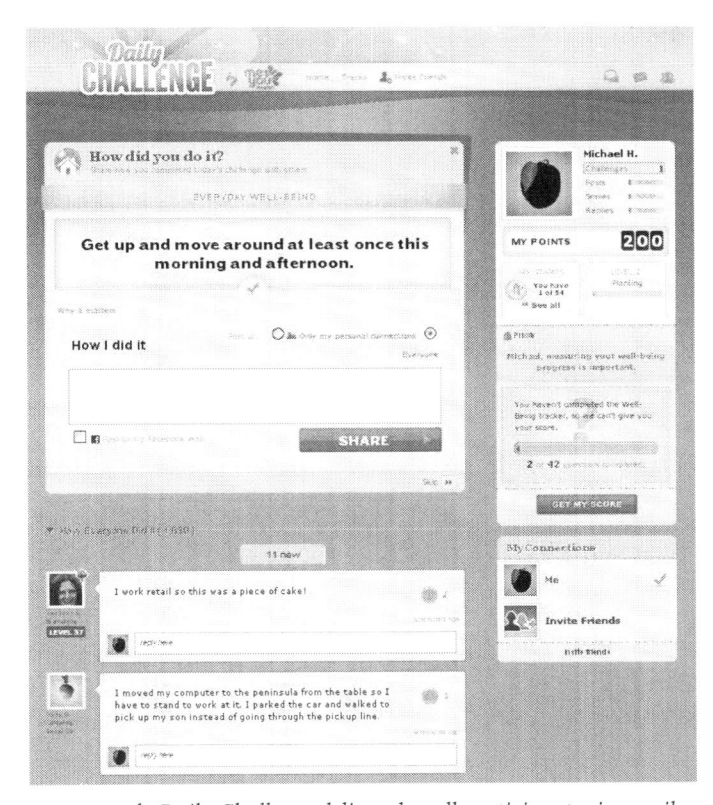

Figure 9-5. A sample Daily Challenge delivered to all participants via email, courtesy of MeYou Health

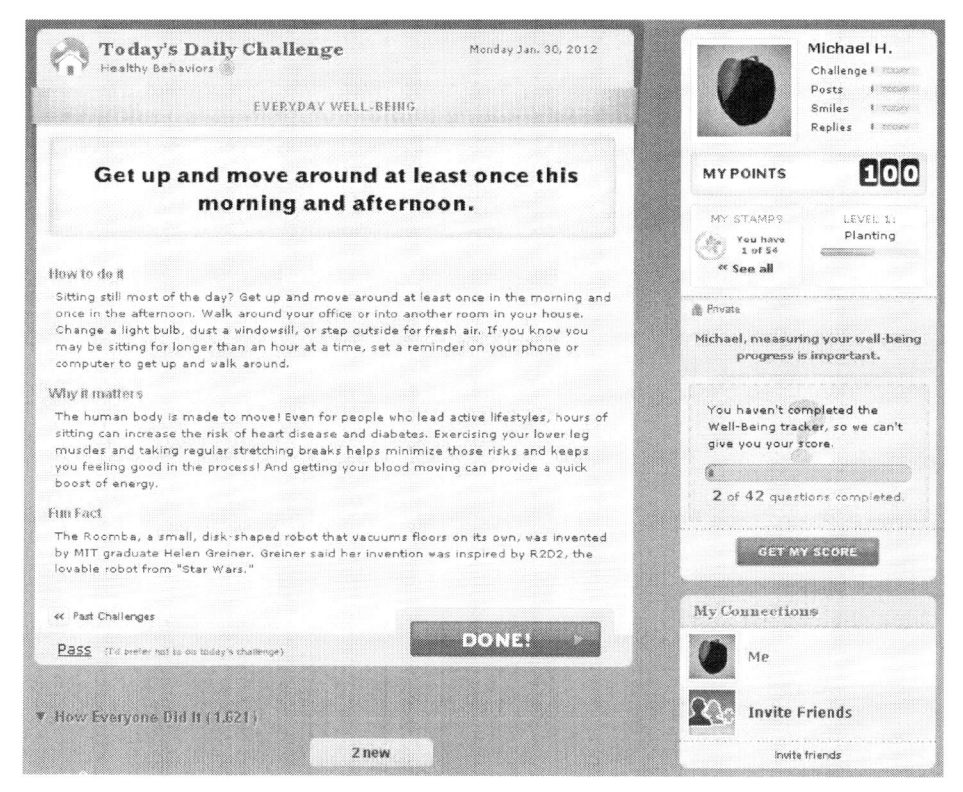

Figure 9-6. Completion of Daily Challenge with the option to share, courtesy of MeYou Health

A Driving Game Called Hypermiling

This is an example of applying one of the most basic game mechanics of all—real-time feedback—to the design of user interfaces used in automobiles. This user interface is designed to encourage and reward drivers who develop behaviors that promote better fuel efficiency.

There are a hundred little adjustments you can make every day, every moment as you drive, and the result will be to increase your gas mileage by 20 or 40 percent or more. We don't need to wait helplessly until somebody invents a car that gets 100 miles per gallon (MPG) or 300 kilometers per liter. Car companies are using game mechanics to make us aware of the moment to moment effects of our driving behavior and to show us ways to drive a little differently and get better results.

I recently spent some time with my brother Andy who lives outside of Albany, NY. He is a levelheaded guy who does not fall for passing fads (he's a financial planner[6] and also a master sergeant in the New York State National Guard who spent a year on duty in Iraq in 2005). When he picked me up at the airport, I noticed something different about the way he was driving. He was accelerating slowly, gliding around corners, and not using the brakes so much. I asked what was going on, and he pointed to a gauge on the dashboard of his Volvo that showed a real-time readout of MPG and average MPG.

He said his goal was to operate the car so as to get the highest possible MPG moment to moment, and over the longer haul his goal was to get the average MPG up to 25.5. He explained that up until a couple of months ago, his average had been around 20.5 and he wanted to see a 25 percent increase to help offset the rising prices he was paying for gas.

I asked a few more questions and he opened up and admitted he was employing a practice known as "hypermiling." While driving, he thought about increasing MPG all the time, and his average MPG was already 24.0 to 24.5, which meant he was saving at least $1,000 annually on gasoline.

This is a great illustration of what simple embedded electronics and data displays can do to change our relationship with our machines, our world, and each other. The effect of a real-time data feed that displays performance data back to an operator allows that person to make continuous adjustments to maximize their efficiency as conditions change. And all those simple adjustments start to add up in significant ways. I'm talking about the performance of cars here, but the same principles apply to the performance of whole companies if they can learn to harness the power of self-adjusting feedback loops.

Devoted hypermilers practice and refine their techniques relentlessly, but that doesn't mean the rest of us can't start learning to do the basic stuff now and level up from there as we get better. It involves applying some principles like pumping up your tires to the maximum rating shown on their sidewalls to reduce rolling resistance; using low viscosity engine oil to reduce engine resistance; keeping your speed down (many cars have a sweet spot at around 40 to 45 MPH where they get the highest MPG) but

---

6 Andy Hugos is a chartered financial consultant, and his firm is Current Assets (*http://www.plansavegrow.com/index.htm*).

going for higher speeds when gliding down hills; avoiding unnecessary braking; and trying to coast to a stop.

One day we took a drive out into the country to a town about 70 miles away, and I started to see the possibilities of hypermiling. The game is infectious. You get caught up in how to play each stretch of road, how to navigate through traffic, and how to time the stop lights so you don't have to use your brakes.

The car itself stores momentum (momentum = mass × speed) and the car chassis has been finely engineered to create minimum friction with the turning wheels. On a straight highway after you get your speed up to 70 MPH or so, you can take your foot off the gas and slip the car into neutral and it will roll for miles before the speed drops below 45 MPH. And if you are driving in the country on hilly terrain, then every moment challenges your skill. You learn to accelerate just enough to glide over the top of a rise up ahead and then pick up speed as you coast down the other side.

When you get the hang of those things, then you start working on more demanding skills like developing a sixth sense about how to play stop lights. Do you use your brakes to stop, or have you timed the light so you can keep rolling right on through?

And then there is the art of acceleration. We all have to accelerate; people used to brag about how fast they could accelerate from zero to sixty, but it's hard for the devoted hypermiler to watch that MPG number drop. The faster you accelerate, the more that number drops (to about 3 MPG or less). Of course you have to balance that reluctance with the likelihood you are going to stir up some irritation from drivers behind you who do not know you are playing the hypermiling game. The day we all start hypermiling as we drive to work, we will look like a bunch of ice skaters as we glide along without the sudden stops and starts that are so much part of our driving style today.

For cars that don't already have readouts showing MPG and average MPG, there is a simple little gauge that aspiring hypermilers can buy and install on any car made since 1996 and get a real-time display of the relevant numbers. Figure 9-7 shows this simple gauge and two other examples of mileage feedback for drivers.

And regardless of the technology used, the main point of the game is to feel the car, feel the road, and understand how your momentum unites you with the world you are passing through. ("Concentrate, Luke; clear your mind... let the Force be with you.")

GAME MECHANICS IN PRODUCTS, SERVICES, AND USER INTERFACES | 115

1. Simple performance monitor attachable to almost any car—produced by ScanGauge.

2. Performance montior for diesel trucks—produced by Bully Dog.

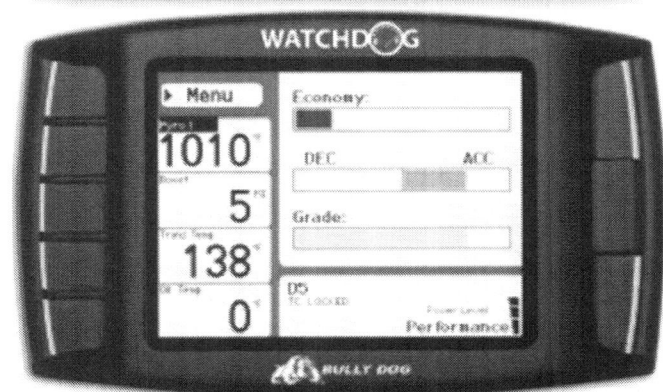

3. Built-in monitor on dashboard display of Ford Fusion car.

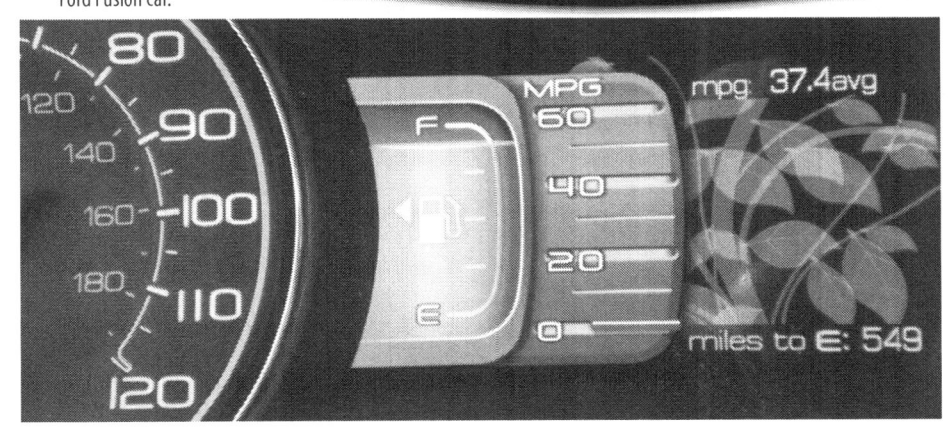

Figure 9-7. Examples of mileage feedback displays

These three games are examples of applying game mechanics to situations so that a self-perpetuating dynamic takes hold. The four traits of a game (goals, rules, feedback systems, and voluntary participation) come into being and people engage with these situations in ways that cause them to learn and increase their skills. The behavior changes that happen because of this result in continuous improvements in the way these operations are performed.

The examples presented here and in previous chapters show that companies can create engaging and effective games using IT infrastructure they already have in place. They can then enhance existing infrastructure with game ingredients such as points, leaderboards, and collaboration platforms as they go and experience substantial benefits from doing so.

In the following chapters, we'll consider what happens when existing IT infrastructure is enhanced with new technology. When this new technology provides additional game ingredients such as 3-D virtual environments and personal representation via avatars, it has the potential to take games in business to a whole new level.

10

Environments of Decision

PROCTER & GAMBLE (P&G) is a multibillion dollar global consumer products company, and over the last few years they have begun using technology in a very game-like manner to enable better collaboration and decision making at many different levels in their organization. They have invested in the creation of what they call "Business Spheres." This is an example of a multinational corporation employing game mechanics at a strategic management level and also at a tactical operating level.

The first Business Sphere was built at their headquarters in Cincinnati, OH, in 2010 and in the following year they built 50 smaller Business Spheres at other P&G offices around the world.[1] The purpose of these Business Spheres is to improve decision making and collaboration by providing people with videoconferencing, real-time product sales numbers, market share data, inventory in the supply chain, and ad spending. Figure 10-1 shows a picture of the Business Sphere in Cincinnati.

Every Monday, P&G's CEO and his management team meet in the Business Sphere to review operations and make decisions. They are immersed in the data. On the walls of the Business Sphere are two 30-foot wide projection screens and six different dashboards and data visualization views can be projected on these screens. At each end of the room are smaller screens that allow remote executives to participate via videoconferencing. These people at remote locations can see what is projected on the different dashboards on their laptops or iPads.

The data displays are designed to be quickly understood. Map views are used to show sales by country and region. Green, yellow, and red indicators show if sales are meeting or exceeding expectations or if they are

---

[1] Big Data I/O Forum, "P&G Investing in Big Data Analytics," March 6, 2012, *http://bigdata-io.org/pg-investing-in-big-data-analytics*.

lagging behind. A data analyst is on hand to help executives get further information about emerging problems. They can drill down to get more granular data showing what is happening in particular countries, stores, and product categories.

The decision-making process is assisted by a set of analytic data models that show what is happening in the business that day, why it is happening, and what the company can do address specific problems. High-level displays quickly show what is happening and focus executive attention on the exceptions and unexpected events. Countries and regions that show up on the map in yellow or red quickly get people's attention. Then, the ability to drill down to get more information shows why these problems are happening. And, finally, predictive models show how different possible actions could affect the problem. People can investigate how best to solve a problem by experimenting with different actions such as changing product prices, advertising, and product mixes.[2]

The point here is to improve the speed and effectiveness of decision making. The Business Spheres at P&G can be thought of as "environments of decision."[3] People have the information they need right there in the meeting. They can investigate options, make decisions, and take actions that day instead of letting problems continue for another week or another month while they gather more data and study possible alternatives.

The four traits of a game—goals, rules, feedback systems, and voluntary participation—are present in this Business Sphere. What P&G has done with its Business Spheres is to dramatically improve its feedback systems by providing near real-time transparency of its operations and sales data. They already have business goals (they announce them at the beginning of each year), and the rules are the rules of business and finance that apply in the countries where they operate. Now voluntary and enthusiastic participation in accomplishing the business goals is greatly increased by the data transparency and feedback systems made possible by Business Sphere.

---

[2] Doug Hanschen, "P&G Turns Analysis Into Action," *InformationWeek*, September 14, 2011, *http://www.informationweek.com/news/global-cio/interviews/231600959*.

[3] The phrase "environments of decision" was coined by Stafford Beer, the British pioneer in operations research and industrial cybernetics. He introduced this concept and describes how it works in his book *Brain of the Firm* (Hoboken, NJ: John Wiley & Sons, 1981), 181. A YouTube video of one of his talks titled "The Cybernetic Paradigm" can be viewed at *http://www.youtube.com/watch?v=7OO9FPHuCQQ*.

Figure 10-1. Procter & Gamble Business Sphere, courtesy of Procter & Gamble

These Business Spheres work so well because the three conditions for creating effective feedback systems (see Chapter 3) are all present: real-time data transparency, people with a stake in the outcome, and people with authority to act within predefined rules to accomplish common goals.

As we have seen from other examples mentioned in this book, such as the IVS System (see Chapter 2) and the Anixter SALE System (see Chapter 8), real-time data transparency brings feedback loops into being and these feedback loops can then be harnessed to steer a company toward its goals even as its environment keeps changing in unexpected ways.

The driving force for success in this real-time global economy is a continuous and effective response to change. Companies that try to maintain their operations based on the industrial model of the last century, which emphasizes efficiency, will find themselves increasingly unable to cope with the fast paced and unpredictable nature of markets today. Efficiency is still important, but it is not the be all and end all of business that it once was. In the real-time economy, responsiveness trumps efficiency. Using game mechanics to create and harness goal-seeking feedback loops is as powerful now as the introduction of the assembly line was at the beginning of the last century.

Harnessing Feedback Loops to Drive the Great Game of Business

We all know the stable and predictable industrial economy of the last century has been replaced with a new real-time economy that is much less predictable and much more volatile, so why do we keep trying to organize and operate businesses as if the world was stable and predictable? Maybe it's because the only model we have for business operations is still the assembly line—that process that served us so well for the last hundred years.

As the world becomes steadily more unpredictable, we need a new process that is more appropriate to the realities of today. This process is based on the feedback loop, and that is what P&G and other companies are experimenting with. Where the assembly line was a strict linear process that put everything in its place and maximized efficiency, the feedback loop is a flexible circular process that drives change and maximizes responsiveness.

Feedback loops come into being when there is real-time data transparency and when people have a reason to care (a stake in the outcome) and have autonomy to act on their own within rules to achieve common goals. In Chapter 3, we saw how game dynamics can be used to drive business agility. Once feedback systems are introduced, people who have a stake in the outcome and authority to act will start to act and learn and respond as events change.

Let's consider a simple model for understanding how feedback loops can be organized to drive business operations. Figure 10-2 shows how three interlinking feedback loops can be employed to drive company operations in a continuous process of sensing and responding to changes in its environment. Companies need to find ways to be agile and responsive without losing control of their operations. That is what the combination of these three feedback loops is designed to accomplish—to enable companies to be agile while still exercising control.

Loop 1 is the executive function; it's where management continually assesses what's happening and makes decisions about what to do. This is what the executives at P&G do in the Business Sphere. Loop 1 highlights the exceptions, or what we could call "nonstandard input." This is what managers need to know about quickly; systems that hide the nonstandard or unexpected data in a mass of routine information are not effective. Nobody has time to wade through volumes of routine data to find out what is important. This is what P&G's Business Sphere does for their executives. Loop 1 is all about creating awareness of changing circumstances and emerging problems.

This awareness gives rise to a game that is always in motion, as is any MMO game. This was the case before, but the reality of it was partly hidden by slow communications and data collection procedures. But no longer.

Depending on what management decides is the reason for an emerging problem or unexpected opportunity, they will then invoke actions that rely on either Loop 2 or Loop 3. Loop 2 is about fixing or improving an existing process and Loop 3 is about creating a new process. Most of the time, problems can be best handled by improving the operation of existing business processes.

This means Loop 2 activity is going on all the time in many different areas of the business. The Six Sigma DMAIC process (Define, Measure, Analyze, Improve, Control) is a well-documented example of how Loop 2 operates.[4] Loop 2 provides continuous adjustments and small changes to existing operations so that they remain in balance with changing business conditions. And these continuous adjustments yield a steady stream of small savings and small earnings realized every day, week, and month. In my personal experience, I have seen this add a steady 2 to 4 percent to gross profits year after year. (An analogy is to think of how the sunflower is able to optimize its photosynthesis with continuous adjustments to its alignment with the sun as the sun travels across the sky.)

Loop 3 is for creating new procedures and products. People build something new to respond to the arrival of a new threat or opportunity. This feedback loop is all about agility because it requires people to move quickly. Creating something new is different from the process of improving existing operations.

---

[4] George Eckes, *Six Sigma for Everyone* (Hoboken, NJ: John Wiley & Sons, 2003), 29.

122 | ENTERPRISE GAMES

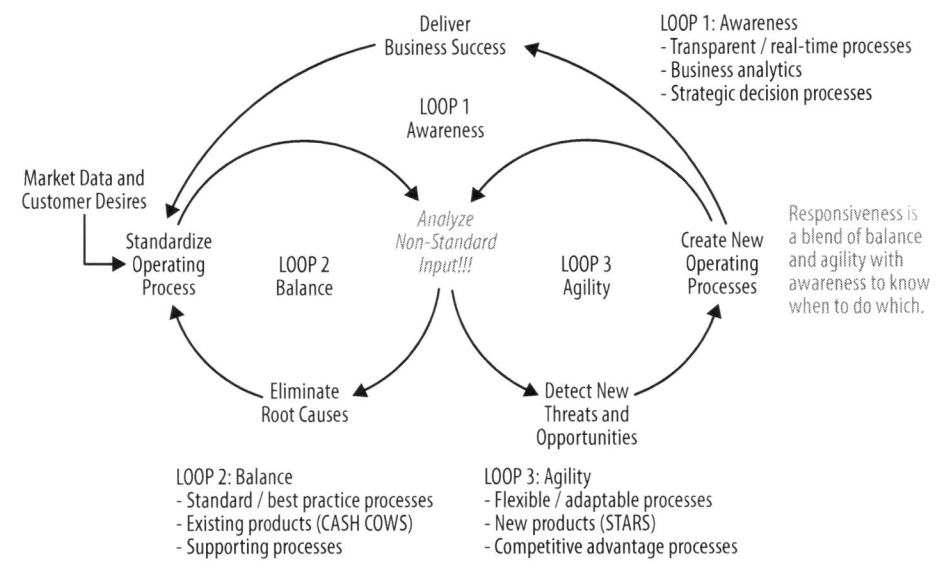

```
                        Deliver              LOOP 1: Awareness
                    Business Success         - Transparent / real-time processes
                                             - Business analytics
                         LOOP 1              - Strategic decision processes
                        Awareness

Market Data and
Customer Desires
                                                              Responsiveness is
    Standardize        Analyze         Create New             a blend of balance
    Operating      → Non-Standard →    Operating              and agility with
    Process          Input!!!          Processes              awareness to know
              LOOP 2              LOOP 3                      when to do which.
              Balance             Agility

            Eliminate              Detect New
            Root Causes            Threats and
                                   Opportunities

    LOOP 2: Balance                   LOOP 3: Agility
    - Standard / best practice processes    - Flexible / adaptable processes
    - Existing products (CASH COWS)         - New products (STARS)
    - Supporting processes                  - Competitive advantage processes
```

Figure 10-2. Three feedback loops drive the responsive organization

Agility is about quickly trying out new ideas to see if they meet the challenge. The agile system development movement has defined a number of methods that can be used to guide the activities in Loop 3. The most popular agile development method at present is called Scrum and it advocates that agile development teams work an iterative process where each iteration typically takes from two to four weeks. At the end of each iteration, a tangible deliverable is produced that is put into operation to get feedback on how well it works. Teams then continue to iteratively build out and improve the system, product, or business process based on what they learn from this feedback. This means people get the first version of a new process or product into operation as soon as possible and if that new process delivers business success, then it becomes part of standard operating procedures and it is continually improved upon to deliver greater success.

The combined effect of these three feedback loops is what creates a responsive and self-adjusting organization. The challenge for companies is learning to embrace these three feedback loops and letting go of practices built around that hallowed tradition called the assembly line. That's a big shift.

The way feedback loops can be used in business is essentially the same as the way games use feedback loops to engage and guide players. MMOs are examples of how such feedback systems work. When all players can see what is happening and when all will be rewarded for achieving certain objectives, then people will work together enthusiastically as long as they believe rules are being fairly enforced. This has potential to generate a new source of steady profits that was once what the efficiencies of the assembly line delivered.

As we look at this new idea of feedback systems, we forget that the assembly line also was once a controversial idea. But when people got over being skeptical, the assembly line was adopted as the organizing paradigm for work in companies from manufacturing to financial services. For its time, it was a powerful innovation and it delivered the productivity that made the consumer economy possible.

Now, business is transitioning out of the predictable assembly line world and is looking for a new operating paradigm. These three feedback loops are simple enough for people to understand (as the assembly line was), and they are flexible enough to control change without stifling it. These feedback loops are about guiding a continuous response to change.

There is certainly more research to be done, and the results delivered by a few companies do not provide conclusive proof of the benefits of a real-time feedback driven business model. Yet one thing is clear: If change is the most predictable thing in a world where so much else is so unpredictable, then companies organized to deal with change will be more successful than companies not organized to deal with change. And harnessing feedback loops to drive responsiveness to change is a powerful innovation for these times.

Loop 1 Awareness: Observe, Orient, Decide, Act

It is in Loop 1 that the game a company plays (its goals and rules) is defined. Skill in Loop 1 activities determines the effectiveness of a company's actions and, ultimately, the outcome of the game it plays. The better people understand and perform in Loop 1, the better a company will perform.

Let's take a closer look at a model for organizing the activities that happen in Loop 1. This model is the work of a former colonel in the US Air Force who was a fighter pilot in the Korean War. His name was John Boyd and he went on to become an influential military thinker whose ideas started out as controversial but have now become accepted doctrine in many military organizations around the world. He carried on a lifelong study of the strategies and tactics that produced successful outcomes in fast-paced and chaotic situations. He summarized his findings in what he called "Observe, Orient, Decide, Act" or the OODA Loop.

The activities that executives at P&G carry out in their meetings in the Business Sphere are well described by the OODA Loop. John Boyd emphasized that the most important step in the OODA Loop was the Orient step. It is in this step that people form a picture of what is happening, and from this they develop their understanding of events and formulate decisions about how best to respond. Everything else flows from this understanding. Figure 10-3 presents a diagram of the activities in the OODA Loop.

The OODA Loop
(Loop 1)

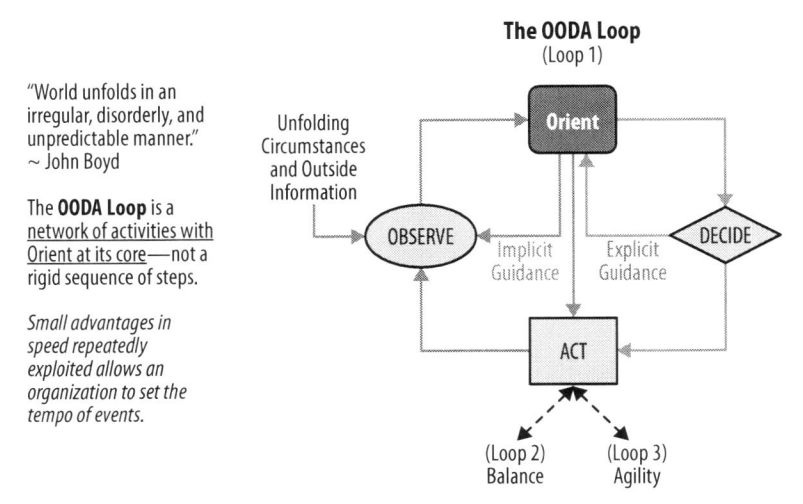

"World unfolds in an irregular, disorderly, and unpredictable manner."
~ John Boyd

The **OODA Loop** is a network of activities with Orient at its core—not a rigid sequence of steps.

Small advantages in speed repeatedly exploited allows an organization to set the tempo of events.

Figure 10-3. John Boyd's OODA Loop

Boyd often pointed out that in the Orient step it was most important to focus on the unexpected or nonstandard events. In any reasonably well-run company, most of the data most of the time will simply confirm that operations are proceeding as expected. But if people allow this to lull them into a false sense of security, they will miss the important information or they will even deliberately turn a blind eye to unexpected events.

In the Orient step, information is organized into a big picture view of what is happening in the company and its environment (an example of how this big picture view can be organized and presented is illustrated by the P&G Business Spheres). A critical part of the Orient activity is to continuously screen incoming real-time data to find the nonstandard inputs or exceptions and bring them to the immediate attention of appropriate persons.

In many cases, exceptions will have been seen before and people will already know how to deal with them. They will act on their own initiative do so. This is what induces the spontaneous self-organizing dynamic that you see in MMO games into business operations. It is a process that John Boyd called "implicit guidance" because everybody knows the drill when it comes to handling these kind of situations. When people see them, they just swing into action; they don't need to be told what to do by any higher authority.

In some cases, the exceptions will be something new that people haven't seen before. That's when executive management and support staff enter the loop and evaluate possible actions before making a decision. Boyd called this explicit guidance, because in these situations, people do not know what to do on their own, and they look to leaders to outline a course of action for them to follow.

The best opportunities lie in creative and effective responses to unexpected events. That is where organizations will find the greatest competitive advantages. Once unexpected events are brought to peoples' attention, the understanding created in the Orient step will largely determine if the unexpected event will be seen as a need to improve an existing process or a need to create a new process.

As people decide how to respond to nonstandard input, there are four things they need to know about the data that generated the exception condition. They need to know if that exception was most likely the result of chance, a transient condition, a slope change, or a step change (this is shown in Figure 10-4).[5] Depending on which cause you assign to this data alert, it will determine if you respond by invoking Loop 2 or Loop 3.

Two statisticians created a forecasting model that can be applied to a real-time data stream in order to determine the most likely cause of an event. This forecasting model is named the Harrison-Stevens model after its inventors.

---

5 William Bolstad, "Harrison-Stevens Forecasting and the Multiprocess Dynamic Linear Model," *The American Statistician*, 40, no. 2 (1986), 129–35, *http://www.jstor.org/stable/2684871*.

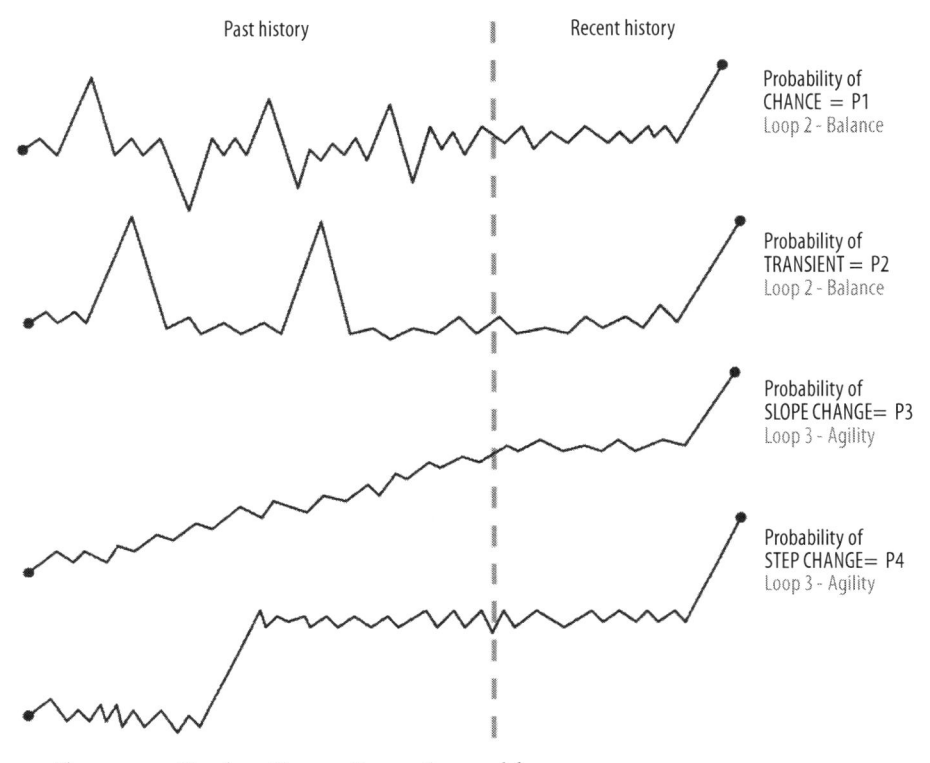

Figure 10-4. Harrison-Stevens Forecasting model

Past history | Recent history

Probability of CHANCE = P1
Loop 2 - Balance

Probability of TRANSIENT = P2
Loop 2 - Balance

Probability of SLOPE CHANGE = P3
Loop 3 - Agility

Probability of STEP CHANGE = P4
Loop 3 - Agility

If the cause of an unexpected event is seen as most likely being caused by chance or by a transient recurring condition, then that indicates a problem in existing procedures, and therefore, Loop 2 is the best course of action.

If it is seen as being caused by a slope change or a step change, then that indicates the appearance of an entirely new situation that has not been seen before and for which existing procedures will not be able to respond effectively. That means invoking Loop 3 is the best course of action.

Dataspaces and Navigating in the Real-Time Economy

As companies harness real-time feedback to guide their operations, they simultaneously have to take on the challenge of finding ways to navigate through massive streams of continuously flowing data. These data streams are known as "big data." Big data is everywhere; it emanates from sources such as on-board computers built into automobiles, industrial and environmental sensor networks, all sorts of social media systems, the click streams of millions of people surfing the Internet, and the moment-to-moment transactions happening in financial and stock trading exchanges around the world, to name just a few.

Jeff Hammerbacker, in his book *Beautiful Data*,[6] talks about creating what he calls "dataspaces." He describes dataspaces as enormous collections of data that are being fed in real time from many different sources. This means that these dataspaces are composed of structured and unstructured data and that the organization of the dataspace itself evolves over time as the data it contains evolve. Jeff goes on to state that dataspaces make their data easily available by providing a rich library of data connections or APIs (application program interfaces) that enable other systems to tap in and download selected data elements.

Dataspaces are designed to enable people to explore and understand the data rather than to do predefined analysis and reporting operations. That is a primary difference between a dataspace and a traditional data warehouse or business intelligence tool. Dataspaces are being created to house and manage what is now called big data.

Big data consists of datasets that grow so large they outgrow the ability of traditional database technology and business intelligence tools to work with them.[7] Difficulties that need to be addressed while working with big data are how the data is captured, how it is stored, how it is searched, and how it is analyzed and visualized. The need for dataspaces is growing because of the benefits of working with larger and larger datasets that allow analysts and organizations to "spot business trends, prevent diseases, and combat crime."[8]

Organizations now have the opportunity to capture and work with big data because the technology to generate data is embedded in everything from websites to sensor networks and video cameras. The sensors in our cars stream real-time data about our cars' performance. Radio frequency identification (RFID) tags attached to cargo containers, and individual products in world supply chains stream data as they pass through sensor

---

6 Jeff Hammerbacker, Tony Segaran, *Beautiful Data: The Stories Behind Elegant Data Solutions* (Cambridge, MA: O'Reilly Media, 2009).

7 *Wikipedia*, "Big Data," http://en.wikipedia.org/wiki/Big_data#cite_ref-3 (accessed March 17, 2012).

8 K. Cukier. "Data, Data Everywhere." *The Economist* (2010), http://www.economist.com/specialreports/displaystory.cfm?story_id=15557443.

networks. The whole world now generates continuous streams of data that thirty years ago was only seen from stock exchanges and financial markets.

Not only does big data outgrow the ability of traditional technology to manage it, big data also outgrows the ability of traditional data analysis tools to visualize it. As companies enter this big data world and create dataspaces to capture and manage the continuous flow of data, there are opportunities to apply video game technology to help us analyze and visualize the data.

In the following chapter, we'll explore how game technology can help us understand and respond to big data in real time.

11

A Novel Encounter with Big Data

TECHNOLOGY AND TECHNIQUES FROM gaming, such as 3-D animation, avatars, and virtual worlds, can be applied to business intelligence and data analytics applications to help us better understand and respond to the massive amounts of data generated by our real-time, unpredictable economy. Operating effectively in a big data world is now critical for success.

Big data is an ocean of data flowing around us. It comes from social media, e-commerce, financial exchanges, supply chains, streaming video, Twitter, and the clickstreams of two billion (soon to be four billion) people surfing the Web and talking to each other at any given moment. There are patterns in the data for those who can see them, and there are signals for those who can hear them, but this calls for a new approach to capture the richness of the data.

We humans are already wired up to comprehend massive amounts of real-time data when it is presented as moving 3-D displays. Our sense of sight is the largest bandwidth sense that we have. And the next largest bandwidth sense is hearing. So, if data is presented within a 3-D space as moving objects with different shapes, sizes, and speeds depending on the data they represent, and if sound is also associated with the different objects, then we can present and comprehend an enormous amount of information.

Multisensory Engagement with the Data

Line graphs, bar and pie charts, and scatter plots all work well enough when there are just a few types of data or relationships to display. But in the ocean of big data, they're overwhelmed like dinghies in a storm. They're limited to a flat world of two dimensions, an X and a Y, a vertical and a horizontal. There's only so much they can show. As Figure 11-1 shows, they're starting to look like finger paintings on a cave wall.

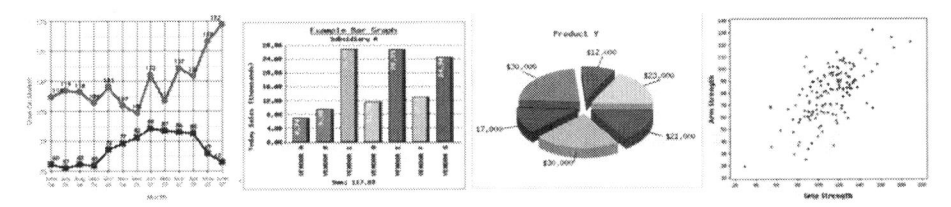

Figure 11-1. Traditional two-dimensional data visualizations

These techniques come from a time when data was scarce, the collection of data happened only occasionally, and we had lots of time to analyze the data because things didn't change that fast. This isn't the case anymore, and these two-dimensional techniques don't handle the richness of the data or the speed with which it comes at us now. These two-dimensional data abstractions cannot handle the richness of big data because they live in Flatland.

In 1884, a British professor and mathematician named Edwin Abbott Abbott wrote a short book titled *Flatland: A Romance of Many Dimensions*.[1] Abbott described what life is like in a two-dimensional world and the characters in the story are two-dimensional shapes such as squares, pentagons, and triangles. Then, one day, the main character in the story (by the name of A. Square) encounters a creature from the third dimension. This creature is a sphere. But A. Square cannot comprehend Mr. Sphere. He can only comprehend a sphere as a circle that changes in size because he can only see two-dimensional slices of a sphere as it passes through the plane of Flatland.

Sphere tries to explain to Square what a three-dimensional world is like, but does not make much progress. Sphere says to Square, "You call me a Circle, but in reality I am not a Circle, but an infinite number of Circles… You cannot indeed see more than one of my sections or Circles, at a time, for you have no power to raise your eye out of the plane of Flatland…" Figure 11-2 shows how Square saw Sphere in Flatland.

---

1 Edwin Abbott Abbott, *Flatland: A Romance of Many Dimensions*, 1884, *http://www.geom.uiuc.edu/~banchoff/Flatland/*.

This is the same problem we have when we reduce big data to two-dimensional representations. We are like Mr. Square trying to understand what Mr. Sphere is like when we can only see small abstractions of the totality of Mr. Sphere.

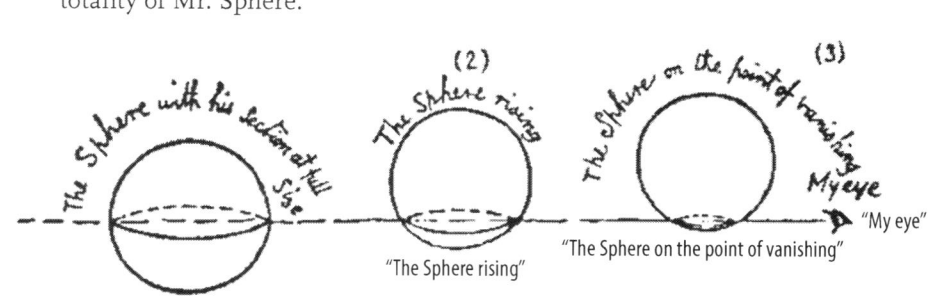

Figure 11-2. Sphere as seen by Square, drawing from Flatland

Finally, Sphere says to Square, "You must go with me—whither you know not—into the Land of Three Dimensions!" And with that, Sphere takes Square into a whole new world to see three-dimensional creatures like cubes and cones and spheres. This new view of the world is a transforming experience for Square. By direct analogy, let's apply this idea to imagine what would happen if we freed ourselves from the need to present big data only in static two-dimensional pictures. What would happen if we presented data in moving three-dimensional animations? Would this be a transformational experience that opens up a whole new world for us to see?

What if we entered a world where big data was displayed as a three-dimensional landscape that we could fly over, as shown in Figure 11-3? What if we could zoom in to see more detail when something attracted our attention? Maybe this is the place we call cyberspace. I offer the following conceptual design as a thought experiment for how we might interact with data and with each other in cyberspace.

Figure 11-3. Display big data as a moving 3-D world that we fly over, courtesy of Center for Systems Innovation [c4si]

We use the word "cyberspace" all the time. Maybe cyberspace is more than just a word. Maybe it is a place and maybe it looks something like this:

> Cyberspace. A consensual hallucination experienced daily by billions of legitimate operators, in every nation, by children being taught mathematical concepts... A graphic representation of data abstracted from the banks of every computer in the human system. Unthinkable complexity. Lines of light ranged in the nonspace of the mind, clusters and constellations of data. Like city lights, receding...

This quote is by William Gibson from his novel *Neuromancer*.[2] He's the person credited with coining the term "cyberspace."

What if you interacted with other people who were there in the places you zoomed in to see? What if you entered these places as an avatar that represented who you were and interacted with other people through their avatars? Figure 11-4 shows what those big data places might look like.

---

2 William Gibson, *Neuromancer* (New York: Ace Books, 1984). A video of an interview with William Gibson where he talks about how video games shaped his conception of cyberspace can be viewed at *http://www.youtube.com/watch?v=WVEUWfDHqsU&feature=related*. A trailer for a movie based on his novel can be viewed at *http://www.youtube.com/watch?v=mFRVPAF2rFo*.

A NOVEL ENCOUNTER WITH BIG DATA | 133

Figure 11-4. Avatars and big data places

The sky and the ground are black, like a computer screen that hasn't had anything drawn into it yet; it is always nighttime in the Metaverse, and the Street is always garish and brilliant, like Las Vegas freed from constraints of physics and finance... The people are pieces of software called avatars. They are the audio visual bodies that people use to communicate with each other in the Metaverse.

This quote is from Neal Stephenson in his novel *Snow Crash*.[3] He's credited with popularizing the term "avatar."[4] The work of Gibson, Stephenson and many video game designers provide creative and thoughtful conceptual designs for displaying and engaging with big data.

---

3 Neal Stephenson, *Snow Crash* (New York: Bantam Dell, 1992). You can read a Wikipedia article on the book at *http://en.wikipedia.org/wiki/Snow_Crash*. A video of a Neal Stephenson talk titled "We Are All Geeks Now" can be viewed at *http://www.youtube.com/watch?v=CwV3x1jZ8oE*.

4 "Here's a point I have to correct based on personal information," writes Noah Falstein (*http://en.wikipedia.org/wiki/Noah_Falstein*), a freelance game designer and producer with many years of experience in the industry. "The term Avatar in its computer usage was coined by Chip Morningstar before the appearance of *Snow Crash*, as documented at *http://en.wikipedia.org/wiki/Avatar_(computing)* and acknowledged by Neal Stephenson, and I happened to share an office with Chip at Lucasfilm Games in the mid-80s when he did it. He's since become a friend of Stephenson."

When you go into those places that attract your attention, you can hear the music that is happening there. Figure 11-5 shows avatars in such a place listening to the music.

Figure 11-5. Avatars listening to the music in this space

And after you heard the music in one place, and learned what you came to learn, then off you'd go. You'd zoom back out and fly over the landscape again (see Figure 11-6), navigating through cyberspace, turning left or right, east or west, looking for the next place you wanted to see. Now where's that place? Ah yes, there it is... you turn in that direction.

A NOVEL ENCOUNTER WITH BIG DATA | 135

Figure 11-6. Navigating in 3-D representation of big data

Something catches your eye. This is the place you were searching for. See how the data streams forth in circular patterns and different colors. You zoom in to check it out. You want to learn more about what's happening here (Figure 11-7 is an illustration of what this place might look like).

Figure 11-7. Data streams forth in spiral patterns and different colors

The size of the circle is the size of demand in this place for your new product. As you watch, you see the circle expanding—driven by growth vectors emanating from customers using your product at this very moment. You decide to talk to some of the avatars in this place to get their feedback on your product.

This is cyberspace—literally. Once this was science fiction; now it is science fact. This is how we will find our way in the real-time ocean of big data. We humans are already wired up to process and respond to a flood of data if we can perceive it as a moving three-dimensional world of sight and sound. This is a world we are born to live in. This is a world where we can engage our senses of sight and sound and even touch to comprehend and respond to real-time flows of big data.

A New Way to Visualize Big Data

In our discussions about how to deal with the flood of data that comes our way every day, we focus on the speed of the computers and the size of the databases, but we're overlooking the most critical element. Yes, computers manipulate and store huge quantities of data, but the main processing is still done by the human mind—the human mind is what turns data into actionable information. So, speed up the link between the computer and the human mind and you'll get much better results.

"We work with the military, big corporations and people frustrated by trying to analyze large volumes of data," said Creve Maples, Ph.D. and CEO of Event Horizon Inc.[5] He explained that when people come to him, they have often tried all sorts of analytic techniques but haven't gotten many useful insights into what the data really means. He described a different approach that his company uses to analyze big data. "What we've learned to do is present data in formats that can be quickly taken in and understood by people." That means they use formats that go beyond traditional line graphs, scatter plots, and bar charts.

According to Maples, the human brain is normally processing about 20 gigabytes of data per second; that's the input from the five senses, and the brain handles this data in real-time. Research at Event Horizon suggests people can track up to 27 different variables as they process their

---

5 Creve Maples, phone interview with author, October 2011. The speaker profile for Creve Maples from a Strata Conference on big data where he presented his ideas on visualizing big data can be seen at *http://strataconf.com/strata2011/public/schedule/speaker/102881*.

20 GB of real-time input. Consider the example of driving a car. The driver can watch the road, operate the car, talk to a passenger, adjust the car heater and radio, and subconsciously be listening to the sound of the engine and feeling the vibrations of the car as it moves. The driver's mind is taking this all in and handling it as a normal matter of course.

But then as soon as there is a slight change in the engine noise or the vibrations of the car, the driver's senses are alerted, and the driver is all over the situation trying to find out what happened to cause this sudden change.

Some years ago, Maples worked with engineers at Penske Racing; Penske was losing races but they couldn't figure out why. They put real-time sensors on their race cars and those sensors streamed data on about 22 independent variables. They collected this data during races and then afterward did all sorts of analysis on it. After two years of effort, they couldn't find answers.

They came to Event Horizon as a last attempt. Maples said he took the raw data but told the Penske engineers he didn't want to see the analysis that had already been done. Maples and his staff wanted to approach the problem from a fresh perspective.

"We displayed the different data variables as cartoon elements. For instance, as tires heated up, we showed them getting bigger, as other variables changed, we changed the shape and color of the cars. We took vehicle data and rendered it visually without showing numbers."

Once they had created these visualizations and ran them as animated sequences, they found the problem on the first day. The response time of the race cars' steering systems was too slow. With moving arrows, they showed visually the direction of the tires and the rotation of the car steering wheel. Animated sequences clearly showed there was a small lag time between when drivers turned the steering wheel and when the car wheels actually turned. So, drivers were constantly making many small adjustments and it slowed them down just enough to lose races.

Maples described another visualization they created when working with a computer chip designer. The designer came to them and said a new chip was overheating and nobody could figure out why; the new design should have been able to dissipate the heat. So they created a 3-D visualization of the chip and let people fly through the circuits of the chip. The circuits were rendered as tubes you could fly through and the walls of the tubes were colored using a range of blue for cool to red for hot with color gradations in between.

Then they brought in the wife of one of the Event Horizon scientists to try out the visualization. She didn't know anything about chip design but she located the point of thermal failure very quickly. The area of the chip that got hottest most quickly was easy to spot as she flew through the chip. And when she examined that area closely she saw there was no way for the heat there to be drained off. It turned out the chip designer had left out a heat-sink connection in that part of the chip.

Figure 11-8. View while traveling inside complex electro-mechanical gear assembly, courtesy of Event Horizon Inc.

Imagine analyzing performance data from a new product by shrinking down and traveling freely inside the device such as this complex electro-mechanical gear assembly shown in Figure 11-8. What better way is there to see how the parts interact and see where the friction builds up?

This is an example of the discoveries and delights that happen when people get a spontaneous human–machine interaction made possible by good user interface design that effectively engages our senses. Maples coined a term for this: it's called "anthropo-cyber-synchronicity."

We would never say "we had fun" as a reason for using a data analytics application. But fun is literally what happens when an analytics system connects with the power of our senses and allows us to suddenly understand and interact with data in a novel way.

Does this seem a bit like a video game? Could game technology help us do analytics? Let's run with this idea of using 3-D environments and moving objects to represent big data. Let's see if there could be software originally developed for creating animation in video games that could be put to the purpose of creating animations of big data.

3-D Design for Visualizing Real-Time Big Data

We need to start doing something like what Creve Maples described in order to see the patterns and hear the signals contained in real-time big data. We need to display big data as moving, three-dimensional images and add sound to the moving images as well. We need to fully engage our senses of sight and hearing if we are going to have any hope of effectively coping with the amount of data inherent in the real-time world.

The question is: how do we get from Flatland to Cyberspace? We need to walk before we try to run. Maples and his company do visualizations that they have learned over many years. How can a newcomer to the world of 3-D animations of big data get started?

Let's begin by noting that any space can be described by a set of three descriptive variables: X, Y, and Z. For this example, let X = Gross Profit, Y = Cost of Sales, and Z = Revenue. These three variables would let us describe a useful market space in which to analyze the performance of companies competing with each other.

Companies in that market space can then be further described by three more variables: x', y', and z'. In this example let x' = Total Liabilities, y' = Net Tangible Assets, and z' = Total Assets. These three variables will determine the size and shape of each company in this market space. This is illustrated in Figure 11-9.

Each company's X, Y, and Z values (its center point) define its position in the market space. The company itself is shown as an octahedron (an eight-sided 3-D object). The size and shape of the octahedron is defined by the values of the company's x', y', z' variables.

140 | ENTERPRISE GAMES

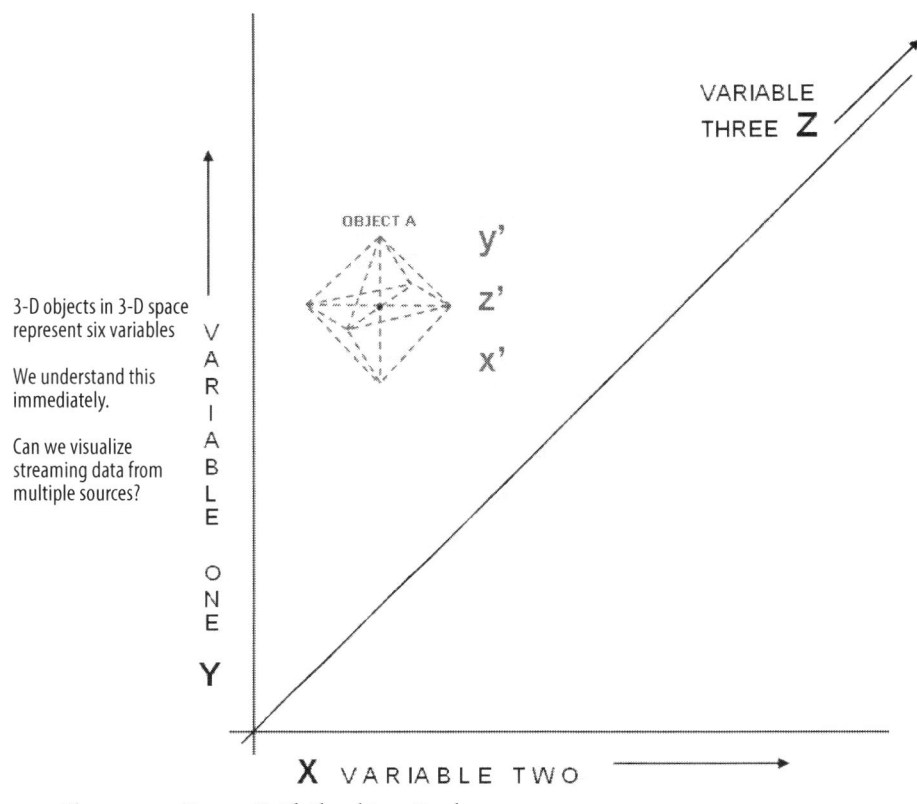

VARIABLE THREE **Z**

OBJECT A

y'
z'
x'

3-D objects in 3-D space represent six variables

We understand this immediately.

Can we visualize streaming data from multiple sources?

VARIABLE ONE Y

X VARIABLE TWO

Figure 11-9. From 2-D Flatland to 3-D cyberspace

If a time series display is made using data collected over time, the position and shape of the companies being displayed will change. This time series display will show company movements within the market space and in comparison to each other. Trends and relationships between the companies will be easy to see. This is illustrated in Figure 11-10.

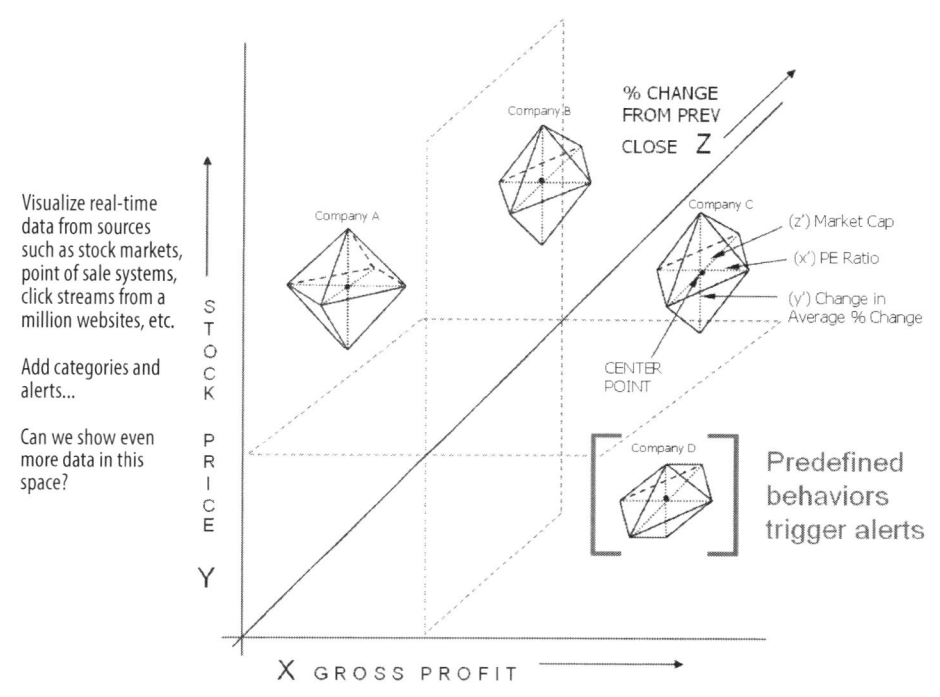

Figure 11-10. Data visualization design to display six different variables

A sample screenshot is shown in Figure 11-11 to illustrate how this data display will look when it is rendered with the visualization engine of a 3-D animation package. There are powerful 3-D animation packages such as the open source Blender[6] package or the Unity[7] game developer package that are low cost and well known in the computer animation industry. These packages can quickly be put to use to provide robust and scalable systems to start experimenting with real-time visualizations of streaming big data from sources such as stock markets, websites, and clickstreams. The example here shows financial data from three publicly traded distribution companies (company names are shown in the figure).

---

6 Blender source 3-D animation software, *http://www.blender.org/*.
7 Unity game developer software, *http://unity3-D.com/*.

142 | ENTERPRISE GAMES

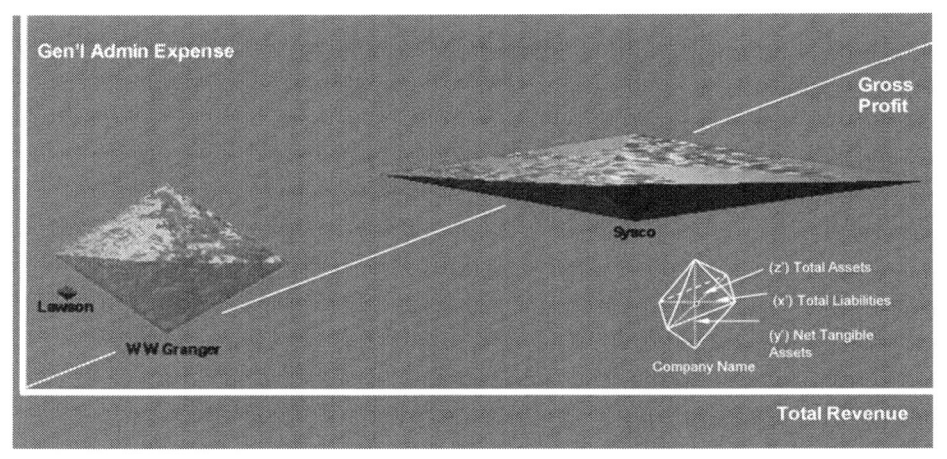

(Image curtesy of Center for Systems Innovation [c4si])

- Sysco is wide and flat; WW Grainger is tall and narrow.
- WW Grainger has a much higher ratio of net tangible assets to total assets.
- Sysco has total assets four times as large as WW Grainger.
- Sysco's net tangible assets are slightly smaller than those of WW Grainger.
- Lawson has asset structure more like WW Grainger than like Sysco.
- Lawson displays a shape similar to WW Grainger but much smaller.

Figure 11-11. Example of 3-D data visualization, courtesy of Center for Systems Innovation (c4si)

This example is just a beginning. There are many other assumptions and analogies that need to be explored. Some assumptions and analogies will prove to be invalid and others will provide amazing insights into the workings of companies and business units within companies as they operate in the real-time world. The key is that we begin to use this type of 3-D visualization as the way to display and make sense of real-time data.

Creating an Interactive Simulation to Explore the Data

In the spirit of fun and adventure, game technology can be even further employed to create an immersive encounter with the data. By combining arcade game and simulator technology, you can quickly build a game unit that can be used to explore real-time streams of big data. Figure 11-12 shows an example. Imagine the big data visualizations shown above were displayed on the console of an arcade game unit that enabled people to literally drive through the environment created by these visualizations.

This is just the beginning of what can be done. It used to cost millions of dollars to experiment with technology like this. Now the technology is readily available, and it is only our lack of imagination that is holding us back.

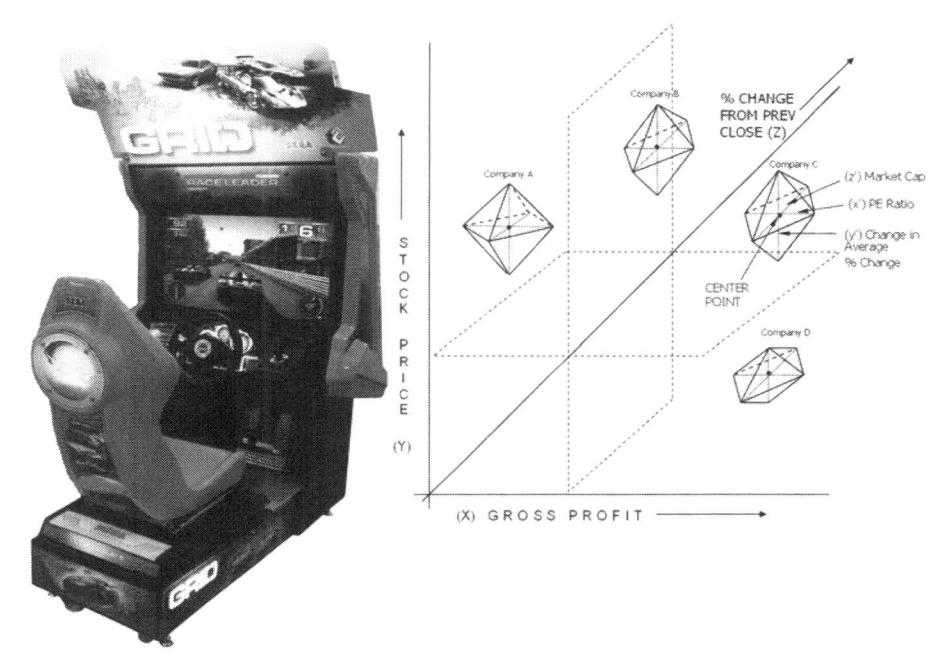

Figure 11-12. Game-based interactive simulators to explore real-time big data, courtesy of Sega Amusements and Center for Systems Innovation (c4si)

The workstation is made from commodity hardware and field-tested, high-performance 3-D graphics software. These units provide immersive environments for stock market traders to interact physically and mentally with trading data presented on a high resolution big screen. In addition to the visual display, traders also get auditory feedback where objects emit sound that rises in pitch as the speed of an object increases, and the traders get tactile feedback as the seat of the unit vibrates at different frequencies depending on predefined qualities in the data being viewed.

I present these ideas partly as tongue-in-cheek humor and partly as an example of how easily we can now construct highly immersive real-time environments with off-the-shelf hardware and software that is not expensive and can be readily assembled. Video games and arcade games over the last 30 years have steadily pushed the technology envelope. They have produced better and better 3-D animations with higher and higher quality visual effects. Video game engines are now capable of driving 3-D animations in simulated worlds where the rules of physics are so well modeled that the actions in these simulated worlds are accurate predictors of what would happen in the real world. And all this technology is available at lower and lower cost.

In the 1990s, and the early years of this century, the kind of simulations and data analysis talked about by Creve Maples at Event Horizon needed multimillion dollar budgets to develop software and assemble high performance computer workstations to run the simulations. Now such simulations can be created for budgets of a few thousand dollars using popular video game animation engines, and they can be run on readily available computer hardware priced for the consumer market (Figure 11-13 is an example of this).

Figure 11-13. Use arcade game technology to drive through real-time big data, courtesy of Sega Driving Simulators

Imagine streaming big data through a video game animation engine to make it visible. This data could be coming from sources like Bloomberg financial data, or the click stream from the online ads your company is running on various websites on any given day.[8]

Imagine presenting this data as moving 3-D displays in real time that people could navigate through while looking for and reacting to patterns and opportunities they discovered in the data. Imagine people could select and trigger combinations of predefined responses when they saw certain patterns. Imagine that the system was programmed to alert people when it saw certain patterns or trends.

Is this just fun and games or serious work? Or could it be both?

---

8 Noah Falstein (*http://en.wikipedia.org/wiki/Noah_Falstein*), game designer and producer, wrote me about a similar experience he had with a client using games to visualize big data. "I have had my own experiences with this in serious games. In 1998 I did some work for Shell Oil and found that they had workstations representing 3-D projections of underground oil and gas fields, and were proud of the computer scientists who had helped build them, including hundreds of thousands of data points. They could even rotate them visually—at a speed of about 1 frame every 2 seconds. An early Serious Game advocate at Shell hired a local Amsterdam game developer to do data-reduction on the mass of data and simplify the model while applying some shortcuts common in simulation games to speed the display, and was able to achieve 15+ frames per second with more visual detail on off the shelf PC's, and instantly features would leap out to the eye that were invisible at the previous glacially slow frame rate on the much more expensive workstations."

12

Game Layer on Top of the World

THE SPREAD OF SOCIAL media is providing the consumer equivalent of the real-time communication networks that previously only large governments and wealthy corporations could afford. For the last decade, Cisco's Visual Networking Index: Global Mobile Data Traffic Forecast has documented the growth of the world's networks and the kinds and amounts of data being transported over these networks.

Here are a handful of findings from the executive summary section of the Cisco report published in February 2012:

- Global mobile data traffic grew 2.3-fold in 2011, more than doubling for the fourth year in a row. The 2011 mobile data traffic growth rate was higher than anticipated.
- Last year's mobile data traffic was eight times the size of the entire global Internet in 2000.
- Mobile video traffic exceeded 50 percent for the first time in 2011.
- Average smartphone usage nearly tripled in 2011.
- Smartphones represent only 12 percent of total global handsets in use today, but they represent over 82 percent of total global handset traffic.
- Global mobile data traffic will increase 18-fold between 2011 and 2016. Mobile data traffic will grow at a compound annual growth rate (CAGR) of 78 percent from 2011 to 2016.
- By the end of 2012, the number of mobile-connected devices will exceed the number of people on earth, and by 2016 there will be 1.4 mobile devices per capita.

What's going on here? What's the significance of streaming video traffic now comprising more than half the data volume on global mobile networks? Who's looking at all this video and could it help us see the world in real time? The numbers show a classic exponential growth curve in the size and usage of the data communication networks that are so quickly spreading around the world. Clearly, something momentous is happening.

The rapid spread of cloud computing, wireless broadband networks, social media, and consumer IT has created the infrastructure we need to make real-time connectivity a reality for billions of people all around the world. This infrastructure is coming online quickly.

And it's waiting for the great game to begin.

Game Layer Leverages the Capabilities of Social Infrastructure

Seth Priebatsch has given himself the title of chief ninja for a prominent social media startup company named SCVNGR[1], which describes itself as building "the game layer on top of the world."

Seth is developing SCVNGR as a cloud-based game platform that is designed to use mobile consumer IT devices (smartphones, tablet computers, etc.) as the user interface. At present, the SCVNGR platform is designed to enable businesses such as restaurants, museums, and stores to set up activities such as scavenger hunts that engage customers and reward them for their participation. Over time, this game platform can be enhanced with new types of games as opportunities arise.

In a manner somewhat similar to the approach taken by Salesforce.com, SCVNGR is encouraging people to codevelop new features and games with them. They provide a user-friendly interface that enables nontechnical people to design and operate their own unique games for specific occasions. As the library of games grows, the value of the SCVNGR game platform also grows. Companies will be able to access predesigned games that are tailored to their needs. And these games can be evaluated and continuously enhanced based on the actual results they produce while in operation. This is a recipe for generating a powerful network effect that could drive exponential value creation.

Seth describes the activity of the last decade as being about building the social infrastructure layer that provides connections between people

---

1 SCVNGR (*http://www.scvngr.com/*).

(think Facebook, Twitter, Yelp, YouTube, etc.). He states that this decade is about the building of what he calls "the game layer."

He explains that, at present, the game layer looks like what the Web looked like in 1997—it's just starting.[2] Gamification techniques like those used by the companies we discussed in Chapter 5 are at present somewhat fragmented and simplistic. But they are a start, and they point to what is coming.

Seth feels the social layer is about connections and the game layer is about influence. The game layer is built upon the social layer, and it is even more powerful than the social layer because it leverages the connections in the social layer to influence people's real world behavior. "At SCVNGR we like to say that with seven game dynamics we can get people to do anything. Four of those dynamics are Appointment Dynamic—like the happy hour appointment at local bars; Influence and Status—like the black credit card issued by American Express; Progression Dynamic—like the progress bar used by LinkedIn; and Communal Discovery—working together to find answers to common problems."

The game layer is different from Facebook in that it needs to be more specifically focused on certain types of activities. Where the generic social connectivity provided by Facebook fits the needs of hundreds of millions of users, the game layer will offer many different game platforms that specialize in the needs of specific customers and vertical markets. Seth believes the game layer will not end up with one dominant platform like Facebook. Because the theory and practices of games is interspersed in so many different areas of business, government, and cultural activities, there will be many different types of games. Figure 12-1 shows the SCVNGR website.

SCVNGR games are in the category called alternate reality games (ARGs). These games are defined by intense player involvement with a plot line that takes place in real time and evolves according to actions of the people in the game. People in the game are actively influenced by the game's designers as the game unfolds. This is unlike a video game where an artificial intelligence provides the interaction with the game's players.

---

2 "Just like DNS connects nodes on the Internet, APIs connect nodes in the Game Layer," is how Seth described it during a phone interview with the author, January 2012. A video of Seth explaining "The game layer on top of the world" can be viewed at *http://www.ted.com/talks/seth_priebatsch_the_game_layer_on_top_of_the_world.html*.

150 | ENTERPRISE GAMES

Players in ARGs interact directly with other players and with characters introduced by the game designers. They solve plot-based challenges and work together with other players to analyze the story and coordinate their activities both in the real world and online. ARGs also use many different media channels to communicate with players. ARGs employ phones, email, regular mail, and social media and use the Internet as the central communication channel to tie all the others together.

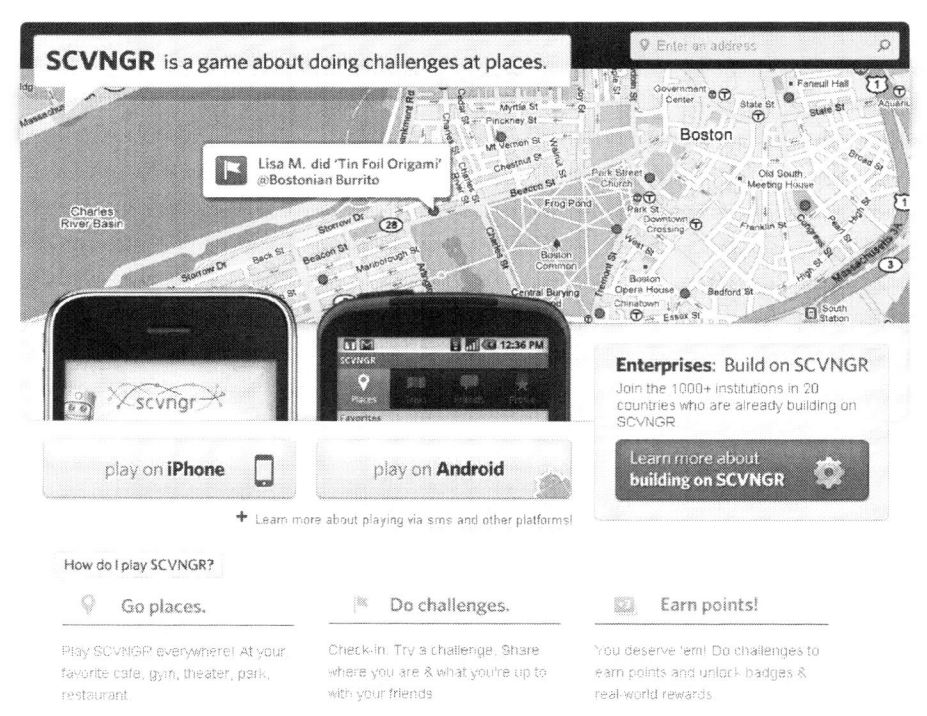

Figure 12-1. The SCVNGR website

The architecture SCVNGR uses to connect the game layer to the traditional IT infrastructure inside companies is based heavily on the use of connecting modules of software known as application program interfaces (APIs). Libraries of APIs are being made available for companies to use to connect their internal systems to the systems of growing numbers of software application providers. These providers' systems are cloud based, and APIs allow customers anywhere in the world to connect with them.

SCVNGR and other service providers are publishing their APIs so that companies can tap into their databases and service offerings. These service offerings range from business applications such as accounting systems to social media and gaming applications.

The Game Layer Is a Coordination Layer

Earlier attempts at industry "hubs" and online markets created in the first decade of this century were expensive to build and complex to connect with. Examples of such industry hubs were Ariba, Commerce One, Covisant, and e2Open.[3] Traditional corporate IT is biased toward complexity and exclusivity because of its revenue model. Corporate IT, over the last 40 years, was built in a world where profit was found in complex software features and the consulting services needed to install those features and train users and system operators. Complexity provided the most profit to providers of IT products and services. And customers also perceived greater value in complexity and were willing to pay extra for complexity.

Now, connectivity via APIs created by social media and SaaS providers is becoming the norm, and connectivity is much easier to accomplish because of the simple nature of the APIs.[4] APIs rolled out by social media and SaaS vendors have a bias toward simplicity because of the revenue model for social media and SaaS products. Revenue rises as customers connect and their participation in the network increases. Profit is found in linking up billions of people in social and business networks and then charging small transaction and advertising fees based on the volume of traffic that runs through a network. So, companies in this area strive to make their social and business networks as easy as possible for others to connect with electronically.

---

3 All these networks have undergone tremendous changes over the last several years and have extensively redesigned their IT infrastructure and refocused on new markets and value added activities. Commerce One is no longer in operation.

4 Software and service providers are stepping up to fill the growing need companies have to connect and merge different kinds of IT architectures (in-house, cloud, game IT). One such company is Snap Logic (*http://www.snaplogic.com/*). Their CEO, Guarav Dhillon, is a serial entrepreneur and earlier, he was a founder of a well-known business intelligence and data services company named Informatica. Snap Logic provides an App Store-like environment where third-party developers can make available for download connectivity apps that leverage APIs written to help companies connect different in-house and SaaS, and social media and game IT apps. They are hosted in the cloud by Snap Logic so they will scale up as connectivity demand grows and companies use what they need on a pay-as-you-go basis.

These networks will morph into "Industry Operating Systems." They will become combinations of technology, standard operating procedures (SOPs), and best practices that have evolved and been proven effective for given industries. Some of these operating systems will become industry standards over time just as some social networks become standards. Everyone will want to be connected with these industry standard networks and they will become very profitable as that happens. The emergence of these trading networks and operating systems fosters organizations that respond to and harmonize with the pulse of the economy.

Feedback loops enabled by the real-time data transparency made possible by these networks will make it possible to operate at levels of efficiency and responsiveness not seen before. This is the business world that is emerging as people get access to up-to-date information, as they get training and authority to act autonomously to achieve performance targets, and as they also get a stake in the outcome so they are motivated to act, adjust, and improve as conditions change.

Real-Time Visualization of Big Data Streaming from the Game Layer

There are growing networks that support functions in the areas of supply chains, agriculture, finance, and electrical transmission to name just a few. These networks are often global in their reach and they exist to collect data and coordinate activities between all the different parties that make up these networks.

Figure 12-2 illustrates the different players in a network devoted to supply chain operations and shows the data that needs to be collected and shared among the players. In all of these networks, there is a common need to connect, communicate, and collaborate. So, even though the functions supported by a network can be different, the architecture and operation of these networks will be very similar—perhaps mostly just variations on a few common themes.

Forecasts, Sales, Inventory, Customer Data, etc.

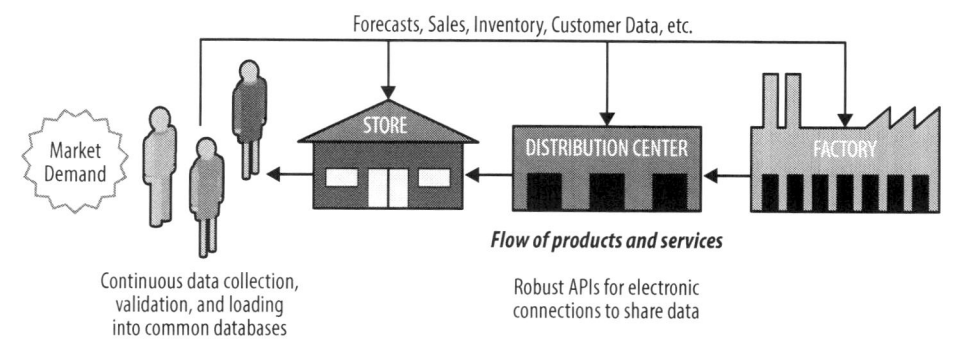

Market Demand

STORE — DISTRIBUTION CENTER — FACTORY

Flow of products and services

Continuous data collection, validation, and loading into common databases

Robust APIs for electronic connections to share data

Big Data provides trasparency—*creates corrective feedback loop*

Figure 12-2. Connect, communicate, collaborate

Supply chains are just one case where information gathering and feedback networks can help us better monitor, visualize, and manage operations. Other operations in the areas of ecosystem management, financial markets, power and communications grids, water distribution, and transportation systems are also ripe for the application of information and feedback networks. What if networks that supported these operations collected real-time data streams and sent alerts to appropriate people when they detected predefined conditions? What if they enabled people to visualize this real-time data in moving 3-D spaces such as those described in Chapter 11? Would companies achieve new levels of efficiency and responsiveness in their businesses?

I discussed these ideas with Brian Gentile, CEO, and Karl van den Bergh, VP Product & Alliances, of Jaspersoft, a fast growing startup in the field of big data analytics. We talked about the technology and processing needed to visualize big data and interactively explore this data in real time. They sketched out the conceptual system design shown in Figure 12-3 and explained how Jaspersoft is providing such systems to clients who want to discover and respond to real-time patterns as they emerge from their big data content.[5]

---

5 Personal interviews with the author on January 15 and March 6, 2012, *www.JasperSoft.com.*

A new generation of databases is coming to market to handle the challenges posed by real-time big data. They are not the relational databases that have become the norm during the last 20 years. Big data databases often do not use relational storage schemes. Databases such as Hadoop, HBase, and many popular NoSQL databases such as MongoDB and Cassandra are nonrelational in nature and are optimized to manage massive amounts of unstructured data. Once captured in these big data databases, the data can be extracted and loaded into relational databases for traditional analysis, or it can be run through in-memory data analytic and visualization engines for real-time exploration.

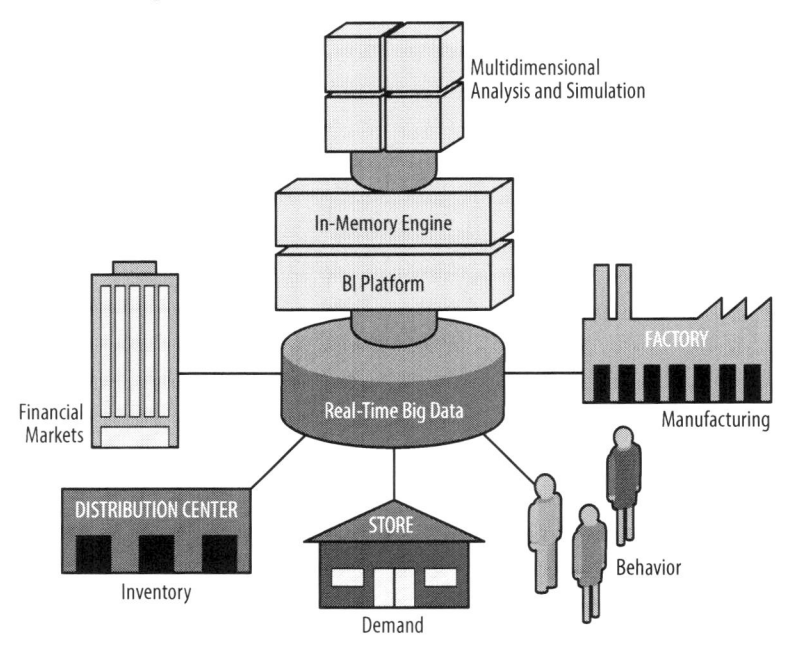

Figure 12-3. Navigating the ocean of big data

Cloud-based big data and data visualization technology is bringing real-time transparency to many activities. And this transparency is creating the feedback systems that combine with goals and rules to create game dynamics. The global game layer is developing rapidly.

Game IT Merges Video Game Technology with Business Technology

Ben Sawyer is an influential game designer and thought leader in the serious games space.[6] He has coined the term "Game IT" to identify and discuss the issues related to merging video game technology with traditional business technology. In an email interview, he explained that Game IT is "a response to the growing use of games largely in corporate enterprises, but also in other large-scale organizations that structure themselves and operate especially against a backbone of information technologies such as streams of data/big data, browser based applications, document creation and dissemination, media creation, etc."

Sawyer went on to question whether companies at present can really make games an inherent and compatible part of the IT infrastructure that they use today. To do that, games would need to be engineered and designed differently than they are now. At the same time, they must still preserve and build on what game designers have learned in commercial games over the last 20 years. "This is a nontrivial process," he observed.

I asked him for his thoughts on how Game IT relates to the existing installed IT infrastructure of a typical $500 million or larger company. Since these companies constitute an enormous amount of business activity and jobs, what are the implications of Game IT for them, and how will it affect the way they use IT in their daily operations?

Sawyer replied that video game technology is not inherently compatible with the web-based, often open source technology stacks used by large enterprises today. He said this needs to change and pointed out that, ironically, with the advent of mobile devices and social media, game companies are starting to feel the need to adjust their closed and proprietary technology on their own, through use of APIs.

He believes the developers of serious games and MMO games need to open up their technology stacks even more than what other game development companies are doing. Game developers (like *EVE Online*, *World of Warcraft*, etc.) need to work with the wider ecosystem of technology

---

6 Ben Sawyer is a cofounder of Digitalmill (*www.dmill.com*), a games consulting firm based in Portland, ME. He has pioneered major initiatives in the field of serious games and has become a nationally recognized leader within the games community and dedicated his professional career to discovering new ways to expand the use of games beyond entertainment. In 2002, he cofounded the Serious Games Initiative, a project of the US Government's Woodrow Wilson International Center for Scholars.

vendors and find ways to embed a game technology stack into the communication pipelines and system processing infrastructures that business organizations have in use today.

"This is a fundamental reshaping of how games are built," he said. "Furthermore, game designers need to redesign around ideas of asynchronous play and short play-times, but with long game-arcs, so as to help companies tackle the types of activities and workflows they have to handle in their businesses." This use of games goes far beyond just training, though training has been and will remain a big part of what companies do with games. What Sawyer is talking about is using computer games to "truly augment the workflow of major organizations through gameplay that is directly compatible with their IT, their workflows, and their data."

Global Game Layers Are Already in Place

An example of a global game layer that is already in place is the Microsoft Xbox Live real-time game network. The Live network has been in operation since 2002, and as of January 2012, more than 66 million Xbox 360 game consoles have been sold worldwide.[7] In addition to Xbox game consoles, the Live network can also be accessed by PCs and mobile consumer IT devices like smartphones and tablet computers.[8] The Xbox Live network allows players to play and compete with each other in MMO games and to download arcade games, game demos, TV shows, music, and movies. The Live network could turn out to be the most valuable asset owned by Microsoft.

Xbox Live incorporates rigorous security to ensure users' privacy and to help prevent hacker attacks. Once a user logs on to the network and is verified, each Xbox device connects to the Xbox Live service through a security gateway that encrypts the data traveling between the individual consoles and the service. This prevents hackers from intercepting and reading data that would reveal what games people are playing and what they are doing in those games. Figure 12-4 illustrates how the network is designed.

---

7   Wikipedia, "Xbox 360," http://en.wikipedia.org/wiki/Xbox_360.

8   Jason Cross, "Microsoft Releases Xbox Live App for iPhone and iPad," *PCWorld*, December 7, 2011, http://www.pcworld.com/article/245653/microsoft_releases_xbox_live_app_for_iphone_and_ipad.html.

Microsoft operates a set of Live datacenters to support services such as player matchmaking, billing, and maintaining consistent gamer IDs. These datacenters also contain data downloads for players, such as new game levels, characters, and statistics. Xbox Live does not host specific MMO games. Third-party MMO game companies are responsible for hosting these games, which can then be connected to the Xbox Live network for billing and other purposes.[9]

The Live network is not alone. There are competing networks from other video game companies, such as Sony's PlayStation Network, and there are competing networks emerging from areas such as entertainment, finance and procurement. These networks and the software that operates these networks are moving (whether consciously or not) toward capabilities that can support the 10 game ingredients and 10 building blocks (introduced in Chapter 7). That means these networks can already, or soon will, support game ingredients such as: player self-representation with avatars, game play in realistic 3-D environments, the management of player reputations and levels, competition under explicit and enforced rules, and real-time reconfigurable communication systems.

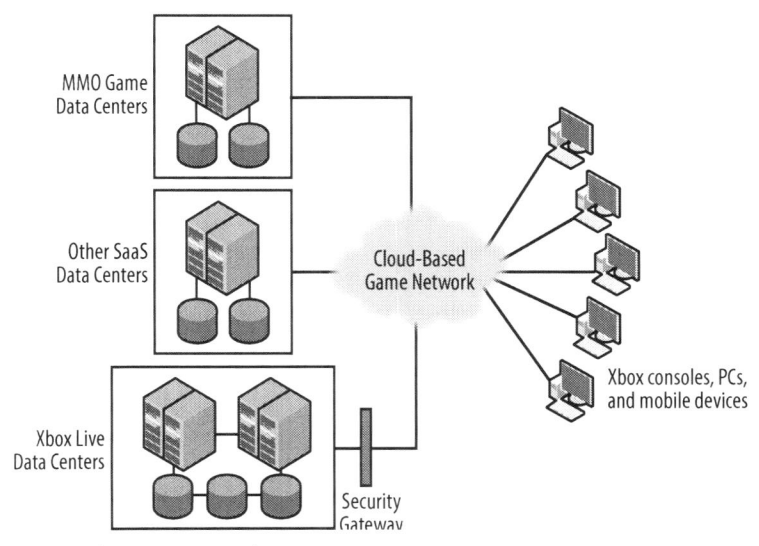

Figure 12-4 Xbox Live Network

---

9 "Xbox Live Architecture and Technology," *Directions on Microsoft*, June 17, 2002, http://www.directionsonmicrosoft.com/sample/DOMIS/update/2002/07jul/0702nvtxs_illo.htm.

158 | ENTERPRISE GAMES

These networks are poised to become the next generation of global business networks, as illustrated in Figure 12-5. Different regional and industry networks can emerge to support the real-time activities that are necessary for their markets. Companies can connect their internal systems to these networks through the use of robust APIs made available by these networks. And, as companies connect, they make use of game layer capabilities provided by the network to collaborate with each other to address common problems. This real-time collaboration is the main reason for companies to join such networks.

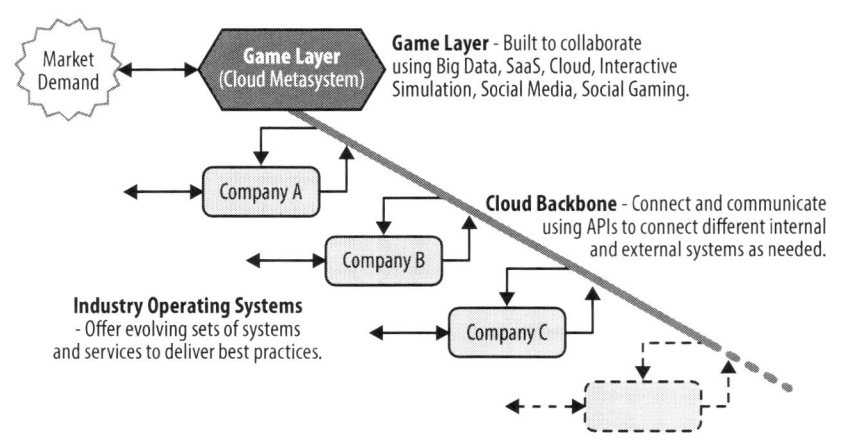

Figure 12-5 Global business networks

MMOs that are currently provided by game networks could morph into real-time business collaboration platforms (see Chapter 7). The technology, to a large extent, already exists. What is still lacking is the widespread understanding of the potential benefits that can be had. Yet, gaming examples provided by MMOs are fueling the spread of these ideas, and as people become more widely aware, it is only a matter of time before something profound happens.

The first decade of this century saw the build out of a global social connection layer composed of social media. The next global technical build out on a scale as large as this will be the spread of game layer technology. The next Facebook will be a company that creates business networks and provides an integrated set of connectivity and game layer features that companies can use to work together and do business in real time.

Networks of Presence—Toward Global Awareness

The whole world is now like a stock market. For decades, financial markets have been generating massive volumes of real-time data; now, much of the rest of the world is also generating massive volumes of real-time data—we have systems operating now that generate continuous streams of data describing everything from weather patterns to air and automobile traffic to electrical power consumption and consumer purchasing activity.

On the one hand, this flood of data can make us feel overwhelmed and unable to cope. On the other hand, it can be our ticket to the next level of understanding and living in the world.

The challenge is to display massive real-time data flows and to do so in a way we humans can understand. As we discussed in the previous chapter, we need to organize and display this data using the same principles that our brain uses when it organizes and processes data that comes through our five senses.

If we start processing and visualizing real-time big data, it will give us the ability to solve some really big problems—like climate change and environmental sustainability (and if it works for these problems, it will work for lots of other problems too). We know we have to do something to respond to how the earth is changing, but the scope of the undertaking is overwhelming and the amount of data is beyond comprehension. Yet we need all that data or we won't know whether our efforts are creating the desired results or not. We need continuous data feedback loops (planetary data feedback loops) to tell us if we are on track and to enable us to make midcourse corrections as needed.

After much posturing and back and forth debate, the nations of the world will have to start the next round of negotiations to deal with greenhouse gases and global warming. These negotiations promise to be exhausting, prolonged, and maybe even fatally flawed by clever negotiating and creative data interpretation. We can be sure that the best experts that can be found will present and spin all sorts of data to prove or disprove all sorts of points. How are we ever going to come up with something that has a chance of actually working?

There is a way if we apply the principle of making the world visible in order to understand it. We need to do two things. First we need to set up an appropriate real-time data stream. Then we need to organize that data as moving 3-D displays so that people can comprehend it and react to it in a timely fashion.

What would happen if the United Nations or some global nongovernmental organization (NGO) set up and operated a worldwide network of environmental sensors that monitored attributes such as air temperature, moisture, air quality, and toxic substances? The data sensors would not be attached to specific buildings but would instead just be placed as a regular grid across the planet and would take readings of the surrounding environment (that way they would not be snooping on individuals or specific facilities).

The real-time data feed from this global network would then be available to everyone over the Internet and would be shown as a moving 3-D display overlaid on a topographic display of the Earth. This would bring transparency to the world's physical environment just as stock markets bring transparency to the world's financial markets. Could it give rise to a widespread understanding and global dynamic that enables us to respond to complex environmental problems as effectively as free market dynamics enable us to respond to complex economic problems?

Such global sensor networks are already coming into being under the efforts of several nations that are building their own networks. One such network of sensors is being built by the American National Aeronautics and Space Administration (NASA) and is called Earth Observatory.[10] NASA and other organizations are collecting real-time data feeds and photographs from a wide range of sensors and cameras mounted on the ground, on satellites orbiting above, and on drones flying over.

It is as if these sensor networks and their real-time flow of images and data are causing us collectively to wake up. Perhaps the constant flow of stimulus they provide to our senses of sight and sound are creating a response in us. Perhaps we are starting to see the world as it unfolds just as people start to see the landscape they live on as the sun rises and day replaces night.

The entire world is connecting in real time via the Internet, electronic trading networks, supply chains, and social media. These real-time data flows are causing the wider world to take on feedback-driven behaviors and dynamics previously only seen in real-time financial and commodities markets. What historical experience with economic models and financial

---

10 National Aeronautics and Space Administration, Earth Observatory sensorweb, *http://earthobservatory.nasa.gov/.*

markets can we draw on for guidance in operating and sustaining ourselves and our real-time world?

Jeremy Rifkin is an American economist, a senior lecturer in the MBA program at the Wharton School of the University of Pennsylvania, and president of the Foundation on Economic Trends. In his recent book, *Empathic Civilization*, he observes:

> We talk breathlessly about access and inclusion in a global communications network but speak little of exactly why we want to communicate with one another on such a planetary scale. What's sorely missing is an overarching reason for why billions of human beings should be increasingly connected. Toward what end? The only feeble explanations thus far offered are to share information, be entertained, advance commercial exchange, and speed the globalization of the economy. All the above, while relevant, nonetheless seem insufficient to justify why nearly seven billion human beings should be connected and mutually embedded in a globalized society. Seven billion individual connections, absent any overall unifying purpose, seem a colossal waste of human energy.[11]

In his book, he makes a compelling case that we are in a race between an approaching environmental catastrophe on the one hand, and on the other hand, our developing abilities to harness information and communication technology to support new ways of living in balance with Earth's ecosystems. He asks, "Can we reach biosphere consciousness and global empathy in time to avert planetary collapse?"

Perhaps the MMOs we play as we interact with each other in the social and business networks that we are a part of are actually the thoughts of Mother Earth as she examines her situation, and considers what to do next. Just as the billions of individual neurons in our brains network together to create something larger than the sum of their parts, there is something similar happening with the billions of us. We network together to create

---

11 Jeremy Rifkin, *The Empathic Civilization: The Race to Global Consciousness in a World in Crisis* (New York:Tarcher/Penguin, 2010), 594. To watch a video of Jeremy Rifkin being interviewed by Charlie Rose go to *http://www.youtube.com/watch?v=Ppw5O-Vtxcs* and to see an animated talk about ideas in his book Empathic Civilization go to *http://www.ted.com/talks/lang/en/jeremy_rifkin_on_the_empathic_civilization.html*

and to be a part of something larger than ourselves.[12] (This is illustrated in Figure 12-6.)

Are we seeing emergence of a global cerebral cortex?

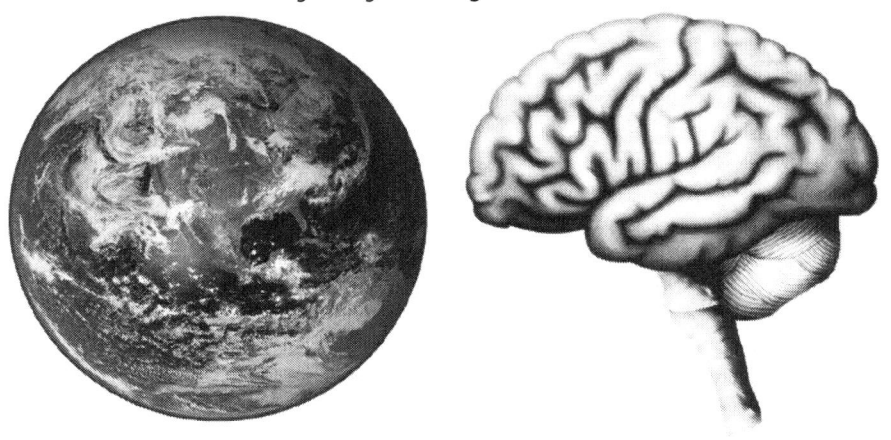

Our bodies are of billions of autonomous cells talking to each other...
Our planet now has billions of us talking to each other...

Figure 12-6. What does it all mean?

I wonder what games are emerging in the game layer of planetary consciousness. What can these games do for us and with us?

---

12 In a conversation a few years ago with Michael Martine, Director of Supply Chain Transformation at IBM, (*http://www.linkedin.com/in/martinemichael*) he made some observations and asked some questions that I think of often when contemplating what the game layer can become. He observed that we leave digital fingerprints all over the Internet containing a rich trove of data about who we are, what we think, and how we behave. Then he asked what would happen if we followed these data trails and collected information about particular people and identified their behavior patterns and applied gaming technology to display this collected information as 3D avatars created from actual pictures and videos of those people? He went on to imagine that perhaps these avatars could be the collected wisdom of famous people or learned experts and we could ask questions of them and interact in real time. Is this a form of immortality for those people? Would their presence help us learn faster, and help us not make the same mistakes over and over again? Or would these avatars be used to manipulate and mislead us?

13

Games for Change

"If you have a problem, and you can't solve it alone, evoke it." So goes the introduction to Jane McGonigal's award-winning game, *Evoke*.[1] Produced by McGonigal, *Evoke* was commissioned by the World Bank Institute, the learning and knowledge arm of the World Bank Group. The game was designed to engage young people and to teach them about ways they can respond to and cope with the kinds of crises that countries will likely go through in the coming decades. In its different challenges, the game leads players to explore everything from sustainable energy systems for the world's cities to how to manage food and water supplies for growing populations.

Evoke uses field-tested game mechanics to get active buy-in from the players and, in doing so, *Evoke* becomes a collaboration platform. It connects people and facilitates to the flow of ideas that enables people to work together to explore ideas and solve common problems. The game's approach is explained as follows:

> When we evoke, we look for creative solutions.
> We use whatever resources we have.
> We get as many people involved as possible.
> We take risks.
> We come up with ideas that have never been tried before.

---

[1] Jane McGonigal, *Evoke: A Crash Course in Changing the World* (Evoke, 2010), *http://www.urgentevoke.com/*.

Waking Up from History

Founded in 2004, Games for Change is a not-for-profit organization that supports the creation and distribution of social impact games, such as *Evoke*, that serve as critical learning tools in humanitarian and educational endeavors. On their website, Games for Change explains its mission as follows: "Unlike the commercial gaming industry, we aim to leverage entertainment and engagement for social good. To further grow the field, Games for Change convenes multiple stakeholders, highlights best practices, incubates games, and helps create and direct investment into new projects."[2]

Games for Change brings together people from government, corporations, civil society, media, academia, and the gaming industry to discuss and investigate the increasing real-world impact of digital games as an agent for social change. They also partner with granting organizations and other foundations to showcase examples of ways that games are supporting philanthropic activities and how games can be used as effective tools for education.

Much of history is a sad litany of repeated mistakes. Yet the good news is this: we are starting to recognize many of the recurring patterns of common mistakes. They've been repeated so often for so many reasons (and they still produce the same dismal results), so researchers and educators are often able to spot these patterns as they develop and understand a lot about their causes. Maybe it's time for us to finally wake up from history.

We need to teach the broad mass of the world's population to recognize and respond to common patterns so as to avoid these common mistakes. And involving people in games is the best way to do this because of the ability of games to engage people so deeply and to communicate on so many levels. This is a huge undertaking, but it is not unprecedented.[3]

It is analogous to the undertaking we faced about a hundred years ago when we resolved to create mass literacy in the world. Teaching billions of people to read and write was never attempted before in human history, and

---

2   Games for Change (*http://www.gamesforchange.org/*)

3   The game *Darfur is Dying* (*http://www.darfurisdying.com/*) has had over 2 million downloads and has arguably been one of the most influential games for change. By playing the game, people understand on an emotional and intuitive level, not just an intellectual level, about the interplay of forces that define the plight and predicament of the refugees in Darfur.

there were (and still are) challenges to this mission. Yet we have largely succeeded in making mass literacy a reality.

Games for Change and similar organizations are embarking on this century's equivalent undertaking to achieve a new level of universal literacy. The opportunity is to use games to engage people and immerse them in learning experiences that enable them to discover common social, economic, and political patterns and to see how they work.

Just as the advent of mass literacy enabled a new level of individual participation in society, the widespread use of games to teach and engage people can enable even more inclusive and more effective participation by larger numbers of individuals.

As we shift from dealing with the problems of the nation-state–oriented Industrial Age (which were complex in their own right) to dealing with the global problems of the age we live in now (which are forcing us to grapple with increasingly complex sequences of cause and effect), we run up against one overriding issue: we absolutely have to get better at dealing with the behavior of complex systems.

The behavior of complex systems is counterintuitive, and that is often the reason why we do the wrong things over and over again. That's how Professor Jay Forrester explains it based on his research in systems dynamics. Jay Forrester is the professor emeritus of Management in Systems Dynamics at the MIT Sloan School of Management.[4] He describes how people see an apparent cause for something that, in reality, is only a coincidental effect.

In complex systems, cause and effect associations are made between variables that are not directly related but that exhibit an action/reaction response because they are moving together as part of the overall dynamics of the system. Because of this, we miss root causes and wind up treating coincident symptoms not related to the problems we are trying to solve. And the results range from ineffectual to disastrous.

As our global problems inexorably press in on us, we need to find a way to "level up" and move beyond the historical predicament of repeating the same old mistakes over and over again. This leveling up will not come from some theoretical state of enlightenment attained by small groups

---

4 Jay Forrester, born 1918, is founder of System Dynamics, which deals with the simulation of interactions between objects in dynamic systems (*Wikipedia*, "Jay Wright Forrester," http://en.wikipedia.org/wiki/Jay_Wright_Forrester).

of experts who will then tell the rest of us what to do. It will come from the emergent effects of mass popular participation in games that we find compelling and that enable us to develop new understandings and new intuitions for dealing with complex systems.[5]

Serious Alternate Reality Games

An alternate reality game (ARG) is an interactive game that takes place in the real world. It usually involves multiple different media such as email, videos, and live chat, as well as a range of game elements. An ARG begins by setting up a situation and telling a story about how this situation came to be. It defines a goal for players to accomplish and it often suggests some objectives for people to focus on achieving right away. The ARG then asks its players to work together in figuring out how the events will unfold going forward.

In the game designing community, there is a widely discussed idea that if ARGs can be used to motivate people to collaborate and solve fictional problems, perhaps they can also be used to rally people to focus on and solve real-world problems. For decades, military and disaster response organizations have been conducting games quite similar to ARGs as ways to field test various responses to different threats or crises. Experience from these games indicates that ARGs can indeed be powerful tools for group problem solving.

A few years ago, I was invited to participate in one such gaming exercise to test the ability of various military and nongovernmental organizations (NGOs) in the United States and Europe to respond to a humanitarian disaster in a fictional African country. The exercise included representatives from the militaries of the United States and other North Atlantic Treaty Organization (NATO) countries, as well as NGOs such as the Red Cross and Doctors Without Borders. The exercise tested procedures for communication and coordination between these NGOs and the military organizations. It was produced and coordinated by the US Transportation Command.[6]

---

5 The Games for Change website lists the games that they have recognized with awards (*http://www.gamesforchange.org/game_categories/g4c-award-winners/*). This list provides a good sampling of the different types and categories of games in this area

6 US Transportation Command, USTRANSCOM, *http://www.transcom.mil/*, Scott Air Force Base, June 2010, at their annual conference.

The producers of the game would periodically send out announcements, news bulletins, and other updates using email, YouTube videos, or live video feeds from interviews of key characters in the game, including the premier of the country in crisis and representatives of various groups trying to work together. The exercise went on all day and at the end of the day, there was a postmortem where all the players convened online and in person to examine what happened and what was learned. For me, it was a powerful demonstration of how games can serve to focus and coordinate the actions of so many different people and organizations, each with somewhat different perspectives and agendas.

ARGs encourage players to compare notes and pool their discoveries. Players do not compete against each other to figure out answers to problems that arise; instead, the game focuses the entire audience of players on solving puzzles presented to them by the game designers. When this kind of cooperation is brought about, it further expands the game because it motivates the existing players to find and bring new people into the game who have skills needed to further the action in the game.

As this happens, ARGs can develop diverse communities of people with a wide range of skills who are able to work together because of their overriding interest in accomplishing a common goal embodied in the game. As McGonigal puts it, "Games are a way to get massively many people to rally around a common goal."[7]

Most ARGs are built to encourage collaboration. And, in this respect, they share many common traits with MMOs, which are also designed to promote collaboration to solve common problems. The necessary skills and the nature of tasks to perform require cooperation and coordination between players.

Finding ways to harness such power has become a goal of organizations such as NGOs that wish to mobilize volunteers and businesses that want to generate viral word-of-mouth marketing campaigns. ARGs are a particular game type that has much potential for organizations that figure out how to employ them effectively.

---

7 Suzie Boss, "Jane McGonigal on Gaming for Good," interview with Jane McGonigal, *World Changing*, February 1, 2010, *http://www.worldchanging.com/archives/010949.html*.

What If Companies Operated as Alternate Reality Games?

Most companies still use traditional hierarchical organization models, and most employees of these companies have their work closely regulated by supervisors and bosses. These companies focus on the traditional industrial concepts of economies of scale and achieving high productivity through the rigorous application of standard operating procedures. There is little incentive for anyone except senior managers in such companies to take any initiative or to try anything different from the norm. This model works well enough in low change and predictable markets, but those kinds of markets are not so common anymore.

The notion that some central person or group of senior managers can do all the thinking for everybody else and tell them what to do and how to do it (no matter how many fancy systems they may have) is fundamentally flawed. No amount of centralized reporting systems and computing power can adequately process the amount of data that needs to be processed in the short time frames now required.

The answer lies in breaking up the data to be processed and the decisions to be made into many smaller jobs that can all run simultaneously—this is swarming dynamics. It is similar to the concept used in the design of massively parallel computer networks (like the Internet itself).

Companies that employ decentralized control structures, that incentivize and train their people to think and act for themselves, and provide them with the real-time performance data they need to make good decisions will outperform their competitors. This is because people working in self-directed teams striving to achieve common objectives find hundreds of ways to make continuous small adjustments to increase their profits and decrease their costs every day, every week, and every month.

Decentralized Coordination Replaces Centralized Control

What would happen if senior managers gave people clear objectives and then got out of the way? What would happen if company regulations were replaced by transparency and personal reputations, and people received a real-time stream of performance data that showed the results of their actions so people could see if their actions were delivering desired results or not? People would know if they were on track to achieve their objectives, and they could act quickly to get back on track when things went wrong (as they inevitably would from time to time).

How fast would people learn to be more productive to save money, increase customer service, and offer new products and services? Would people soon learn to regularly meet or exceed the performance objectives given to them? Would they evolve ways of working together that turn out to be orders of magnitude better than what we have seen from companies up until now?

Organizations that adopt this mode of operation and learn to harness its power would develop the ability to act as a highly coordinated entity but without the complications that arise when a small body of experts tries to do all the thinking for everybody else.

An apt analogy for this is the human body; it can be seen as a swarm of cells that continually sense their environment and act on their own without waiting to be told what to do. We may say that our brains are still that central body of experts who do the thinking and tell all the other cells what to do, but that analogy is not accurate. Our brains are not aware of everything that our bodies are doing nor do they need to be. Individual cells and organs know how to act on their own. And the overall effect of these self-motivated cells is to produce the coordinated behavior that makes our lives possible.

Unlike the slower and more predictable industrial economy of the twentieth century, we live in an unpredictable global economy and the best efficiencies come from individual dynamics that make hundreds of small adjustments to respond quickly as situations change. Organizations operating like this are structured as networks of many self-directed operating units (like organs and limbs of the body) that respond quickly without waiting to be told what to do.

Massively Multiplayer Alternate Reality Role Playing Games

A terrible thing is something that happens to others, but a real tragedy is something that happens to us individually. And things in the world seem to be happening a lot faster than we might have figured they would even a few years ago. Polar ice caps are melting faster than we thought. Developing countries like India and China and Brazil are growing faster than we thought. And there is increasing competition for oil, food, water, and other natural resources.

The complexity and urgency of the issues we are facing as a planet continue to increase and give no indication of going away if we just ignore or deny them. How are we going to respond to this challenge? Here's a thought: what would we get if we combined Google Earth with the NASA Earth Observatory[8] SensorWeb system and then added in *Second Life*[9] and the game *SimCity*?[10]

We would get a collaboration platform we could use to figure out how to deal with global issues from climate change and natural resources management to energy and land usage. We would get a way to use our collective creativity and innovation to try out different courses of action and see what specific combinations work best out of thousands of possible actions.

We would also get the chance to find out what doesn't work. And we could find this out by making our mistakes in virtual worlds instead of in the real one. We would get to learn from our failures and mistakes without destroying ourselves in the process.

Serious games are the games pilots play in flight simulators where they learn how to fly their airliner through a storm after their left engine conks out. Serious games are what soldiers and generals use to plan and execute battles and try different strategies and tactics to see what works best. Serious games are what surgeons play when they try out new surgical procedures and equipment to see if they will help the patient or kill the patient. They make lots of mistakes on the way to finding the right way, but unlike in the real world, they don't die and other people don't die, and they keep trying different actions until they find something that works.

As serious games and computer simulations get more sophisticated and more and more lifelike, their usefulness as serious research and learning tools grows exponentially. Figure 13-1 shows how SensorWeb gathers and processes environmental data.

---

8 NASA Earth Observatory: "The vision for NASA's sensorweb system for Earth science is to enable "on-demand sensing of a broad array of environmental and ecological phenomena across a wide range of spatial and temporal scales, from a heterogeneous suite of sensors both in situ and in orbit." *http://earthobservatory.nasa.gov/.*

9 *Second Life, http://secondlife.com/.*

10 *SimCity, http://www.simcity.com/en_US.*

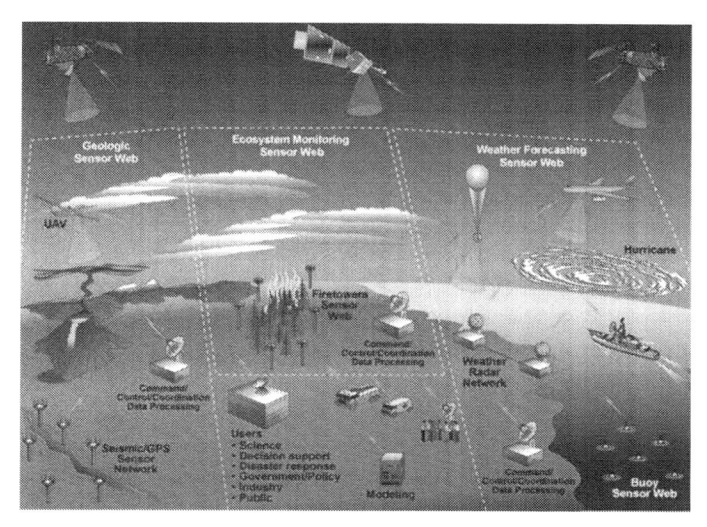

Figure 13-1. SensorWeb Earth monitoring system courtesy of NASA

In this massively multiplayer alternate reality game, we get to try a lot of different approaches and see what will work and what won't. We can try different combinations of technology and lifestyles and see which of those combinations actually work. We get to see vivid and educational simulations of what happens as we try different courses of action. We can see our cities crumble in the face of hurricanes, droughts, and rising ocean levels; we can see military adventures that spin out of control and destroy our world in those many scenarios that don't work out.

Big pieces of this "World Game" already exist. Yes, there are technical problems to address in building this game. But the good thing about technical problems is that they have technical answers. And we are getting better and better at solving technical problems. Look at the rate of change in our technology over the last decade. The pace of change is directly related to our ability to handle greater and greater technical challenges.

To build the World Game, we start by merging Google Earth with the database created by NASA's Earth Observatory SensorNet. This will exhibit real-time data about the earth and about specific locations on the planet. We can create a bunch of virtual Earths and start testing out different strategies for responding to situations such as humanitarian disasters like the Haiti earthquake as well as longer term problems caused by deforestation, the accumulation of greenhouse gasses in the atmosphere, the growth of populations, and the scarcity of natural resources like food and water.

Once we have our World Game 1.0 system set up, then we port over the software used to create and animate the men and women avatars in *Second Life*. That software allows each person to have different behaviors and to act autonomously as situations evolve. All we have to do is scale it up a bit to create six or seven billion virtual people to populate our virtual Earth.

Then we drop in *SimCity*. *SimCity* lets us build cities in the World Game, and we get to try out different approaches. We'll choose actual places in the world and build cities, suburbs, or whatever we want. And as the simulation plays out, we'll get to see what happens.

Then we port over a good 3-D animation and game engine to simulate airplanes, cars, trains, buildings, and bridges and we are good to go. We can also use the Wii game console interface for those who want a more realistic and interactive way to operate the game. And we can use mobile consumer IT devices like smartphones and tablet computers to let people access and interact with the World Game from anywhere. Imagine what you could do if you could combine selected features and capabilities of the applications shown in Figure 13-2.

Figure 13-2. The "World Game" is created by combining existing applications, courtesy of NASA, SimCity, Second Life, *and Google Earth*

GAMES FOR CHANGE | 173

Of course there are technical issues to tackle here, but technical problems are easy compared to political and cultural problems. And since we are getting so good at solving technical problems, let's use that ability to build simulation gaming systems that help us explore and resolve the more difficult political and cultural problems.

There is a way to pull this off. We figured out how to launch satellites and land on the Moon, we figured out how to build computers and construct the Internet, and we can solve our global problems too. As we start using simulation gaming to identify technology and lifestyle combinations that deliver good results (we would use the World Game to crowdsource possible solutions), we could create those worlds in the game and people could visit them and see what it would be like to live in them. We would then be able to tweak them and refine them to smooth off the rough edges before we actually build such worlds in real life.

Let everyone join in. Let everyone see what happens when you do things like cut down rain forests, drain swamps, burn fossil fuel, and expand urban sprawl. Make the game logic open to inspection by everyone. Invite panels of distinguished scientists as well as industry lobbying groups. Let people check the simulation logic and propose different logic if they feel the logic is flawed.

If certain courses of action require highly suspect or unrealistic logic in order to produce the results claimed by their proponents, then we should probably think twice before we embark on those courses of action. If other courses of action consistently produce desirable outcomes in simulation after simulation, then those are probably the courses of action we should follow.

Let us all be gamers then until the games shall free us!

| 14

The Future of Work

TRADITIONAL HIERARCHIES IN BUSINESS and government are structurally designed to ignore anything that does not feed into their established operating models. They are good at doing the same things over and over. That's why so many big government and corporate hierarchies are having so much trouble these days in spite of their claims to embrace innovation. Hierarchies are motivated to maintain the status quo simply because that is where their money and support comes from, not because the people in them are any less imaginative or intelligent.

Networks, on the other hand, are great at promoting new ideas and getting things done quickly. Networks of players working together on project focused teams are shown time and again to be the best sources for continuous innovation. Clearly the demand for things networks are good at is going to soar in the coming years. This means there is a tremendous opportunity for self-organizing networks of workers who operate in a game-like manner to come together in project teams and to get things done.

Already we are seeing examples of large corporate hierarchies actively fostering relationships with wide networks of external business partners. An example of this is Procter & Gamble. In 2000, their CEO at that time realized that the traditional invent-it-ourselves model was not capable of sustaining high levels of top-line growth. So, he launched an initiative called "Connect + Develop"[1] with the stated goal of setting in motion a process of continuous innovation.

---

1 Larry Huston and Nabil Sakkab, "Connect and Develop: Inside Procter & Gamble's New Model for Innovation," *Harvard Business Review*, March 20, 2006. Download a PDF of this white paper at *http://www.proinno-europe.eu/sites/default/files/1_1_von_Heimburg_a7986.pdf.*

The aim of this initiative was that 50 percent or more of the product innovation that came about would result from collaboration with external partners. The program has thrived and, more than 10 years later, the P&G Connect + Develop website makes this statement: "We're very proud that more than half of new product initiatives at Procter and Gamble involve significant collaboration with those outside our walls. We partner with small companies, multi-nationals, individual inventors, and in some cases, even our competitors, to bring game-changing innovations to market. Connect + DevelopSM is at the heart of how P&G innovates."[2]

In a white paper titled "Innovation by Collaboration,"[3] Deloitte Consulting released findings from an extensive study of more than 400 manufacturing firms over the last decade. "The traditional path to innovation through internal R&D efforts is not likely to turn things around," they report. The reason is that internal R&D efforts often suffer from a lack of diversity; there just is not enough variety of ideas inside one company.

Business success these days lies in spinning out a steady stream of products that coevolve with the evolving needs and desires of your customers. P&G is an example of this in the way that they continually evolve their lines of consumer products. It is important to remember that innovation is not just an occasional event. The competition brought about by the real-time economy results in shorter product life cycles and a need to continuously improve existing products while also bringing out entirely new products. In the consumer electronics industry, many products now have life cycles measured in months, not years, and life cycles in most other industries are shrinking dramatically also.

Companies will evolve networks of trusted contractors who they turn to on a regular basis for input and assistance in their continuous evolution of products and processes. People in these networks will (and already do) earn their reputations based on verifiable skills and objective reporting of the outcomes of the projects they participate in. Game dynamics can be used to orchestrate these networks so that workers and projects are brought together much more quickly and effectively than what we have experienced up until now.

---

2 The Proctor & Gamble Connect + Develop website, *http://www.pg.com/connect_develop/index.shtml* (accessed July 4, 2012).

3 Duane Dickenson, Atanu Chaudhuri, and John Ofori, "Innovation by Collaboration: A Blueprint for Action," Deloitte Consulting LLP, 2011. Download a PDF of this whitepaper at *http://www.deloitte.com.mx/Borderlink/11/6/innovationbycollaboration_03092011.pdf*.

Capitalism Reinvented for This Century

Capitalism has always assumed that personal drives for power and money were the most important motivators, but perhaps this is only true for a small minority of people. What would happen if the other motivators that games appeal to (social connection, satisfying work, hope and experience of success) were effectively harnessed to engage more people more productively in company operations?

The traditional capitalist model handed down to us from the last century is promoting the concentration of money in the hands of fewer and fewer people and larger and larger corporate structures. And, furthermore, this model of capitalism is simply unable to generate the number of jobs needed to absorb the ever growing numbers of people entering the labor market.

Large modern corporations are often very efficient, but the value of efficiency alone is no longer what it was a hundred years ago when this focus on efficiency was ushered in to great effect with inventions like the assembly line. "It raises the question of whether in the pursuit of efficiency have we neglected the principle of access to the market and egalitarianism?" This is how the award-winning business journalist Robert Neuwirth defines the issue.[4]

In his newest book, *Stealth of Nations: The Global Rise of the Informal Economy*, he explores what is happening in economies and labor markets around the world.[5] He describes the rise of an informal economy he calls "System D," which is a slang phrase that comes from French speaking Africa and the Caribbean. The French have a word they use to describe particularly effective and motivated people: *debrouillards*. It means people who are resourceful and ingenious at finding ways to make a living. So, System D translates as "the ingenuity economy, the economy of improvisation and self-reliance, the do-it-yourself, or DIY economy."[6]

---

4 Robert Neuwirth (*http://www.ted.com/speakers/robert_neuwirth.html*) is a business journalist and investigative reporter whose work has appeared in the *New York Times, Forbes, Fortune,* and *Wired* to name a few publications. His work has received grants and awards from the Fund for Investigative Journalism, the John D. and Catherine T. MacArthur Foundation, and the Nation Institute.

5 Robert Neuwirth, *Stealth of Nations: The Global Rise of the Informal Economy* (New York: Pantheon Books, 2011). His Stealth of Nations blog is located at *http://stealthofnations.blogspot.com/.*

6 Ibid, 18.

In 2009, the Organization for Economic Co-operation and Development (OECD), a research organization sponsored by governments of 30 of the most powerful capitalist economies in the world, estimated in a report that half of the world's workers (about 1.8 billion people) were working in System D. And they reported that System D is the fastest growing segment of many countries' economies and that growth has increased due to the effects of the economic crisis of 2008. OECD projects that by 2020 two thirds of the world's workers will be employed by System D.[7]

System D is another manifestation of new business models being brought into existence because of the confluence of economic necessity and the spread of social technology. People are being resourceful and ingenious and figuring out how to use social technology to respond to economic realities and new opportunities.

System D is a network-based business model instead of a traditional hierarchy-based model. And because of its network structure, it shares many of the same dynamics that you see in ARG or MMO games. The new wave of social technology (mobile consumer IT, SaaS, cloud computing, social media) fits this networked organization structure well and enables fast and effective communication between people in these networks. The time is ripe for the emergence of new game-like business models.

In an ongoing conversation over the last several years with Mike Chakos, I have discussed with him what a business looks like that is optimized to deal with the uncertainty and rapid rates of change that are now the norm in our real-time economy. From his experience in starting and growing businesses, Mike has formulated five characteristics that define agile and successful companies.

These five characteristics embody the qualities of agility and responsiveness needed for success. They are also very game-like in that they are an accurate description of how teams and guilds operate now in popular MMOs like *World of Warcraft* and *EVE Online*. These five characteristics seem to be applicable to any business. I've added a few refinements to Mike's five traits, and I offer them here for you to consider.[8]

---

[7] Ibid, 19

[8] I explored these five characteristics and how they operate in *Business Agility: Sustainable Prosperity in a Relentlessly Competitive World* (Hoboken, NJ: John Wiley & Sons, 2009). A link to this book is on my website at *http://michaelhugos.com/business-agility/*.

Five Characteristics of an Agile and Responsive Enterprise

The agile enterprise is more than just an attempt to apply technology to create speeded up versions of traditional organizations from the last century. Technology is necessary but not sufficient. To create agility, a new game-like business model is needed before technology can really be employed to best effect.

The first characteristic of an agile and responsive company is that it is populated with entrepreneurial employees. Agile organizations replace command and control with training and trust. They train their people and give them authority to decide and act on their own within broadly defined parameters set by senior management. People are empowered to do whatever is legal and not expressly prohibited instead of only doing what is specifically permitted.

The second characteristic is a network organization structure that enables a large degree of autonomy and freedom of action for people and individual business units. The organization structure of an agile enterprise doesn't look much like the traditional pyramid-shaped hierarchy of a twentieth-century industrial corporation. Hierarchies move way too slowly because pyramids inevitably create decision-making bottlenecks as information gets passed up the chain of command (see Figure 14-1). In a fast-paced world (regardless of how many information systems are installed), a few people at the top simply can't do all the thinking for everybody else.

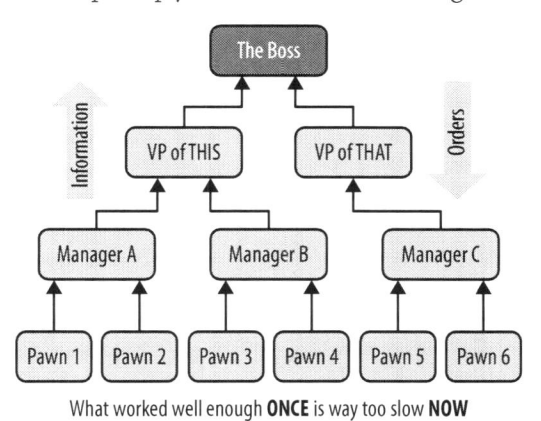

Figure 14-1. Traditional business model

180 | ENTERPRISE GAMES

This characteristic—a network organization structure—is so important because it promotes coordination over control. A network structure allows for decentralized decision making and more freedom of action for autonomous business units. Senior management makes sure people are well trained, and then management trusts people to act without having to ask permission first (see Figure 14-2).

Network of autonomous business units

Coordination replaces control

Enterprise Coordinator says **WHAT**
Business Units are free to choose **HOW**

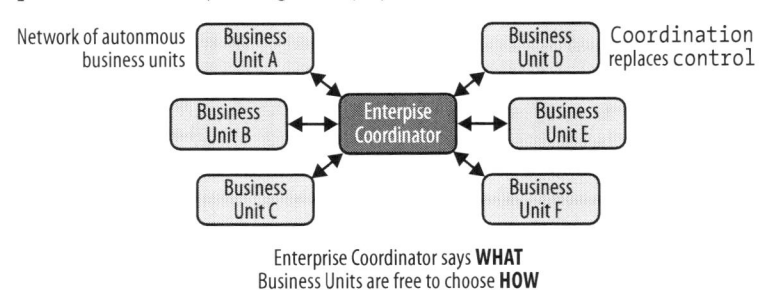

Figure 14-2. Agile business model

A network organization structure of autonomous business units acts like a school of fish, a flight of birds, or a swarm of bees. The business units coordinate with each other, yet people think and act for themselves within the parameters defined by senior management. And if an opportunity proves to be a big one, then new business units are created to grow into those new markets instead of letting any one business unit get too big. Network organization structures promote organic growth like that illustrated in Figure 14-3.

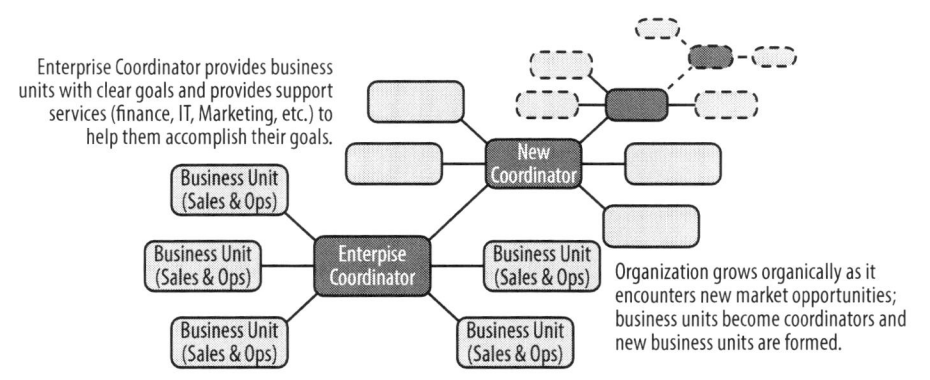

Enterprise Coordinator provides business units with clear goals and provides support services (finance, IT, Marketing, etc.) to help them accomplish their goals.

Organization grows organically as it encounters new market opportunities; business units become coordinators and new business units are formed.

Figure 14-3. Growth of agile business

Characteristic number three is that agile enterprises employ transparency, and people are trained to read balance sheets and income statements.

They get access to updated operating and finance information every week. People quickly learn to read financial reports (whether they have an MBA or not) because people can always figure out things that interest them. Since agile organizations are composed of entrepreneurial employees who earn a portion of their compensation from quarterly performance bonuses, that means real money is riding on business results, so everyone from senior managers to brand new hires has skin in the game and everyone is interested in the financials.

The fourth characteristic is financial fluency. Everyone understands balance sheets and income statements and everyone understands breakeven points. Everybody in the company is able to do a breakeven analysis on their projects or the support activities they perform. This simple calculation tells employees the minimum activity level necessary to pay for themselves and anything else they or the company might do. It allows people to size up situations and determine which ones are worth pursuing and which ones are not.

Every person understands how to apply breakeven analysis so they can do things such as:

- Calculate the sales level at a given gross margin percentage that would be needed to pay for a new investment
- Translate sales into relevant business terms, such as the number of billable hours or production levels they need to achieve to fill given sales targets
- Calculate the breakeven level for their work unit given normal billable hours or production levels after subtracting out their variable costs
- Calculate their share of the profits that would result from exceeding their breakeven points
- Know how much money they would lose if they do not reach their breakeven points

People at each level of an agile organization know their operating numbers and their breakeven points better than senior management does. Because of this, performance targets necessary for higher profits become clear to everyone and people see what their share of the profits (or the losses) would be. This common understanding is extremely powerful; it is what creates consensus and guides effective entrepreneurial behavior. It enables the decentralized decision making that agile organizations depend on.

The fifth characteristic of agile organizations is that they have "participatory senior management." That means that the leaders of the company participate in the financial ups and downs of the company. They prosper when the company prospers, and they do not pay themselves enormous bonuses when the company does not do well. Participatory senior managers have real money at stake in the company and are highly motivated to see the entire company do well as a condition of their own personal success.

In every agile enterprise there are ongoing conversations about where to centralize certain functions like finance, marketing, logistics, and selected IT functions to get economies of scale. But at no time does the notion of centrally controlled economies of scale ever become the main business strategy or the dominant operating policy. Centrally controlled hierarchies optimized for economies of scale were the model for industrial corporations in the relatively slow moving and predictable twentieth century, but they don't work as well in the fluid and unpredictable economy of this century.

Business models for this century must embrace uncertainty. Agile organizations focus on building and harnessing the entrepreneurial energy of their members; that is the main driver of their business strategies. They understand that in the competitive and unpredictable world we live in now, responsiveness driven by the entrepreneurial energy of autonomous business units is the more profitable course.

Because only autonomous business units with local decision-making authority can move fast enough to capitalize on opportunities or respond to threats in a timely manner.

Events unfold in bewildering and unpredictable ways. The agile enterprise embraces this state of affairs and learns to use it to its advantage. Agile and responsive organizations generate better profits because of their ability to make many small adjustments every day to improve their performance as conditions change and because of their ability to move quickly to seize profitable new opportunities that come their way.

These five characteristics are much like the behavior of guilds and corporations that arise in MMOs. They are very game-like. And this gives them great ability to handle uncertainty. That is why the five characteristics of an agile enterprise and the game-like business practices that promote them are the basis for sustainable prosperity in this economy.

If We Can't Find Full-Time Jobs, Let's Try Games Instead

Given that more and more people enter and reenter the workforce every day, and given that more and more people work as temps and contract workers because companies are reluctant to hire full time employees, perhaps it's time to come to terms with some trends that are accelerating year after year.[9] Instead of trying to entice companies to create full-time jobs (with all the fixed cost and risk that this implies), what if we focus on efficient and effective ways for companies and people to come together to get things done?

The concept of "a full-time job" is a concept from the last century when the growth of the industrial economy produced mass markets and predictable business environments that made it profitable for companies to enter into the long-term commitments implied in the traditional full-time job with a career path, benefits, and a pension.[10]

But now instead of predictable mass markets, we have an economy of rapidly evolving products and massive market uncertainty. Now, in the space of a few years, new companies come out of nowhere and established companies fade into oblivion. We all know examples of both, and those examples keep coming faster and faster. OK, you think, perhaps we do need to consider something more aligned with the realities of this century, maybe full-time jobs are becoming relics of the last century. Well then, what other models could we use for examples of how people can earn a living?

The way people interact in massively multiplayer online role playing games (MMOs) is also a model for how people can interact and earn a living in business. Popular MMOs like *World of Warcraft* or *EVE Online* and many others provide people with a central theme and goals of a game, a set of rules that guide the players and a rich multimedia online real-time environment that provides a feedback system and a place where people interact. Otherwise the games are unscripted and what happens is the result of the interactions of the players—just like the way the real world happens.

---

9   Jackson, Cheryl V., "Temporary workers carve out alternative careers," *Chicago Tribune*, August 27, 2012 (*http://www.chicagotribune.com/business/ct-biz-0827-temp-workers-20120827,0,282846.story*).

10 Portions of this section were first published on my blog at CIO.com in a post titled "If We Can't Find Full-Time Jobs, Let's Try Games Instead" on August 23, 2011 at *http://blogs.cio.com/careers/16469/if-we-can%E2%80%99t-find-full-time-jobs-let%E2%80%99s-try-games-instead*.

In MMOs, players come together to form corporations and guilds and those organizations make plans and go on missions. They solicit the participation of other players who have the skills and experience they need to make their missions successful. Interested players apply to go on those missions, and they are accepted based on their reputation within the game community. Figure 14-4 shows screenshots from some popular MMOs to illustrate these ideas.

Players can see the skill levels and experiences of other players and the outcome of missions that players participate in builds their reputations. Players who have certifications in sought after skills and who have successful reputations can stay as busy as they want. And when they want to take a break after finishing a mission, they do so.

How is this so different from the realities of that activity we call work? Companies hire people with desirable skill sets who have the experience they want for particular projects. There is not much difference between full-time employees and contract employees anymore. Full-time employees are routinely terminated when business needs change just as contract employees leave when their contracts expire or their projects are finished.

- Players form guilds and corporations.
- Missions require the right mix of skills and close coordination to succeed.

Figure 14-4. Collaborative game play, courtesy of World of Warcraft *and* EVE Online

An MMO for the Game of New Product Development

oDesk is a company offering a web-based set of services to match up companies with projects and contractors with relevant skills.[11] The way oDesk operates has much in common with the MMO approach to getting work done.

To illustrate this MMO style of working, I'll use a project that I've been running with a team of people over the past year or so. We've been developing the SCM Globe supply chain simulation system that is mentioned at several points in this book. oDesk provides rules and a real time feedback system, and the people on the project team and I use it in a game-like manner to transact business and get things done.

When I started the SCM Globe project, I registered my company as a hiring company with oDesk and I described the project and the kinds of skills I was looking for on the project team. Over the next couple of days, contractors responded to my project posting. From each contractor, I got a short pitch with their skills and experience and their requested pay rate.

Working with two other people at my company, we scanned the responses and picked out a handful of interesting contractors. We then checked their experience in more detail. Their oDesk profiles contained lots of information about them and the other projects they have worked on for other oDesk hiring companies. For every project that oDesk contractors work on, they get a ranking from one star to five stars by the company that hired them. In addition to the ranking there are also comments about their work from the hiring companies. These rankings and comments are believable because they are made by people who hired them and who have no reason to give false praise or exaggerate their skills.

In addition to the job history and ratings provided for contractors, I could also see each contractor's pay rate history and the total amount of money they have earned on oDesk. What I saw was that people just starting out worked for lower rates and then, as they built up their reputations, they raised their rates. I saw that lots of contractors from all over the world have been working on oDesk for several years or more and plenty of them are making significant amounts of money by doing so.

---

11 oDesk (*https://www.odesk.com/*) calls itself "the world's largest and fastest growing online workplace."

This is important because it is part of the feedback system that makes the game work. This feedback system encourages contractors to apply only for jobs where they think they will do well because that's how they build their reputations and that's how they earn the ability to raise their rates. Contractors don't want to apply for jobs they aren't qualified for because they will get bad ratings and comments from people who hire them (and therefore, they won't be able to build their reputations or raise their rates). This is the same dynamic that operates in MMOs and induces players to work long and hard to build their reputations and level up in those games.

The longer a contractor has been on oDesk and the more money a contractor is able to earn through oDesk, the more valuable their oDesk reputation becomes. This is good because it reassures me as the hiring company that I will mostly get a self-selected group of qualified contractors who apply to work on my projects. I will not be bombarded by replies from anyone and everyone.

I want experienced developers with certain skills and a solid reputation, so I will pay more for those people because they are worth more (and other hiring companies will pay their asking rates if I don't). And for companies that mostly want just low price, then they accept lower skilled people with less of a reputation because those people work for less (in order to get started and build up their reputations).

After we researched contractors of interest to us, we set up some Skype calls to talk to them in person. Pretty quickly we put together our extended project team of developers and system administrators. The team included people in the United States, India, Pakistan, and Indonesia.

With each contractor, we discussed the work we needed from them and agreed on an hourly rate and a maximum number of hours each week that they could bill on the project. We also set out a weekly work schedule and specified the deliverables we needed from each contractor each week.

During the week, contractors on our project clock in to our virtual team room on oDesk, and oDesk starts taking screen shots at random showing what is on their screens. Every hour, six random screenshots are recorded and I can see them. Contractors can review these screenshots and delete any of them before I see them, but they must also delete 10 minutes of billing for each screenshot they delete. These screen shots give me verification that contractors were actually working on my project during the time they are billing me.

On our project, we use a program code library and management system named GitHub[12] and an issues tracking system named Redmine.[13] Our extended project team has access to these systems. As developers finish their program code, they upload it to GitHub and they and the system administrators upload documentation and other information to Redmine. Then we check the deliverables. Each week, we talk with our contractors and schedule that week's work and deliverables. If we are not pleased with a contractor's work, we discuss it, and if they don't improve then at the end of any given week we can end our contract with them.

oDesk guarantees payment to the contractors each week for their scheduled time as long as their screenshots show they were working on my project. I put my company credit card on file with oDesk and every week they pay my contractors for the previous week's work and charge the amount to my card. This further strengthens the contractor's loyalty to oDesk, which is good because it attracts and retains good contractors and reinforces the value of their reputation on oDesk. Like players in an MMO, contractors are motivated to work hard to build and protect their reputations—and that's good for hiring companies.

The collaborative work environment my company uses is illustrated in the screenshots shown in Figures 14-5 through 14-7. There are so many useful and well-designed apps to help companies assemble and collaborate with extended networks of people. The apps I show here are just a small sample of what is available.

---

12 GitHub (*https://github.com/*) describes its product as "an extremely fast, efficient, distributed version control system ideal for the collaborative development of software."

13 Redmine (*www.redmine.org/*) is a "flexible project management web application." It is a cross-platform, open source application.

| ENTERPRISE GAMES

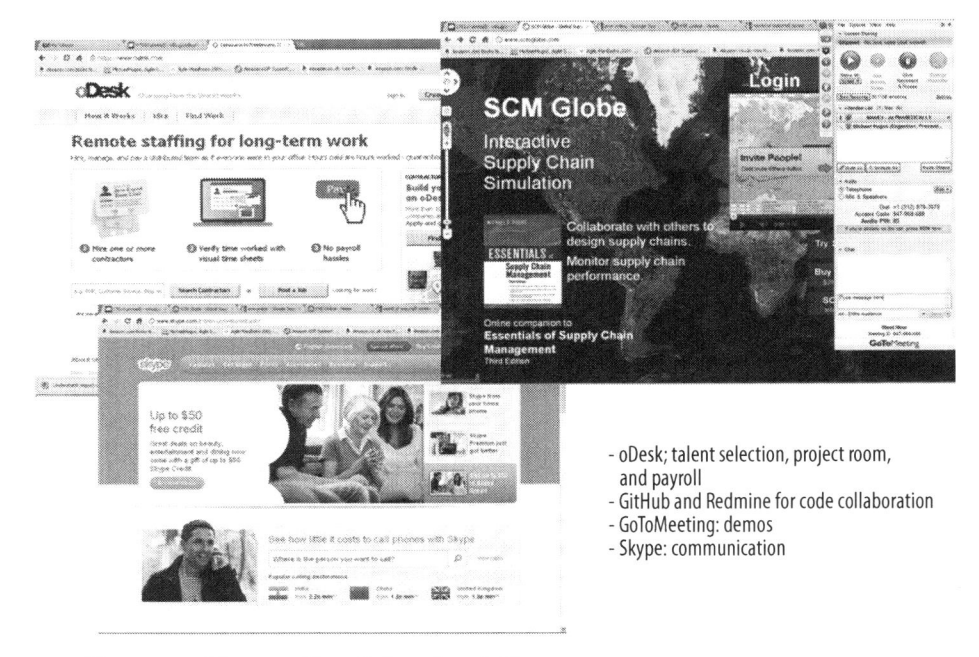

- oDesk; talent selection, project room, and payroll
- GitHub and Redmine for code collaboration
- GoToMeeting: demos
- Skype: communication

Figure 14-5. My game-like collaboration platform

In the upper left of Figure 14-5 is the oDesk home screen, and my company's SCM Globe home screen is shown on the right. Overlaying the SCM Globe screen is the GoToMeeting conference call control panel.[14] We pass control of the conference call from one participant to another and whoever has control can show the rest of us what is on their screen. Below these two screens is the Skype home screen.[15] We use Skype for global calls and video conferences.

---

14 GoToMeeting (*www.gotomeeting.com/fec/*) describes its products as "easy web conferencing and online meeting tools."

15 Skype (*www.skype.com/intl/en-us/business/*) offers Internet-based voice and video communication.

THE FUTURE OF WORK | 189

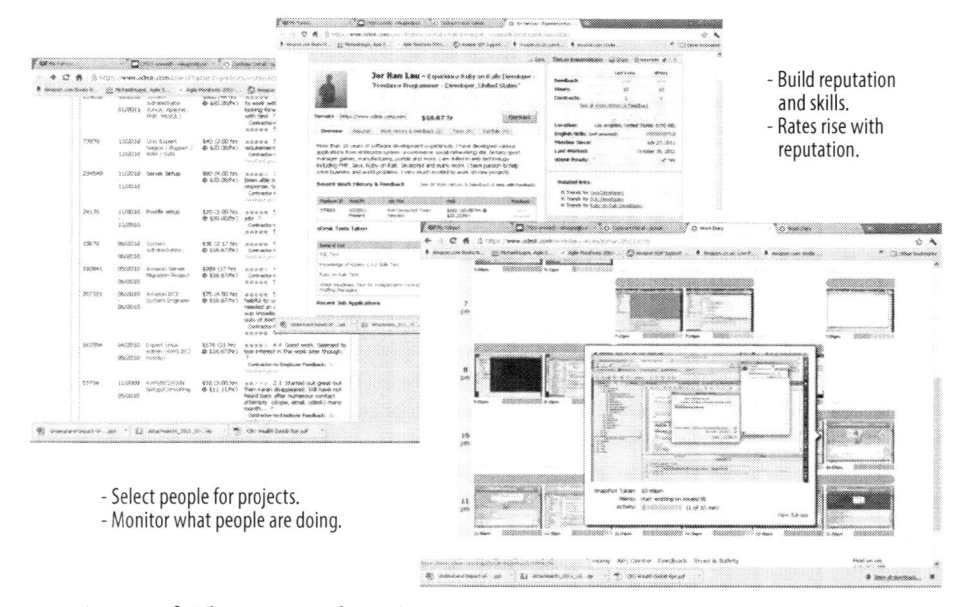

Figure 14-6. The game (work) environment

The screenshots in Figure 14-6 are from our project that we are running on oDesk. The screen on the left shows a list of applicants who responded to a project listing. The screen above and to the right shows the personal profile of one of the contractors we are working with on the project. And the screen below that shows the random snapshots that oDesk took of our contractor's PC screen while he was working on our project.

The two screens in Figure 14-7 are also from oDesk. The first shows different categories of skills that are available for contractors and hiring companies, and the second one shows high level profiles and rates of contractors available in one of the skills categories.

I wonder if this model would work in other areas as well? It seems like it works for everything from launching a new marketing campaign to designing a new consumer electronics product or doing an environmental impact assessment. This model would be useful to organize and do work in any industry where work was project oriented and the demand for labor rose and fell depending on the number of projects under way.

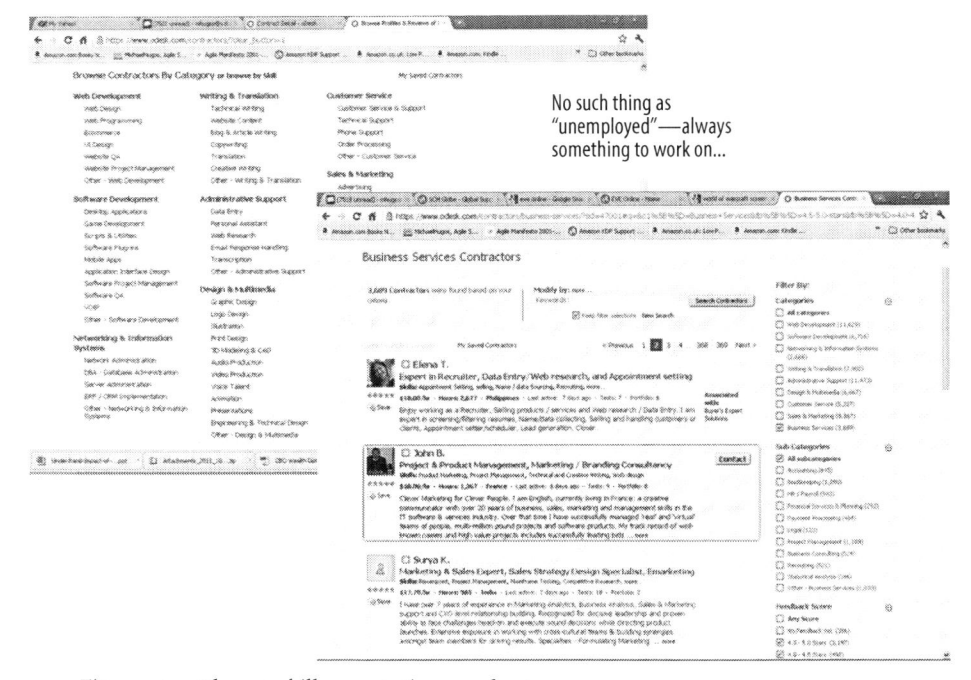

Figure 14-7. Players: skills, reputations, and rates

In addition to oDesk, there are other similar companies responding to the need to bring together contractors and hiring companies. Another company, somewhat similar to oDesk, is Freelancer.com.[16] And there are other companies such as Gigwalk[17] and TaskRabbit[18] that specialize in particular types of short-term jobs. This is just a beginning.

The Times They Are A-Changin'

If the old days of full-time jobs are relentlessly disappearing, then it's a losing proposition to stubbornly cling to that vanishing way of life. For good or for bad, the world is changing in ways we never imagined (at first), and in ways that can be disorienting and sometimes scary.

---

16 Freelancer (*www.freelancer.com/*) describes itself as "the world's largest outsourcing marketplace."

17 Gigwalk (*www.gigwalk.com*) offers capabilities to "instantly mobilize people to do work anywhere."

18 TaskRabbit (*www.taskrabbit.com*) offers services to "get just about anything done by safe, reliable, awesome people."

The MMO model of working has a lot to offer; it responds quickly to people who need to get things done. It's an effective way to find and hire people who can do the work, and it offers a way for people to build their skills and reputations and earn a good living. Perhaps we are already experiencing the early stages of the transition to a new way of working, a way of working based on the use of game-like operating models.

This transition isn't going to be easy. And this isn't going to be painless. Like other big transitions, such as what happened one hundred years ago when employment in North America and Europe shifted from farms and small businesses to factories and big corporations, this is going to stretch our imagination and test our strength.

Yet something similar to this game-like model of employment is steadily gaining ground in the world economy. This is what Robert Neuwirth calls the System D economy. Others call it the "informal economy." Estimates indicate it will employ something like two thirds of the world's workers by 2020. It is happening because of the responses of billions of motivated and ingenious people who cannot find employment in traditional corporations and who must still find a way to make a living.

We will do ourselves a great favor if we find ways to help this trend. We need to find ways for people to have access to affordable healthcare without depending on employers to do that for them. And we need to find ways for people to create pension and benefits funds without depending on employers to do that for them (I'm sure there are great ideas that can be crowd sourced in these areas).

It was often said that the success of the British Empire was won on the playing fields of Eton, because in playing those games, its leaders learned the values of team play, sportsmanship, and perseverance.

Perhaps the next empires will be won on new kinds of playing fields.

So, let the games begin.

Index

Symbols
3-D environments
   importance of, 86
   visualizing dataspaces, 139–142

A
Abbott, Edwin, Flatland: A Romance of Many Dimensions, 130
accounts payable, 105–108
actions, defined, 88
agile development method
   Business Spheres, 122
   KPI scorecard system, 20
agile enterprises
   benefits of, 31
   feedback, 30
   five characteristics of, 179–182
agility dividends, 31
airplanes, simulations, 68
alternate reality games, *See* ARGs
America's Army game, 74
Anixter International, 94
anthropo-cyber-synchronicity, 138
APIs, 151
ARGs (alternate reality games)
   about, 149, 166
   companies operating as, 168
   multiplayer role playing, 169–173

autonomy, defined, 25
avatars
   origin of, 133
   self-representation with, 86
awareness
   Business Spheres, 121
   decision-making environments, 123–126

B
badges, sharing, 109
black boxes, defined, 88
Blender, open source game developer package, 141
Bogost, Ian, on gamification, 56
bonus plans
   goals and rules, 26
   Mike Chakos, 9
   trust and participation, 28
bonus programs, feedback systems, 25
boredom, source of, 2
Boyd, John, OODA Loop, 123
Bunchball, 56
business, game dynamics applied to, 14
Business Spheres, 117

C

capitalism
   as shared opportunity, 6
   reinvented, 177
Card, Orson Scott, Ender's Game, 71
cause and effect associations, 165
Chakos, Mike
   business philosophy, 8
   on five traits that characterize successful companies, 178
   on sharing the reasons behind bonus payouts, 29
Chatfield, Tom, on the learning potential of simulations, 66
Chinese People's Liberation Army game, 76
chip design, 137
CityOne, 58
Coffman, Curt W., on work satisfaction survey, 2
communications systems, importance of parallel communication systems, 87
continuum of functionality, 63–78
   America's Army game, 74
   Chinese People's Liberation Army game, 76
   game capabilities, 64
   multiplayer online games, 78
   pilots, soldiers and surgeons, 66
   pilot training, 68
   simulation of serious games, 71
   soldier games, 69
   surgery game, 70
   use of serious games, 73
controversy, gamification, 56
coordination layer, game layer as, 151
corporate IT, 151
cyberspace, 131, 136

D

data entry task, 105
dataspaces, 129–145
   3-D design, 139–142
   interactive simulation, 142–145
   multisensory engagement, 129–136
   navigating in the real-time economy, 126–128
   spreadsheets, 18
   visualizing
      3-D design, 139–142
      about, 136–139
decentralized control structures, 168
decision-making environments, 117–128
   awareness, 123–126
   dataspaces and navigating in the real-time economy, 126–128
   feedback loops, 120–123
decision trees, 99
demographics, video game players, 48
drone aircraft, 71

E

Earth Observatory, 160
electronics industry
   supply chain, 32
elegant simplicity principle, 95
Ender's Game (Card), 71
engagement engines, 12

entrepreneurship, Mike Chakos, 8
EVE Online, 81
Evoke, 163
executive function, Business Spheres, 120

F

F-15 Strike Eagle, 97
Facebook, Miss Social application, 52
feedback, 11–22, 23–36
   bonus plans, 26, 28
   business agility, 30
   decision-making environments, 120–123
   defined, 7, 88
   game dynamics applied to business, 14
   importance of, 86
   information technology, 13
   oDesk, 186
   IVS system, 17–22 supply management game, 31–36
   video games, 11
financial fluency, 181
Flatland: A Romance of Many Dimensions (Abbott), 130
Flight Simulator, 64
forecasting model, 125
Forrester, Jay, on cause and effect associations, 165
Foursquare application, 51

G

Game IT, 155
game layer, 147–162
   as coordination layer, 151
   global game layers, 156
   networks, 159–162
   social infrastructure, 148
   video game technology, 155
   visualization of data streaming from, 152–154
Games for Change, 163–173
   ARGs
      about, 166
      companies operating as, 168
      multiplayer role playing, 169–173
   decentralized coordination, 168
   history, 164
gamification, 47–61
   beyond gamification, 57
   CityOne, 58
   concepts and techniques, 49
   controversy, 56
   defined, 47
   Foursquare application, 51
   future of, 60
   Plantville, 59
   Playboy application, 52
   Salesforce.com application, 54
   Samsung Electronics, 53
   trend of, 13
   why gamification?, 48
Gamification Cup, 106
Gibson, William, on cyberspace, 132
GitHub, 187
goals
   bonus plans, 26
   defined, 7
   feedback systems, 24
   objectives, 88
growth, game-like operating models, 8

H
Hammerbacker, Jeff, on dataspaces, 127
Harrison-Stevens model, 125
health and wellness, 108–112
Herger, Mario, on motivation and teams, 106
Hypermiling game, 112–116

I
IBM, CityOne, 58
informal economy, 177, 191
information technology, feedback, 13
interactive simulation, dataspaces, 142–145
intuitively obvious principle, 95
Inventory system, 15

J
jobs, trying games instead, 183

K
KPI scorecard, the IVS System, 20

L
leadership, MMOs, 80

M
management incentive plans (MIPs), 26
Maples, Creve
    anthropo-cyber-synchronicity, 138
    on visualizing big data, 136
Markelz, Trapper, on using game techniques, 109
market places and economies, 86
massively multiplayer online role playing games, *See* MMOs
mastery, defined, 25
McGonigal, Jane
    on gameplay's effect on people, 3
    on the four defining traits of games, 1
    on the four essential human cravings, 5
MeYou Health, 108
Microsoft, Xbox Live real-time game network, 156
MIPs (management incentive plans), 26
Mission of Honor, 77
Miss Social application, 52
MMOs (massively multiplayer online role playing games), 79–92
    about, 36
    game ingredients and building blocks, 85–90
    as a model for business, 183
    product development, 185–190
    supply chain games, 90
    when serious games become massively multiplayer online games, 81–85
motivation
    elements of, 25
    teams, 106
multiplayer games
    multiplayer online games, 78, 79–92
        game ingredients and building blocks, 85–90
        product development, 185–190
        supply chain games, 90

when serious games become massively multiplayer online games, 81–85
IVS system, 17–22
supply management game, 31–36

N

narrative context, 86
NASA, Earth Observatory, 160
National Gamers Survey, 41
networks
 expansion of, 147
 game layer, 159–162
 organization structure, 180
Neuwirth, Robert, Stealth of Nations: The Global Rise of the Informal Economy, 177
North American Coatings, 28

O

objectives, 88
oDesk, 185
OECD (Organization for Economic Co-operation and Development), 178
OODA Loop, 123
outcomes, defined, 88

P

paradigms, 37–45
 all the world's a game, 43–45
 games, gamers and new business strategies, 41
participation, bonus plans, 28
pilot training, 68
Plantville, 59
PLA (People's Liberation Army), 77
Playboy application, 52

player profiles, 88
Procter & Gamble, 117, 175
products and services, 105–116
 accounts payable, 105–108
 health and wellness, 108–112
 Hypermiling game, 112–116
 product development, 185–190
profits, game-like operating models, 8
purpose, defined, 25

R

racing cars, 137
Read, J. Leighton
 on ten game ingredients to guide real work, 85
 on work and play, 3
Reeves, Byron

 on MMOs and team work, 80
 on ten game ingredients to guide real work, 85
 on work and play, 3
reputations, ranks and levels, 86
resistance, defined, 88
resources, defined, 88
Rifkin, Jeremy, on the purpose of communications, 161
rules
 bonus plans, 26
 defined, 7
 role of in games, 87

S

SaaS, APIs, 151
sales, 93–104
 as a game, 43
 Ian Bogost on gamification, 57
 sales design system, 94–101
 system rollout, 102–104

Salesforce.com application, 54
SALE system, 96
Samsung Electronics, 53
SAP, 106
Sawyer, Ben, Game IT, 155
SCM Globe, 32, 185, 189
Scrum, Business Spheres, 122
SCVNGR, 148
Semco, 6
senior management, 182
SensorWeb, 170
serious games
   about, 73
   examples of, 170
services, *See* products and services
Siemens, Plantville, 59
SimCity, 172
simulation modeling, 63–78
   about, 64
   interactive simulation and dataspaces, 142–145
   learning potential of, 66
   merging with real world, 71
   multiplayer online games, 78
   SCM Globe, 185
   serious games, 73
   war games, 74
Social Fabric platform, 54
social infrastructure, game layer, 148
social media, business-to-business network and real-time feedback system, 39
social technology
   about, 37
   effectiveness of, 41
   potential of, 6
soldier games, 69

spreadsheets
   sharing data, 18
   simulation modeling, 64
Springfield ReManufacturing, 6
Stealth of Nations: The Global Rise of the Informal Economy (Neuwirth), 177
Stephenson, Neal, avatar, 133
supply chains
   electronics industry, 32
   games, 90
   SCM Globe, 185
supply management game, 31–36
surgery game, 70
surveys, work satisfaction, 2
System D economy
   about, 178
   Robert Neuwirth on, 191

T
teams
   about, 87
   MMOs, 80
   motivation, 106
time pressure, importance of, 87
trends, visualizing, 140
trust, bonus plans, 28

U
Unity game developer package, 141
Unreal Engine, developed by Epic Games, 74
user interfaces
   F-15 Strike Eagle simulator, 97
   Hypermiling, 112
   mileage feedback displays, 115
   multisensory engagement, 129
   SALE system, 100
   SCM Globe and oDesk, 189

V

VBS2 (Virtual Battlespace 2), 73
video games
    feedback loops, 11
    game layer and business technology, 155
    popularity of, 41
    serious games in the military, 73
VisiCalc, 64
visualization
    3-D design, 139–142
    dataspaces, 136–139
    data streaming from game layer, 152–154
voluntary participation, defined, 7

W

war games
    about, 67
    America's Army, 74
    serious games, 73
    training soldiers, 69
work
    boundaries of, 4
    satisfaction survey, 2
World Bank Institute, Evoke, 163
World of Warcraft, 80

X

Xbox Live real-time game network, 156

About the Author

Michael Hugos is an author, speaker, award-winning CIO and principal at Center for Systems Innovation [c4si]. He works with clients to find elegant solutions to complex problems with a focus in supply chains, business intelligence, and new business ventures. Earlier, he spent six years as CIO of a national distribution organization, where he developed a suite of supply chain and e-business systems that transformed the company's operations and revenue model. For this work, he won the CIO 100 Award, the InformationWeek 500 Award, and the Premier 100 Award. He earned his MBA from Northwestern University's Kellogg School of Management with a joint major in finance and information systems. He is author of eight other books, including the popular *Essentials of Supply Chain Management* (Wiley), now in its third edition.

Made in the USA
Lexington, KY
04 June 2014